KU-714-572

JACK HOLLAND was a highly respected author and journalist known particularly for his commentary about Northern Irish politics. He grew up in Belfast (where he was taught by Seamus Heaney), and worked with Jeremy Paxman and other outstanding journalists at BBC Belfast, during a period of seminal current affairs programming. Jack published four novels and seven works of non-fiction, most of the latter relating to politics and terrorism in Northern Ireland, including the bestselling *Phoenix: Policing the Shadows*.

Sadly, Jack died of cancer in 2004, just after finishing the manuscript of *Misogyny*. On his death, his family received letters of respect from statesmen including Ted Kennedy and Hillary Clinton, who had come to rely on his balanced analysis of Irish politics.

Other titles in this series

A BRIEF HISTORY OF

MISOGYNY

The world's oldest prejudice

JACK HOLLAND

ROBINSON
London

Constable & Robinson Ltd
3 The Lanchesters
162 Fulham Palace Road
London W6 9ER
www.constablerobinson.com

This edition published by Robinson,
an imprint of Constable & Robinson Ltd, 2006

Copyright © Jack Holland 2006

The right of Jack Holland to be identified as the author of this
work has been asserted by him in accordance with the
Copyright, Designs and Patents Act 1988

All rights reserved. This book is sold subject to the condition
that it shall not, by way of trade or otherwise, be lent, re-sold,
hired out or otherwise circulated in any form of binding or cover
other than that in which it is published and without a similar condition
including this condition being imposed on the subsequent purchaser.

A copy of the British Library Cataloguing in
Publication data is available from the British Library

ISBN-13: 978-1-84529-371-0
ISBN-10: 1-84529-371-1

Printed and bound in the EU

3 5 7 9 10 8 6 4 2

This book is dedicated to the memory of its author.

It is also dedicated to the women who raised him – his mother, Elizabeth Rodgers Holland, his grandmother Kate Murphy Holland and his aunt 'Cissy' Martha Holland, as well as to his sisters – Katherine, Elizabeth and Eileen.

CONTENTS

ACKNOWLEDGEMENTS

Thanks are due to a number of people in our quest to get this book published posthumously. For their moral and/or practical support, we would like to thank Stephen Davis, Don Gilbert, Susan Phoenix, Marcia Rock and Michelle Stoddard. We are particularly grateful to Brad Henslee, David Goodine and Mike Myles for creating, developing and maintaining *www.jackholland.net*.

We especially wish to thank Sappho Clissitt, our London literary agent, who had the courage and foresight to take on this project, when many other agents would not.

They all have our heartfelt thanks.

Mary Hudson and Jenny Holland

FOREWORD

My father loved history and he loved women. These are the two factors that brought him to the topic of misogyny, one substantially different from the Northern Irish political matters on which he had built a career.

He began work on *Misogyny: The World's Oldest Prejudice* in 2002. The topic was quite a conversation starter. A common response from other men, when my father told them what he was working on, was an assumption that he was writing some sort of defence of misogyny, a reaction he found startling. Another common response was surprise that such a book should be written by a man. To this, his answer was simple. 'Why not?' he would say. 'It was invented by men.'

While he was writing, he became consumed by the astonishing list of crimes committed against women by their husbands, fathers, neighbours and rulers. My mother and I would shudder as he recounted them: from the mind-boggling torture of suspected witches in early modern Europe, to the horrendous cruelty suffered by women in North Korean prisons. He clipped newspaper articles; he read myriad histories; he turned to poetry and plays in an attempt to find cultural explanations.

My father felt that this was his most important work. In it, he turned his journalist's eye to a daunting question: how do you explain the oppression and brutalization of half the world's population by the other half, throughout history?

The tools he used in tackling that question were the same ones he employed to make other more contemporary conflicts tangible to his readers – his ability to condense difficult, inaccessible material; his considerable knowledge of Western culture and history; his sympathy for the oppressed; and his lyrical prose style. With these at his disposal, he created a history which, despite its often brutal subject matter, is remarkably pleasurable to read.

In March 2004, a month after he finished *Misogyny*, my father was diagnosed with cancer. He died that May of NK/T cell lymphoma, an extremely rare form of cancer that is almost always fatal. Although weakened by illness and treatment, he remained absorbed by the project, and continued working on the final edits while in his hospital bed.

The father–daughter relationship occupies an important place in this book, for it is in this most intimate of connections that misogyny's pernicious effects are carried forward, or broken. It is also a central relationship in any girl's life – and as a father, mine approached his parental role with lightness, admiring without fawning, accepting the arrival of my womanhood with grace and tactful approval. Most of all he always asked me for my thoughts. He encouraged me to be argumentative, to challenge him. Occasionally, he would chuckle and poke fun at my youthful convictions; other times our debates would become quite heated. I knew from what he said that he prized my intelligence. I knew from the soft look in his eyes that he cherished my womanliness.

It is difficult to measure the importance of that acceptance, especially now that it is gone. As I read what my father wrote about the treatment that so many women have endured, for centuries and across continents, I become aware of an irony. I was spared the effects of misogyny. Exceptionally, I was able to live, at least at home, free from its shackles.

My most tender memory of my father, out of a lifetime of tender memories, is from three days before he died. He and I were sitting alone in one of the patient lounges of a Manhattan hospital, going through the manuscript together. I read aloud, and he wanted to know if I had any suggested changes. I was flattered that he – professional author, expert, adult, father – was asking me – newbie reporter, expert on nothing, young woman, daughter – for my opinion.

It was a golden moment, now burnished by recollection. It felt as though the quiet task we were engaged in was greater than his illness. In the sun-drenched room where we sat overlooking the Hudson River, for a brief moment, we were keeping at bay the suffering and fear that surrounded us in that cancer ward.

We were not long at our task when I realized that my father's doctor, a kind, soft-spoken man who barely two weeks earlier had informed my mother and me that my father's death was imminent, was standing by watching us, clearly moved. His expression told me that he did not see scenes like this very often.

Jack grew up in Northern Ireland in the 1950s and came of age in the socially and politically turbulent 1960s. From early on, he was surrounded by capable women. He was raised primarily by his grandmother Kate Murphy Holland, a formidable matriarch from the wilds of County Down, and his aunt 'Cissy' Martha Holland, a woman of considerable beauty who never married and worked in one of Belfast's many linen mills. His own mother, Elizabeth Rodgers Holland, grew up so poor that she could afford to attend school only sporadically. She would serve as an inspiration to him throughout his career. He used to say that his aim as a writer was to give people like her, uneducated but endowed with intelligence, access to complex ideas.

He was always concerned with the female experience. When he came to write his first non-fiction account of the Troubles, then at their height, he mined the letters and stories of his mother and aunt and used them to great effect in *Too Long a Sacrifice: Life and Death in Northern Ireland Since 1969*, published in 1981. His first novel, *The Prisoner's Wife* (1982), explored the suffering endured by women when men engage in war.

The most important woman in my father's life was my mother, Mary Hudson, a formidable intellect in her own right, and a gifted linguist and teacher. They enjoyed a productive and happy thirty-year marriage, invaluable to each other both personally and professionally. Growing up, I was privy to countless discussions at the dinner table about how to develop this or that aspect of whatever book he was writing at the time. *Misogyny*, as well as most of his other books, was improved by her editing.

Without her perseverance over the last two years, this book would have never seen the light of day. The US publisher with whom my father had a contract, and with whom he had closely collaborated throughout the writing process, oddly claimed after his death that the manuscript was not publishable. My mother knew this was untrue, and was determined that a home for the book should be found, because it was a story that had to be told. It is because of her resilience that this important and thought-provoking work will now reach its audience.

We now live in an age that is relatively enlightened, when finally the phenomenon of misogyny has been identified not only as a source of oppression and injustice, but also as an obstacle to human development, and to social and economic progress. Yet on the whole women continue to be paid less than their male counterparts, and in the United States reproductive rights won decades ago are being eroded. True sexual equality still eludes us. And in many parts of the world, where issues of gender are compounded by poverty, ignorance, fundamentalism and disease, women's lot has scarcely improved over the centuries.

Jack Holland, my father, was acutely aware that such problems could not be solved by a single book, or indeed by many. But this book, his last, shall stand as an important tool in the struggle against the world's oldest prejudice.

INTRODUCTION

her shaved head
like a stubble of black corn
her blindfold a bandage
her noose a ring
                    Seamus Heaney,
                    'Punishment' from
                    North (1975)

On 22 June 2002, in a remote area of the Punjab, a Pakistani woman named Mukhtaran Bibi was sentenced on the orders of a tribal council to be gang raped because allegedly her brother had been seen in the company of a higher-caste woman. Four men dragged her into a hut ignoring her pleas for mercy.

'They raped me for one hour, and afterwards I was unable to move,' she told reporters. Hundreds witnessed the sentencing but none offered to help.

On 2 May 2002, Lee Sun-Ok, a defector from North Korea, testified before the House International Relations Committee in Washington DC about conditions in the Kaechon Women's Prison in North Korea where some 80 per cent of the prisoners are housewives. She witnessed three women giving birth on a cement floor. 'It was horrible to watch the prison doctor kicking the pregnant women with his boots. When a baby was born, the doctor shouted, "Kill it quickly. How can a criminal in the prison expect to have a baby?"'

Nigeria, 2002. Amina Lawal was sentenced to death by stoning for having a child out of wedlock. She was sentenced to be buried up to her neck and rocks thrown at her head until her skull was crushed.

Fayetteville, North Carolina. In Fort Bragg army base, over a period of just six weeks in the summer of 2003, four women died at the hands of their enraged husbands. One was stabbed more than fifty times by the man who once claimed he loved her.

East Africa. In an area stretching from Egypt to Somalia, it is estimated that between 80 per cent and 100 per cent of all women have suffered genital mutilation. Some have fled to the United States seeking asylum. The women have argued that they are entitled to the same protection as refugees escaping political oppression. But the struggle in which they are engaged is far older than any campaign for national, political or civil rights.

I grew up in Northern Ireland, a world away from the Punjab, North Korea and East Africa. But it was a place where the word 'cunt' expressed the worst form of contempt one person could feel for another. If you loathed or despised a person, 'cunt' said it all.

The word was scrawled on the walls of rubbish-strewn back alleyways or in public toilets reeking of urine and faeces. Nothing was worse than being treated like a 'cunt' or nothing so stupid as a 'stupid cunt'.

Belfast, Northern Ireland, the city where I grew up, had its own peculiar hatreds. Its sectarian animosities over the years have made it a byword for violence and bloodshed. But there was one thing on which the warring communities of Catholics and Protestants could agree: the contemptible status of cunt.

Belfast was little different in this way from other poor, industrialized parts of Britain where a mundane form of contempt for women, wife beating, was a fairly regular occurrence. Men would step in to defend a dog from being kicked around by another man, but felt no obligation to do the same when faced with brutality being inflicted on a wife by her husband. Ironically, this was because of the 'sacred' status of the relationship between man and wife, which barred intervention.

When political violence broke out in the late 1960s, misogynistic behaviour expressed itself more publicly. Catholic girls who dated British soldiers were dragged into the street, bound and held down (often by other women), while the men hacked and shaved off their hair, before pouring hot tar over them and sprinkling them with feathers. They were then tied to a lamp post to be gaped at by the nervous onlookers, with a sign hung around their necks on which was scrawled another sexual insult: 'whore'.

Perhaps we were imitating the French, to whom the English-speaking nations usually defer in matters sexual, having seen those news pictures as France was liberated of what befell women found guilty of going out with German soldiers. But we were also following the inner logic of our own powerful feelings, the same rage which we articulated with monosyllabic concision in the word 'cunt'.

It was a logic that had been articulated some 1,800 years earlier by Tertullian (AD 160–220), one of the founding fathers of the Catholic Church, who wrote:

> You are the devil's gateway; you are the unsealer of that forbidden tree; you are the first deserter of Divine law. You are she who persuaded him whom the devil was not valiant enough to attack. You destroyed so easily God's image, man.

Misogyny, the hatred of women, has thrived on many different levels, from the loftiest philosophical plane in the works of Greek thinkers, who helped frame how Western society views the world, to the back streets of nineteenth-century London and the highways of modern Los Angeles, where serial killers have left in their wake a trail of the tortured and mutilated corpses of women. From the Christian ascetics of the third century AD, to the Taliban rulers of Afghanistan in the late 1990s, it has directed its rage at women and tried to suppress their sexuality. At least once, during the witch-hunts of the late Middle Ages, it has launched what amounted to a sexual pogrom, burning hundreds of thousands – some historians say millions – of women at the stake throughout Europe. It has been expressed by some of the greatest and most renowned artists that civilization has produced, and celebrated in the lowest, most vulgar works of modern pornography. The history of misogyny is indeed the story of a hatred unique as it is enduring, uniting Aristotle with Jack The Ripper, King Lear with James Bond.

At the most private level of all, the sex act itself became a form of humiliation and shame – humiliation for the woman who experienced it and shame for the man who perpetrated it. In Belfast slang the verb 'to stiff' someone can mean two things: 'to make love to' or 'to kill'. But death here does not imply the French sense of '*la petite mort*', which describes the abandonment of self in the ecstatic swoon of orgasm. 'I just stiffed that cunt' can mean 'I just shot him dead' or 'I just fucked her'. Either way, the victim is now discarded, discountable, essentially dehumanized.

I know that tracing the history of any hatred is a complex matter. At the root of a particular form of hatred, whether it be class or racial hatred, religious or ethnic hatred, one usually finds a conflict. But, on the depressing list of hatreds that human beings feel for each other, none other than misogyny involves the profound need and desires that most men have for women, and most women for men. Hatred coexists with desire in a peculiar way. This is what makes misogyny so complex: it involves a man's conflict with himself. Indeed, for the most part, the conflict is not even recognized. In Ireland, as in the rest of the Catholic world, this is expressed in what looks at first like a paradox. Women might be held in contempt on the street, but walk into any Catholic church and you find a woman on a pedestal being revered, even worshipped.

Our church in Belfast was a nondescript structure, typical of Irish churches, most of which were built in the late nineteenth and early twentieth centuries – that is, long after the glorious phase of Catholic architecture had ended and been replaced by one of sentimental piety. It was built of red brick, like the little rows of houses around it. Its only flourishes of beauty were a pseudo-Gothic doorway and a porphyry holy-water font at the entrance. By the last mass on a Sunday, tiny black clumps of furry dirt had coagulated at the bottom of the little basin.

Upon entering the darkened interior, one's attention was arrested by the statue of a young woman in a blue mantle, a halo of stars around her head, her pale, dainty feet trampling on the head of a writhing serpent. The serpent's forked tongue was thrust out menacingly from a garish red, gaping mouth. But its poisonous wrath is rendered impotent: 'And that great dragon was cast out, that old serpent, called the Devil, and Satan, which deceiveth the whole world.' (Revelations 20:2).

A woman who was a virgin had vanquished the Devil through her purity, which was unassailable in its perfection. We were made to understand that the evil over which she stood in triumph, and for which she was exalted, was the evil of the flesh, of lust, the desire to commit unmentionable acts. But we were distracted by the fact that the snake was too obvious a sexual symbol to be ignored. In celebrating the triumph of purity over bodily desire, the statue instead asserted a latent sensuality – the way her garment was slightly lifted up to reveal her dainty, feminine feet in such intimate, physical contact with the slithering, writhing snake. We would one day learn that repression of sex is just another form of sexual obsession, like pornography.

By fifteen, my friends and I all knew what it was she was really trampling into the dust. This was the role that women in our society were expected to perform – to deny desire in others and crush it in themselves.

It took no training in philosophy to decipher the misogyny behind the use of the word 'cunt'. But the exaltation of the Virgin Mary as Mother of God proved that misogyny can push a woman upwards as well as downwards. In either direction, the destination is the same: woman dehumanized.

Though misogyny is one of the most tenacious prejudices, it has changed and evolved over the centuries, moderated or exacerbated by prevailing social, political and, above all, religious currents. A dramatic transformation in the history of the hatred of women occurred with the rise of Christianity and the promulgation of the doctrine of Original Sin.

As explained in this book, the doctrine was a product of the confluence in Christianity of three powerful currents in the ancient world: Greek philosophical Platonism; Judaic patriarchal monotheism; and Christian revelation, as expressed in the assertion that Christ was the Son of God, and that in him God himself became incarnate and intervened directly in human affairs. This unprecedented convergence of philosophical, mystical and historical claims helped create a powerful ideological underpinning for the world's oldest prejudice when it made conception itself a sin – Original Sin. Woman, even as she was exalted in the form of the Virgin Mary, was at the same time held responsible for perpetrating this sin, the falling away of man from the perfect state of grace with God into the horror of the reality of being.

The story of how this dual process of dehumanization – upwards and downwards – might have occurred takes us far beyond the cult of the Virgin Mary. In effect, it is the story of the oldest prejudice. It has survived in one form or another over immense periods of time, emerging seemingly unchanged from the cataclysms that have engulfed empires and cultures, and swept away their other modes of thought and feeling. It persists after philosophical and scientific revolutions have seemingly transformed permanently how we look at the world. When social and political upheavals have refashioned relationships between citizens and the state, and democracies vanquished oligarchies and driven absolute monarchs from power, it comes back to haunt our ideals of equality, with the persistence of a ghost that cannot be exorcised. It is as up to date as the latest porn website and as old as civilization itself.

For we are the inheritors of an ancient tradition, going back to the origins of the great civilizations of the past which have so profoundly shaped our consciousness, and fashioned the dualism that lies behind our efforts to dehumanize half the human race. 'The duality of the world is beyond comprehension,' wrote Otto Weininger, the twentieth-century Austrian thinker, and perhaps the last Western philosopher ever to attempt to justify misogyny on philosophical grounds, 'it is the plot of man's fall, the primitive riddle. It is the binding of eternal life in a perishable being, of the innocent in the guilty.'

Understanding the history of this 'riddle' may help us unravel it. But to trace its roots, it is necessary to look at what may have preceded it. If for centuries women have been an object of contempt, was there a women's history BC – 'before contempt', before misogyny? That is the question.

It is the question at any rate that has exercised the thoughts of many, mostly feminist historians and scholars who have sought to go beyond the conventional history of women, which consists largely of the history of their relationship to men. Indeed, in scholarly terms, until very recently, women have been seen in relation to precious little else.

History has been (and to a large extent remains) 'his story' – the story of men's impact upon the world around them in all its complex aspects, religious, political, militaristic, social, philosophical, economic, artistic and scientific. Many besides feminists have characterized history as, in effect, the product of a patriarchal society in which women's roles and contributions have been discounted or ignored. Throughout that history, misogyny has manifested itself in different ways at different times. Indeed, for some, what we call history is merely the tale that patriarchy wants to tell, and misogyny is its ideology, a system of beliefs and ideas the aim of which is to explain the domination of men over women.

Many feminists, frustrated with this historical form of confinement, have turned to prehistory for relief, and constructed a remoter past in which matriarchy prevailed and the higher status it accorded to women presumably protected them from the kind of contempt that would later blight their lives and distort how they are viewed.

In one version or another, beginning in the nineteenth century, the matriarchal model has exercised at times an intense appeal to a remarkably wide range of individuals, from Friedrich Engels and Sigmund Freud to members of the spiritualist feminist movement of the late twentieth century. It has been espoused by such serious scholars as the archaeologist Marija Gimbutas, and popularized in such best-selling books as *Who Cooked The Last Supper: The Women's History of the World* by Rosalind Miles. The latter states:

> For in the beginning, as humankind emerged from the darkness of prehistory, God was a woman. And what a woman! . . . The power and centrality of the first woman-God is one of the best-kept secrets of history.

Miles gives a chronology of the worship of the Great Goddess (which is equated with the prevalence of matriarchal societies) and claims that 'the sacred status of womanhood lasted for at least 25,000 years – some commentators would push it back further still, to 40,000 years or even 50,000. In fact, there never was a time at this stage of human history when woman was not special and magical.'

The problem is finding evidence for the existence of matriarchy. And even if there were proof that it existed, this would not in itself change the fact that women's relationship to men defines their role in history: matriarchal history merely replaces a role that is subordinate with one that is dominant. For much of the time matriarchy is supposed to have prevailed, written records do not exist. Artefacts such as the so-called Venusian figurines of Palaeolithic origin, and found from southern France to Siberia, are frequently cited as proof of the widespread worship of the Great Goddess. However, they are notoriously difficult to interpret. To some exponents of the matriarchal interpretation, they are proof of the awe and veneration accorded women at the time; but others have interpreted the figurines as grotesque, inspiring not awe and veneration but horror. However, even if it could be proved that the figurines represent a Great Goddess cult, history demonstrates that there is no necessary link between goddess worship and a high social status for women – the cult of the Virgin Mary, for instance, was in the ascendant during the witch burnings of the Middle Ages.

In Europe, it is much later than the Palaeolithic and only when we come to the Celts that we find a pre-Classical culture offering some textual basis for claims that, before the Greeks and Romans stamped their hegemony on history, a form of matriarchy prevailed. The evidence comes both in the form of the Celtic myths and sagas, and in the writings of the Greeks and Romans of the time about what seemed to them the shocking freedoms the Celts accorded their women.

The temptation to believe in an Arcadia, a lost golden age when the relations between men and women were without conflict, is very strong, but must be resisted. The most we can hope for, in Celtic society at any rate, is evidence of a more balanced relationship between the sexes. *Misogyny* will show that this balance was lost with the rise of Greece and Rome, and will examine the dualism, identified by Weininger, that those civilizations created. In this dualism, men were the thesis, and women the antithesis.

It is in the nature of dualism (unlike the dialectic) that there be no synthesis – the sexes are doomed to perpetual conflict. Women were faced with a battery of philosophical, scientific and legal arguments aimed at proving and codifying their 'inherent inferiority' to men. Later, Christianity added a theological one, with such profound impact that its ramifications are with us today.

The rise of liberal democracy in the post-Enlightenment era saw the beginning of the long struggle for political and legal equality for women. But misogyny has never let progress get in its way. When political and legal equality in the West was followed by the sexual revolution, this produced a backlash from both fundamentalist Protestants and conservative Catholics. In many Third World nations the drive for women's rights threatened deeply held religious ideas and social customs. This culminated in Taliban-ruled Afghanistan – a state with the suppression of women as a primary aim. It legislated women out of public life, denying them basic rights – comparable to the way the Nazis' Nuremberg Laws turned German Jews into non-persons. Rarely, if ever, has the aim of misogyny, to dehumanize half the human race, been made more explicit.

The hatred of women affects us in ways that no other hatred does because it strikes at our innermost selves. It is located where the private and public worlds intersect. The history of that hatred may dwell on its public consequences, but at the same time it allows us to speculate on why, at the personal level, man's complex relationship to woman has permitted misogyny to thrive. Ultimately, such speculation should allow us to see how equality between the sexes will eventually be able to banish misogyny and put an end to the world's oldest prejudice.

I

PANDORA'S DAUGHTERS

It is hard to be precise about the origins of a prejudice. But if misogyny has a birthday, it falls sometime in the eighth century BC. If it has a cradle, it lies somewhere in the eastern Mediterranean.

At around that time in both Greece and Judaea, creation stories that were to acquire the power of myth arose, describing the Fall of Man, and how woman's weakness is responsible for all subsequent human suffering, misery and death. Both myths have since flowed into the mainstream of Western civilization, carried along by two of its most powerful tributaries: In the Jewish tradition, as recounted in Genesis (which a majority of Americans still accept as true)[1] the culprit is Eve; and in the Greek, Pandora.

The Greeks are the first colonists of our intellectual world. Their vision of a universe governed by natural laws that the human intellect can uncover and comprehend is the basis on

which our science and philosophy rest. They created the first
democracy. But in the history of misogyny, the Greeks also
occupy a unique place as the intellectual pioneers of a pernicious view of women that has persisted down to modern times,
confounding any notion we might still have that the rise of
reason and science means the decline of prejudice and hatred.

The myth of Pandora was first written down in the eighth
century BC by Hesiod, a farmer turned poet, in two poems:
'Theogony' and 'Works and Days'. In spite of Hesiod's considerable experience as a farmer, his account of mankind's
creation ignores some of the basic facts of life. The race of
men exists before the arrival of woman, in blissful autonomy,
as companions to the gods, 'apart from sorrow and from painful
work/ Free from disease . . .'[2] As in the Biblical account of the
creation of man, woman is an afterthought. But in the Greek
version, she is also a most malicious one. Zeus, the father of the
gods, seeks to punish men by keeping from them the secret of fire,
so that, like the beasts, they must eat their meat raw. Prometheus,
a demi-god and the creator of the first men, steals fire from
heaven and brings it to earth. Furious at being deceived, Zeus
devises the supreme trick in the form of a 'gift' to men, 'an evil
thing for their delight', Pandora, the 'all giver'. The Greek phrase
used to describe her, *'kalon kakon'*, means 'the beautiful evil'.
Her beauty compares to that of the goddesses:

> From her comes all the race of womankind
> The deadly female race and tribe of wives
> Who live with mortal men and bring them harm.[3]

The gods give her 'sly manners, and the morals of a bitch'.
Pandora is presented to Epimetheus, Prometheus' younger
brother. He is enchanted by 'this hopeless trap, deadly to
men' and marries her. Pandora brings with her a large sealed

jar, which she has been told never to open. The jar is an earthenware vessel, womb-like in shape and primarily used to store wine and olive oil. In earlier times, it was also used as a coffin.[4] Pandora cannot resist seeing what is inside:

> But now the woman opened up the cask,
> And scattered pains and evils among men.[5]

Since then, according to Greek mythology, mankind has been doomed to labour, grow old, get sick, and die in suffering.

One of the functions of mythology is to answer the sort of questions we asked as children, such as 'Why do the stars shine?' and 'Why did grandad die?' Myths also justify the existing order of things – both natural and social – and account for traditional beliefs, rituals, and roles. One of the beliefs most central to the Greek, and later the Judaeo-Christian, traditions was that man was fashioned by the gods, or God, separately from the creation of animals. (The persistence of this belief among conservative Christians is why Darwin's theory of evolution continues to meet with such resistance.) The possession of fire was proof that man was different from the animals, and also further up the hierarchy of species. But fire's acquisition brought man too close to the gods for their comfort. Woman, it was said, is his punishment for this hubris, a reminder that man, regardless of his origins and aspirations, comes into the world as does a lowly beast. Today, some have turned this attitude of contempt on its head, celebrating woman because of what they see as her closer links to nature. But to the Greeks, nature was a threat and a challenge to man's higher self, and woman was nature's most powerful (because most alluring) embodiment. It was necessary to dehumanize her, even though she made it possible for the human race to continue. Contempt was her due for exciting the lust that leads us into the cycle of birth and death, from which we can never break free.

As well as burdening Pandora with responsibility for the mortal lot of man, the Greeks created a vision of woman as 'the Other', the antithesis to the male thesis, who needed boundaries to contain her. Most crucially, Greece laid the philosophical–scientific foundations for a dualistic view of reality in which women were forever doomed to embody this mutable, and essentially contemptible world. Any history of the attempt to dehumanize half the human race is confronted by this paradox, that some of the values we cherish most were forged in a society that devalued, denigrated and despised women. 'Sex roles that will be familiar to the modern reader were firmly established in the Dark Ages in Athens,' wrote the historian Sarah Pomeroy.[6] That is, along with Plato and the Parthenon, Greece gave us some of the cheapest sexual dichotomies of all, including that of 'good girl versus bad girl'.

Hesiod was writing some five centuries after tribes who would become the Greeks had swept into the eastern Mediterranean as conquerors, establishing themselves not only on the Greek mainland but also in the islands around it and on the shores of Asia Minor (modern Turkey). By the sixth century BC, the Greeks had spread as far west as Sicily, the coasts of southern Italy, and the southeast coast of Gaul (now France). They brought with them their pantheon of warrior gods of whom the most powerful was Zeus, the Thunderer. Having violent warrior divinities, however, is not necessarily an indication of a misogynistic culture. In the older civilizations the Greeks encountered, such as those of Egypt and Babylon, there was an abundance of war gods, but no equivalent of the Fall of Man myth. In Mesopotamia, the Sumerian poem 'The Epic of Gilgamesh', which dates back to the third millennium BC, has a hero who like Prometheus aspires to rival the gods. Gilgamesh does so by seeking to share in their immortality; but women are not made the instrument of revenge by some vindictive deity seeking to punish man for challenging his mortal lot. Nor does Gilgamesh castigate women for being to blame for 'the lot of man'; the gods are to blame for our mortality. The goddess who rules Paradise tells him:

> Gilgamesh, where are you hurrying to? You will never find that life for which you are looking. When the gods created man they allotted him death but life they retained in their own keeping. As for you, Gilgamesh, fill up your belly with good things, day and night, night and day, dance and be merry, feast and rejoice; let your clothes be fresh, bathe yourself in water, cherish the little child that holds your hand, and make your wife happy in your embrace; for this too, is the lot of man.[7]

In the later culture of the nomadic Celts, which dominated northwestern Europe, myths of paradise found and lost abound, but there is no myth of the Fall of Man. The Celtic version of paradise is, like that of the Sumerians and Jews, a fruitful garden where beautiful women rule and lure men to a life of bliss. But the only conflict is between the men's nostalgia for home and their desire for the women of the garden. Desire exists, but the evil consequences do not. There is no Celtic equivalent of Pandora or Eve.

The gods of the Athenian pantheon – traditionally located on Mount Olympus – became the national gods of Greece, with several prominent characteristics. Four of the five major goddesses are either virginal or asexual. The most important of them, Athena, is as androgynous as the Statue of Liberty in New York harbour. She is usually shown holding a shield and spear, clad in helmet and long thick robes that conceal her body. The fifth goddess, Aphrodite, the goddess of love, behaves at times like a celestial airhead. The sexlessness of most of the female deities is in startling contrast to the violent, predatory nature of the males. Most significantly, the Athenian pantheon established a serial rapist, the sky-god Zeus, as the father of them all. Zeus' numerous offspring are nearly all the product of the rape of mortal women. The two exceptions are Athena and Dionysus, to whom Zeus gives birth himself. Athena springs from his head, fully armed, carrying her spear and shield; and Dionysus emerges from his thigh.

All religions ask us to believe the impossible. The fantasy of male autonomy, in which men are seen as somehow free from dependence on women, expresses itself in the creation myth of Pandora, where males can come into existence without females. In the Athenian pantheon, this impossibility expresses itself in the claim that males can make females redundant in the very sphere where they are indispensable – that of reproduction. Ludicrous as it might seem, the myth of the father of the gods becoming the mother of the gods was given force by the science of Aristotle, in which the role of the mother in pregnancy was determined to be merely nutritive. She was the passive receptacle of the male seed, which contained everything needed (except the environment) for the development of the foetus. Whatever the female can do, it seems, the male can do better – though there is no evidence of any Greek males rushing to experiment with impregnation and giving birth.

The rise of misogyny in the eighth century BC Greece occurred just as the influence of family-based dynasties was on the decline; instead power was invested in the body politic of the city-state. One historian has suggested that:

> Where political power was rooted in the royal household, the boundary between the domestic and the political, between the private and the public, is not nearly so rigid. The roles of men

and women overlap, and it is for this reason that a woman can come close – in the absence of her husband – to the exercise of political power.[8]

Alliances between noble families were of vital importance and women's role in forging such bonds was essential. This is reflected in the work of Homer, Hesiod's more gifted contemporary. In *The Iliad*, the story of the siege of Troy, Menelaus, the king of Sparta and Helen's husband, owes his throne to his wife. For Menelaus it is essential to get his wife back after she has eloped with Paris to Troy not just for her unrivalled beauty, but because his kingship depends on it.

Homer based both *The Iliad* and *The Odyssey* (the latter recounting the long journey home of Odysseus, one of the Greek kings) on material which dates back to the earlier dynastic period. In these works, women are generally portrayed sympathetically; they are complex and powerful, and among the most memorable characters in all literature. The end of this era was accompanied by a move from a pastoral to a labour-intensive agricultural economy, one concerned about the conservation of property. But the expressions of hostility to women, not only in Hesiod but in other extant eighth-century writings, cannot be entirely explained by changing political and social structures: no deep-seated hatred can. They provided, however, the context in which men felt comfortable in expressing misogyny.[9] And the woman against whom they felt most comfortable expressing it was an eighth-century creation: Helen of Troy, Greek misogyny's centre-fold, the face 'that launched a thousand ships/ And burned the topless towers of Ilium'.[10]

Helen's mother Leda was one of Zeus' rape victims, whom he violated when he was in the form of a swan. But Helen, in her remarkable career as a complex icon inciting both desire and loathing, is more truly a daughter of Pandora. Like Pandora's, her beauty is a trick. It arouses extraordinary desire in men. But to desire her is to uncork the evils of bloodshed and destruction. In *The Iliad*, Helen expresses self-loathing, describing herself as a 'nasty bitch, evil-intriguing'.[11] She echoes the description of Pandora. At the peak of Athens' most creative period, when self-loathing becomes a generalized feeling among the female characters of some of the great dramas, Helen is the focal point of misogyny. She is the man-slaughterer, man's curse, bitch, vampire, destroyer of cities, the poisoned chalice, devourer of men – almost every misogynistic epithet imaginable is thrown at her. In Euripides' *The Trojan Women*, Hecuba the widow of Priam, the slaughtered king of Troy, cries out to Menelaus the victorious Spartan King:

> I bless thee, Menelaus, I bless thee,
> If thou wilt slay her! Only fear to see
> Her visage, lest she snare thee and thou fall!
> She snareth strong men's eyes; she snareth tall
> Cities; and fire from out her eateth up
> Houses. Such magic hath she, as a cup
> Of death![12]

Hecuba's pleas are in vain. Menelaus both needs and desires Helen too much to punish her. He carries her back to Sparta where they resume their married life, while the other women, reduced to the status of the victors' slaves, are left to lament their lost husbands, fathers, and sons.

Like that of Pandora, the story of Helen is an allegory that inextricably links desire with death. In the Pandora story, her loss of virginity – the uncorking of the jar – lets death into the world, just as Paris' desire for Helen brings war and all its horrors. Such allegories are expressions of what Sigmund Freud called 'the eternal struggle between Eros and the destructive or death instinct' – Thanatos.[13] In the culture of contempt, women are made to feel overwhelming guilt because their beauty causes desire, starting the cycle of life and death.

Other mythologies and cultures have mediated this complex dance of Eros and Thanatos but primarily as an inescapable act of life. In the mythology of the Celts, goddesses are typically identified with the principles of both life and death. These dual roles are not, however, seen dualistically; that is, as two principles of life and death, forever at war. The Celts portray their goddesses as unselfconsciously reconciling the forces of life and death in the way every mother does in reality: by bringing life into the world, she also brings death. This life/death reconciliation is, to them, simply in the nature of things, not a cause for blame or condemnation. But to the Greek dualistic mentality, nature embodies man's limitations and weaknesses, and woman embodies nature. Woman serves as a constant and resented reminder of those limitations. This is the sin of Pandora and her daughters, for which misogyny, from its fairy tales to its philosophies, seeks to punish all women.

'One constant rule of mythology,' wrote the poet Robert Graves, 'is that whatever happens among the gods above, reflects events on earth.'[14] Relationships and attitudes which are given mythological sanction are usually reflected in laws and customs. During the sixth century BC, this became evident with the growth of democracy and city states such as Athens, which quickly developed restrictive codes to regulate women's behaviour.

To modern minds, the notion that the rise of democracy should lead to a diminishing of women's status might seem to be something of a contradiction. But the notion of universal suffrage or even of equality, as it is understood now, did not inspire the democracies of Greece and Rome. They were slave-owning states where democratic rights were severely restricted to adult male citizens. In a slave-owning economy, the idea that all people are born equal would have contradicted a blatant reality, one that was as self-serving as it was universal. Slavery was the 'natural' outcome of inherent inequalities. In a society where one form of gross inequality is institutionalized, it is easier for other forms of inequality to flourish as well.

Laws regulating women's behaviour and opportunities give the most graphic and pertinent examples of how Hesiod's allegory of misogyny became a social fact. Legally speaking, Athenian women remained children, always under the guardianship of a male. A woman could not leave the house unless accompanied by a chaperone. She seldom was invited to dinner with her husband and lived in a segregated area of the house. She received no formal education: 'Let a woman not develop her reason, for that would be a terrible thing,' said the philosopher Democritus. Women were married when they reached puberty, often to men twice their age. Such a difference in age and maturity, as well as in education, would have enhanced the notion of women's inferiority. The husband was warned: 'He who teaches letters to his wife is ill advised: he's giving additional poison to a snake.'[15]

A husband's adultery was not considered grounds for divorce. (This view prevailed in England up until 1923, a reflection of how deeply the classics permeated upper-class English culture.) But if a woman committed adultery or was raped, her husband was obliged to divorce her or lose his citizenship. With these threats, women in the world's first democracy were worse off than in the autocracy of ancient Babylon. There, under the laws of King Hammurabi compiled in 1750 BC, the husband of a woman convicted of adultery at least had the power to pardon her.

Having consensual sex with another man's wife in ancient Greece was regarded as a more serious offence than raping her.

During the trial of a husband accused of murdering his wife's lover, the clerk of the court reads from the laws of Solon (the great Athenian lawgiver of the sixth century BC) regarding rape:

> Thus, members of the jury, the lawgiver considered violators deserving of a lesser penalty than seducers: for the latter he provided the death penalty; for the former, the doubled fine. His idea was that those who use force are loathed by the persons violated, whereas those who have got their way by persuasion corrupt women's minds, in such a way as to make other men's wives more attached to themselves than to their husbands, so that the whole house is in their power, and it is uncertain who is the children's father, the husband or the lover.[16]

The defence of the husband was that he had the right to kill his wife's lover because he had caught them *in flagrante*. A raped woman suffered the same penalties as one accused of adultery, and was forbidden to take part in public ceremonies or to wear jewellery. As in many conservative Moslem societies today, the rape victim was regarded as responsible for her own violation. She became a social outcast, a terrible fate in the small, close-knit community of the city state.[17]

Solon imposed further restrictions on women: he circumscribed their appearance at funerals (where traditionally they had provided contingents of paid mourners) and at feasts, as well as limiting their public displays of wealth. In addition, they were banned from buying or selling land. Solon also enacted a law forcing a woman without brothers, on the death of her father, to marry his nearest male relative. The sons born of that marriage would inherit any land. In this way, woman became 'the vehicle through which the property was kept within the family'.[18] Even after her marriage, an Athenian woman remained under the control of her father, who retained the power to divorce her from her husband and wed another if he decided that it was advantageous. Another law attributed to Solon forbade any Athenian citizen from enslaving another Athenian citizen (the enslavement of non-citizens was allowed) with one notable exception: a father or head of the household had the right to sell his unmarried daughter into slavery if she lost her virginity before marriage.

Having ensured that the 'good' girls were safe from any taint of sexual indiscretion, it was necessary to supply the 'bad' girls to cater for men's sexual appetites. Solon legalized state brothels, staffed by slaves and aliens. While the good girls composed a single category (wives cum mothers), the bad girls were graded from the high-maintenance *hetaera* – the equivalent of the mistress – to the low-end street walker, who could be picked up for a few dollars near the city dumps where people went to defecate. The whore's sexuality was a public convenience; she was viewed in terms of a sewer that drained off men's lust.[19]

'We have *hetaerae* for our pleasure, concubines for our daily needs, and wives to give us legitimate children and look after the housekeeping,' Demosthenes, the greatest of the Athenian orators, is reported to have said. This demarcation associating female virtue with sexlessness has been used to dehumanize women to this day.

It is not surprising, given the number of boundaries circumscribing women, that men developed something of an obsession with women as boundary-crossers. This fascination is graphically illustrated by the Greek interest in the Amazons, the legendary tribe of warrior women who invaded the most male of sanctuaries, organized warfare. The Amazons are a recurring presence in Greek history; this theme has persisted down to modern times. First mentioned by the fifth-century historian Herodotus (the 'father' of history), they were depicted as dwelling on the borderlands of civilization, devoted solely to warfare; they sought men only when they needed to mate, and exposed all their male babies, rearing only the females. They are the mirror image of patriarchal Athens. With the Amazons, the fantasy of the autonomous male meets its nightmare opposite, the autonomous female.

Men's fascination with warrior women has a long history, from Classical Athens to today's comic book heroine Wonder Woman and professional women wrestlers. The Amazons are like these wrestlers in that their combat is fantasy. But for men the fascination, edged with anxiety, is real. Among the Athenians, it reached obsessive proportions. Representations of battles between men and Amazons are among the most popular depictions of women in Antiquity. Over 800 examples survive, the bulk of them Athenian in origin.[20] They decorate everything from temples to vases and drinking bowls. Wherever a citizen looked, his eye would inevitably fall on a scene showing a man, sword or spear raised, hauling a woman by her hair off a horse; or stabbing and clubbing her to death, a javelin pointed at her nipple, as invariably her tunic slips to reveal a breast, and her short skirt rolls up to reveal her thighs. The greatest temple in Athens, the Parthenon, was erected in 437 BC to honour Athena, the city's ruling deity, and to celebrate the Greek victory over Persian invaders. But the battle scene chosen to decorate the shield of Athena was not based on any historical event. It was a depiction of the legendary victory of the hero Theseus, the mythological founder of the city, over an invading army of Amazons. The popularity of this scene cannot be explained merely by the fact that it was the only theme that allowed the artist to portray women naked or partially naked. (Convention in fifth-century Athens permitted only men to be depicted nude.) The scene reoccurs with the repetitiousness of pornography.

But like pornography, the repetition cannot assuage the urge and the anxiety that lies behind it.[21]

Male anxiety about women boundary-crossers manifests itself most powerfully and memorably in Greek tragedy. All the tragedies that have survived were written by Athenian playwrights during one relatively brief period of the fifth century. Only one of them, Sophocles' *Philoctetes*, has no woman character. The titles of over half of all the tragedies include either a woman's name or some other female reference.[22] Women were centre-stage and in a state of ferocious rebellion.

The tragedies nearly always take their characters and much of their plotting from the epics of Homer and his Bronze Age heroes, heroines and villains. It is as if modern novelists followed a convention which obliged them to base all their characters and plots on the legend of King Arthur and his Knights of the Round Table. Questions have therefore been raised about how much these dramas can tell us about the lives and problems of real women. However, the question is not how accurately they reflect the behaviour of real women but how truly they express society's anxieties about relationships between men and women. No one has doubted that they do.[23]

In Euripides' *Medea*, the eponymous heroine slaughters her children to take revenge on her husband, the Greek mythological hero Jason, when he abandons her to marry another woman. In Aeschylus' *Agamemnon*, Clytemnestra takes a lover when her husband sails for Troy; she assumes state power and murders him when he returns. In Sophocles' *Electra*, Agamemnon's daughter goads her hesitating brother Orestes into revenging their father's death by murdering their mother Clytemnestra. *Antigone* is the story of a woman who defies her uncle Creon, the king, to bury her brother, when he has forbidden it on pain of death. She pays for her rebellion by being walled up alive. Euripides' *The Bacchae* tells how the women worshippers of the orgiastic wine-god Dionysus are transformed into Amazons. They rampage around the countryside, sack villages for plunder, defeat a contingent of soldiers in battle, and in ecstatic frenzy, tear King Pentheus limb from limb, when he tries to spy on their activities.

The tragedy in each case results when women defy the patriarchal order, breaking temporarily free from the confinement that it imposes upon them. The women do so while asserting the claims of 'nature'. Their rebellion is often in the name of the family, which predates, and supersedes, the demands of the state. 'We'll have no woman's law here while I live,' Creon asserts when Antigone declares that her love for her brother obliges her to bury him decently, in defiance of the law.[24]

In rebellion, the tragic heroines cross the boundary between what is acceptable female behaviour and what is not, thereby becoming masculine, even Amazon-like. As Antigone challenges the law, Ismene warns her defiant sister: 'We were born women . . . we were not meant to fight with men.'[25]

The message is mixed, if not contradictory. While the playwrights often convey sympathy with women for the suffering and the oppression that goads them into rebellion, the resulting violence and savagery reinforces the underlying anxiety that women are wild and irrational creatures, eruptions of nature who are a threat to the civilized order created by men. This expresses itself in one of the most powerful pieces of misogyny ever penned: In Euripides' *Hippolyta*, Hippolytus declaims:

> Go to hell! I'll never have my fill of hating
> Women, not if I'm said to talk without ceasing,
> For women are also unceasingly wicked.
> Either someone should teach them to be sensible,
> Or let me trample them underfoot.[26]

While the injustices that women suffer are recognized, so is the necessity for maintaining the patriarchal order that perpetrates them.

The sense of woman as 'the Other', the antithesis of man, emerges powerfully from the dramas. This sexual dualism has been a characteristic of Western civilization ever since, partly thanks to Plato and Aristotle, who gave it philosophical and scientific expression.

Plato (429–347 BC) has been called the most influential of all philosophers – ancient, medieval, or modern. His ideas about the nature of the world have spread wherever Western civilization and its most crusading catalyst, Christianity, have taken root, shaping the intellectual and spiritual development of continents and nations that were undiscovered or unexplored at the time those ideas were formulated. Plato's contribution to the history of misogyny is a by-product of this extraordinary impact but it is, in some ways, a paradoxical one.

Some have hailed Plato as the first feminist because in *The Republic*, his vision of Utopia, he advocated that women receive the same education as men. At the same time, however, his dualistic vision of the world represents a turning away from the realm of ordinary, mutable existence. This existence he held was an illusion and a distraction to be scorned by the wise man. It included marriage and procreation, lowly pursuits with which he identifies women.[27] He himself never married, and exalted the 'pure' love of men for men higher than the love of men for women, which he placed closer to animal lust. His is a familiar enough dualism – identifying man with spirituality and woman with carnal appetites. But Plato gave it a kind of philosophic fire-power never seen before.

No philosopher's speculations take place in a vacuum; however abstract or obtuse the thought, there are circumstances, real enough, to help explain it. 'Plato was the child of a time that is still our own,' wrote Karl Popper.[28] His search for a higher, more perfect world beyond that of the senses took place against the background of years of starvation, plague, repression, censorship, and civil bloodshed. The events that shook the Greek world when Plato was a young man profoundly shaped him. Born into a wealthy Athenian family, he grew up during the Peloponnesian War between Athens and Sparta that lasted almost continuously from 431 BC to 404 BC. Few wars have had such long-term consequences. The impact of the Peloponnesian War on Greece can be compared with that of the First World War on Europe. It led to the ruin of Athens and its empire. It brought about the end of one of the most extraordinary periods of intellectual and artistic achievement that civilization has ever enjoyed. It exhausted Greece, paving the way for conquest first by the Macedonians, and then by Rome. In the turmoil and confusion that followed defeat, a vengeful democratic regime forced Plato's beloved mentor Socrates (469–399 BC) to commit suicide. The Peloponnesian War profoundly influenced Plato's view of the world – this alone makes it a turning point in history. It bred in him a profound distrust, and indeed contempt, for democracy.

When Plato envisioned the first Utopia, it was as a totalitarian state, rigidly ruled by a permanent elite, the Guardians, with an underclass whose only role was to maintain society's economic and agricultural basis. In the world of *The Republic*, frivolous pleasures such as love poetry and dancing are forbidden. The Guardians are allowed no wealth, and no form of personal adornment such as make-up. Plato, who viewed the body as essentially evil, often voices contempt for the mutable world of the senses.[29] In the *Symposium* he calls personal beauty a 'trifle', and speaks of 'the pollution of mortality'. 'So when the current of a man's desires flows towards knowledge and the like,' he asserts in *The Republic*, 'his pleasure will be entirely in things of the mind, and physical pleasures will pass him by – that is, if he is a genuine philosopher and not a sham.' Nothing must be allowed that will distract the elite from contemplating Absolute Beauty and Absolute Goodness – surely a recipe, if ever there was one, for Absolute Dullness.

All of Plato's work takes the form of dialogues between Socrates and his pupils. In *The Republic*, Socrates advocates the integration of selected women into the ruling elite (the Guardians) with responsibilities equal to those of men, based on his claim that women and men differ only in their biological roles and physical strength. They will be trained and educated alongside their male compatriots. Men and women Guardians 'will live and feed together, and have no private home or property'.[30] Mutual attraction between men and women Guardians is inevitable but 'it would be a sin either for mating or for anything else in our ideal society to take place without regulation. The Rulers would not allow it.' The aim is 'to have a real pedigree herd' so the best must breed with the best. The offspring of their unions will be taken away from their mothers immediately upon birth and reared in a communal nursery. The mothers will be spared the time-consuming and exhausting business of breast-feeding their babies. State nurses will do that for them. 'No parent should know his child, or child his parent.' By eliminating private property there will be no need for the father to know his son, since there will be nothing to inherit.

In Plato's work, equality for women has been achieved by the denial of the full range of their sexuality. They have become, in effect, honorary men. The only biological distinction acknowledged for them is that of reproduction. (Several thousand years later, some radical feminists would make the same claim – that men and women differed solely in their genitalia, and that all else was learned behaviour.) The female Guardians are permitted merely to breed and not to bond. Their offspring will be 'mothered' by the state. The control of sexuality is the key to the state's domination of its citizens. It becomes an instrument of state policy. By breaking the bonds of the family, especially the relationship between mother and child, Plato's Utopia attacks the notion of individuality itself. All totalitarian ideologies seek to erase individualism in order to ensure that the needs of the state are paramount.

The disparaging of mundane pleasures is among the aspects of Plato's Utopia that can be found in the totalitarian states of the twentieth century. Seeing sex merely in terms of the task of reproducing the 'pedigree herd' foreshadows Nazi Germany's obsession with the breeding of a master race. The sexless status of female Guardians would be duplicated by attempts in Maoist China to make men and women indistinguishable in their boiler suits. Most forms of poetry and music were actually banned during the fanatical censorship of the Taliban in Afghanistan, in their efforts to create a pure Islamic republic. During their rule, it was even a seditious act to open a hairdresser's salon. From Plato onwards, it has been the goal of every totalitarian regime to stop women from putting on make-up.

The Republic also makes it clear that 'the Other' can take different forms, in this case racial. Socrates advocates that the 'natural enemies' of the Greeks are the barbarians, just as women are 'natural enemies' of men. The division of the world into warring principles makes it easy to develop exclusive categories of persons. It is no accident that misogyny and racism are often found in the same social environment.

Plato's dualism takes on its most powerful philosophical expression in his Theory of Forms. The Guardians are expected to grasp it as their guiding wisdom and the most essential part of their education. Without understanding it, they will not know how to distinguish true Reality from false. For Plato, the true Reality is grasped only by the mind.

In *The Republic* he writes regarding the Theory of Forms:

> We distinguish between the many particular things which we call beautiful or good, and absolute beauty and goodness. Similarly, with all other collections of things, we say there is corresponding to each set a single, unique Form, which we call an absolute reality.[31]

Plato also equates this higher 'Reality' with the Good, which is timeless in its perfection. In a discussion about the nature of God, he defines God as the supreme realization of this perfection, scorning the Homeric pantheon in which the gods change themselves into different beings like magicians. 'Any change must be for the worse, for God is perfect Goodness.'

Plato's Theory of Forms is the philosophical basis for the Christian doctrine of Original Sin, in which the very act of conception is viewed as a falling away from the perfection of God into the abysmal world of appearances, of suffering and of death. It provided the allegory of Pandora and the Fall of Man with a powerful philosophical basis. Before this Fall, autonomous man lived in a state of harmony with God. A falling away from God is, inevitably, with the intervention of woman, a falling away from the highest good. This dualistic vision of reality denigrated the world of the senses, placing it in an eternal struggle with the achievement of the highest form of knowledge: the knowledge of God. This vision profoundly influenced Christian thinkers in their view of women, who literally as well as figuratively, embodied what is scorned as transient, mutable and contemptible.

If Plato's Theory of Forms made misogyny philosophically respectable, Aristotle (384–322 BC), Plato's pupil, made it scientifically respectable. Because much of Aristotle's science appears to the modern mind as ludicrous, it is easy to forget that his doctrines dominated Western thinking about the world for close to 2,000 years. It was not until the scientific revolution of the seventeenth century that his ideas were overthrown. 'Ever since the beginning of the seventeenth century, almost every serious intellectual advance has had to begin with an attack on some Aristotelian doctrine,' observed Bertrand Russell.[32]

Aristotle has been described as one of the most ferocious misogynists of all time. His views on women take two forms: scientific and social. Although at times Aristotle was a precise observer of the natural world – his descriptions of various species impressed Charles Darwin – his observations of women were decidedly warped. As a sign of women's inferiority, he referenced the fact that they did not grow bald – 'proof' of their more childlike nature. He also claimed that women had fewer teeth than men, about which Bertrand Russell is said to have commented: 'Aristotle would never have made this mistake if he had allowed his wife to open her mouth once in a while.'[33]

Aristotle introduced the concept of purpose as fundamental to science. The purpose of things, including all living things, is to become what they are. In the absence of any knowledge of genetics, or of evolution, Aristotle saw purpose as the realization of each thing's potential to be itself. In a sense, this is a materialistic version of Plato's Theory of Forms: there is an Ideal Fish of which all the actual fishes are different realizations. The ideal is their purpose.

When applied to human beings, notably to women, this has unfortunate but predictable results; it becomes a justification of inequality rather than an explanation for it. The most pernicious example is seen in Aristotle's theory of generation.

This assumes different purposes for men and women: 'the male is by nature superior and the female inferior; and the one rules, and the other is ruled; the principle of necessity extends to all mankind.' Therefore, according to Aristotle, the male semen must carry the soul or spirit, and all the potential for the person to be fully human. The female, the recipient of the male seed, provides merely the matter, the nutritive environment. The male is the active principle, the mover, the female the passive, the moved. The full potential of the child is reached only if it is born male; if the 'cold constitution' of the female predominates, through an excess of menstrual fluid in the womb, then the child will fail to reach its full human potential and the result is female. 'For the female is, as it were, a mutilated male,' Aristotle concludes.[34]

Much of Aristotle's discussion of women takes place in the context of his treatment of slaves. Slaves, like women, are purposed by nature to be the way they are. Aristotle argues, however, that slaves lack the 'deliberative faculty', whereas this *is* granted to women. Nonetheless, this faculty is 'without authority'. Obedience is seen as a woman's natural state, in which she achieves her purpose. And women and slaves are similar in one important respect: their inferiority to their ruler – a master in the slave's case, and a husband in the woman's – is permanent and unchanging.

The consequences of seeing females as mutilated males could be heard at night, in the world of Classical Antiquity, when newborns' cries disrupted the silence. 'If – good luck to you! – you bear offspring, if it is a male, let it live; if it is female, expose it,' wrote Hilarion to his wife Alis, in 1 BC, testifying to a custom that lasted until Christianity became the dominant religion of the Roman Empire.[35] Unwanted infants were abandoned on rubbish dumps. The majority of those exposed were deformed or sickly males or 'mutilated males' (baby

girls). It was such a common practice that the cries of the
abandoned babies are unlikely to have disturbed the citizens'
repose. Archaeologists studying burial remains in Athens of
the seventh century BC made the startling discovery that there
were twice as many men as women interred in the plots. By 18
BC, the historian Dio Cassius was lamenting that there were
not enough women for upper class men to marry. Females, one
scholar wrote, were 'selectively eliminated'. When combined
with high mortality rates during childbirth and abortion, this
practice ensured that men always outnumbered women, in
significant ratios.[36] But not all the exposed daughters died.
Because abandoned infants were automatically reduced to
slave status, brothel owners frequented dumps, searching
for baby girls to raise as prostitutes. We will never know
how many millions of Pandora's daughters ended up on the
rubbish dumps of Greece and Rome – some dying of hunger
and cold; others, more 'fortunate', destined for a life of
prostitution.

A population imbalance in favour of men has been associated with lower social status for women. Today, we find this
in parts of India and China, where the selective abortion of
female foetuses has meant fewer women than men, and
women's status suffers accordingly. Women become 'scarce
goods' and are confined to the narrow roles of marriage and
child-rearing.

Where females outnumber males, on the other hand, they
enjoy a corresponding rise in status.[37] Sparta has been cited as
proof of this phenomenon. The victor of the Peloponnesian
War, and the model for Plato's Republic, Sparta was something of an anomaly: It practised infanticide, but did not
discriminate between males and females, only between healthy
and sickly babies. All healthy babies were raised and, since
males tend to be sicklier than females at birth and have more

complications, fewer females were exposed than males. The fact that Sparta was a militaristic state and frequently at war further drastically increased the male mortality rate. Moreover, Spartan women married at an older age than was typical at that time, so they had a better chance of surviving pregnancy. Because women were expected to be strong in order to be fit mothers of Spartan warriors, their health was of concern to the state. To the horror, and no doubt fascination, of the rest of Greece, they exercised naked, took part in athletic games, and generally tended to be stronger and fitter.

> Dear Spartan girl with a delightful face,
> Washed with the rosy spring, how fresh you look,
> In the easy stride of your sleek slenderness.
> Why, you could strangle a bull.[38]

Much to the outrage of Aristotle and other conventional moralists, Spartan women even wore short, revealing tunics. They were able to inherit their husband's property and manage it. By the fourth century BC they possessed two-fifths of all Spartan land. The result was a seeming paradox – a militaristic society where women enjoyed greater freedoms and higher status than in Athens, the home of democracy.

Sparta faded into oblivion, its treatment of women cited only as an unnatural folly. Plato and Aristotle, on the other hand, survived to become the twin pillars of philosophic and scientific thinking in the Western world, supporting the massive edifice of Christianity. Plato's Theory of Forms, with its inherent contempt for the physical world, and Aristotle's biological dualism, in which females were seen as failed males, provided the intellectual apparatus for the centuries of misogyny that were to follow.

2

WOMEN AT THE GATES: MISOGYNY IN ANCIENT ROME

Roman women were the Greek male nightmare come true. They defied the misogynistic dictate (attributed to the Athenian statesman Pericles) that a good woman is one who is not talked about, even in praise. Obeying this had consigned the good women of fifth-century BC Athens to complete oblivion; today, not a single one is known by name. But the women of Rome made themselves known; a few have been talked about ever since. Messalina, whose name became synonymous with sexual excess; Agrippina, the woman of ruthless, 'unnatural' ambition who murdered her way to the top; Sempronia, the intellectual who abandoned the female sphere to enter the dangerous male world of conspiracy and revolution; Cleopatra, the brilliant seductress who plotted to rule the Empire and plunged it into civil war; and Julia, the emperor's rebellious daughter who defied her father's plans and threw the state into crisis. They emerge from the pages of Rome's historians and poets as flesh-and-blood examples of how men viewed women. Much of what is said about them is far from flattering. But men's vitriol proves as powerful a historical preservative for women as does their desire. These recorded sentiments are an indication of the impact women made and the obstacles they overcame, including some of the most fearsome misogynistic laws ever codified.

The Romans were not original thinkers. They did not produce a new theory or philosophy to justify the oppression and dehumanization of women. The stereotypes that evolved in Greek culture were good enough for them (as they have been for many succeeding cultures, including our own). But Roman writers allow us to see behind them. In the literary and historical portraits of the handful of extraordinary women who helped shape one of the greatest civilizations the world has ever seen, we get a glimpse of their struggle to assert themselves.

A difference quickly emerges between the misogyny of the Greeks and that found in Rome. Greek misogyny is based on fears of what women might do if they were free to do it. However, as far as is known, if women challenged men, these actions were confined to their private world and only made public through the realm of the Greek imagination. But from the start, Roman women openly challenged the prevailing misogyny and made public their feelings and demands. Roman women protested their fate and took to the streets. In Rome, the veil of their anonymity was lifted. Women entered the public sphere, and made history. They intervened in wars and stopped them; they took to the streets in protest at government policy and changed it; they murdered their husbands; a few trained and fought as gladiators in the arena (evoking worrying images of Amazons); they subverted the authority of their fathers; they even sought personal satisfaction in their relationships, and rejected their role as breeders of rulers; and, perhaps most disturbingly of all, they came tantalizingly close to political power. They provoked a backlash which mustered some of the biggest guns that literature and history have ever aimed at them.

The context in which this battle was waged was the greatest and most successful empire the world has ever produced, an empire of some sixty million people that at its peak stretched from Scotland to Iraq and embraced a bewildering variety of cultures and peoples. Rome, its capital, was the largest city that had ever existed, with a population in the first century AD of between one and two million. It was the New York of its day, a city of savage spectacles and immense grandeur, teeming with people of different races from every corner of the vast, sprawling Empire.

Of those millions, only a comparatively few names have been preserved. They are, overwhelmingly, the names of those who made up society's upper echelons, contending for honour, power and wealth in a theatre every bit as dangerous and bloody as that of the arena, where gladiators fought to their deaths under the burning Roman sun to the cheers and howls of the Roman mob.

It is in this arena of the ruling class that, over 2,000 years later, we find the names of nearly all of the Roman women still known to us. They were defined by their relationships to men: as daughters, sisters, mistresses, wives, and mothers. Like the heroines of the Greek tragedies, they fought to promote the interests of their kith and kin. But this was no play. In Rome, it was a matter of life and death.

As in Greece, the first major obstacle that a woman faced in life was the threat of being deprived of it at birth. In Rome, this threat was codified in a way that encouraged female infanticide. Laws attributed to Romulus, the city's mythological founder, decreed that only 'every male child and the first-born female' be reared – an invitation to expose other daughters born afterwards.

Marriage was the next hurdle for women, which they faced upon reaching puberty. In early Rome, circa the seventh century BC, they were subject to some of the most oppressive marriage laws imaginable. As a wife, a woman was placed under the absolute rule of her husband, who had the power of life or death over her. Sitting in judgement with his wife's relatives, a husband was 'given power to pass sentence in cases of adultery and . . . if any wife was found drinking wine Romulus allowed the death penalty for both crimes.'[39] If ever there was a law that actively encouraged wife battering, this was it. Egnatius Metellus, the bearer of one of the great aristocratic names in Roman history, was held up as a sterling example of how a man should act in a good marriage. Once, he arrived home to find his wife drinking wine. He promptly took a cudgel and bludgeoned her to death. According to the historian Valerius Maximus:

> Not only did no one charge him with a crime, but no one even blamed him. Everyone considered this an excellent example of one who had justly paid the penalty for violating the laws of sobriety. Indeed, any woman who immoderately seeks the use of wine closes the door on all virtues and opens it to vices.[40]

Valerius Maximus also quotes with approval Gaius Sulpicius Gallus, who divorced his wife because he caught her with her hair uncovered in public. In words that could have been uttered by a twenty-first century Saudi Arabian prince, he explained: 'The law prescribes for you my eyes alone to which you may prove your beauty. For these eyes you should provide the ornaments of beauty, for these be lovely . . .'[41]

Another example is given of the man who divorced his wife when he saw her talking to a woman friend who was an ex-slave on the grounds that such female liaisons nourished potential wrongdoing and it was better to prevent the sin from being committed than to punish it afterwards.[42] The laws also allowed the death penalty to be imposed on a daughter-in-law for striking her father-in-law. Needless to say, the power of divorce was granted only to the husband.

The Romans inherited the Greek preoccupation with female virtue, and linked it to the honour of the family and the welfare of the state. The most famous example of an early Roman matron's virtue in action was that of Lucretia, a model of female behaviour much alluded to by moralists in the later, 'decadent' years of the Empire. She remains an example of the dangers women faced when expected to live up to moral standards based on the misogynistic notion which equates sexual purity in women with goodness. Lucretia's husband Collatinus made the mistake of boasting about her goodness to the lustful king of Rome, Tarquinius Superbus. Reverence for something is frequently accompanied by the urge to defile it: symbols of sexual purity probably arouse lust more often than pornographic images. Driven by the urge to profane this example of matronly virtue, Tarquinius threatens Lucretia that if she does not sleep with him, he will murder both her and her slave and leave their naked corpses in the same bed. Knowing the humiliation and horror that would fall upon her husband and family if it were thought she had made love to a slave, Lucretia chooses the lesser of the two evils. Even though clearly forced to endure Tarquinius' lust, under Roman law she is still guilty of adultery. After telling her story to her husband and her family, she stabs herself to death. Like so many women who have suffered rape, Lucretia blamed herself, and (as St Augustine so wisely pointed out) punished herself for the wrongs inflicted by others.[43] Misogyny always confronts women with the same dilemma. Whether they are 'good' girls or 'bad' girls, they are forced into the same conundrum: they still arouse lust in men for which they, not those who desire them, are held responsible.

The story had a happy ending for Rome, if not for poor Lucretia. Enraged, Romans overthrew Tarquinius and ended the rule of kings. They established the Republic, which was to last nearly five centuries before it gave way to imperial autocracy. But Lucretia has continued to be used as an example throughout the centuries to bully women into accepting that they are worth nothing more than their virtue.

Early Rome also presents us, on a massive scale, with the first example of date rape in human history. Moreover, the 'rape of the Sabine women' set the precedent for future acts of political intervention by women. Short of women, the founders of Rome invited people from the neighbouring Sabine tribe to a party. At a given signal from Romulus, the Romans seized the best-looking young women and carried them off. According to the historian Livy, the Romans treated the captive women with delicacy. Romulus persuaded them to stay and marry their captors. The most unbelievable part of the entire story is that he did so by reading them the Roman marriage laws to show how superior their laws were to those of the Sabines. A war ensued between the Sabines, intent on revenge, and the Romans. At one point in the battle, not wishing to see their new husbands fighting with their brothers and fathers, the Sabine women thrust themselves between the ranks and brought hostilities to a halt.

The Romans accepted this tale as part of the city's early history, crediting the women with achieving in reality what Aristophanes portrayed only as fantasy in his comedy *Lysistrata*, where he tells how the women of Greece went on a sex strike to stop the Peloponnesian War.

Until the time of Julius Caesar, a temple dedicated to the fortune of women stood on the Via Latina that runs south out of Rome. It commemorated women's intervention in another war, after Rome had banished one of its most successful generals, Coriolanus, because of his overweening arrogance. In revenge, he led an army of the city's enemies against his home. As he approached the city, ready to shed the blood of his fellow citizens, all seemed lost until a delegation of Roman women (including his mother and wife) blocked his path and persuaded him to turn back. The city was saved, and thanks to women, again a costly war was ended.

Though they lived under oppressive laws, Roman women were never kept in the Oriental-style seclusion to which Greek women were subjected. Greek visitors to Rome commented with some amazement on the differences. One such was Cornelius Nepos, who journeyed to Rome in the first century BC and observed:

> Much that in Rome we hold to be correct is thought shocking in Greece. No Roman thinks it an embarrassment to take his wife to a dinner party. At home the wife holds first place in the house and is the centre of its social life. Things are very different in Greece, where the wife is never present at dinner, unless it is a family party, and spends all her time in a remote part of the house called The Women's Quarter, which is never entered by a man unless he is a very close relation.[44]

In an even more shocking display of their freedom, Roman women extended their tradition of public intervention to protesting on the streets. They launched the first recorded public protest movement ever organized by women. In 205 BC, during a war with the Carthaginian general Hannibal, Rome passed the Oppian Laws, legislation curtailing the amount of gold women could possess and restricting public displays of decoration and luxury in women's dress. Ten years later, with Carthage safely vanquished, Roman upper-class women demanded to know why the Oppian Laws were still on the statute books. After much agitation to abolish them, the Senate decided to debate the issue. On the day of the debate, the women flocked into the Forum, where the senate house – the ancient seat of government – still stands, to lobby for their demands.

The main opponent to the repeal was Cato the Elder, the most formidable orator of his time. Cato was a *nouveau riche*, but he identified with Rome's founding fathers and old aristocracy, expounding the ancient virtues of hard work, abstemiousness, and plain living which, he claimed, had made Rome great. Like many a professional puritan, he paraded his simple life style with great ostentation. According to the historian Livy, as recorded in *The Early History of Rome*, in a misogynistic *tour de force* Cato declared:

If every married man had been concerned to ensure that his own wife looked up to him and respected his rightful position as her husband, we should not have half this trouble with women en masse. Instead, women have become so powerful that our independence has been lost in our own homes and is now being trampled and stamped underfoot in public. We have failed to retrain them as individuals, and now they have combined to reduce us to our present panic . . . It made me blush to push my way through a positive regiment of women a few minutes ago in order to get here. My respect for the position and modesty of them as individuals – a respect which I do not feel for them as a mob – prevented my doing anything as consul which would suggest the use of force. Otherwise I should have said to them, 'What do you mean by rushing out in public in this unprecedented fashion, blocking the streets and shouting out to men who are not your husbands? Could you not have asked your questions at home, and have asked them of your husbands?' [. . .]

Woman is a violent and uncontrolled animal, and it is no good giving her the reins and expecting her not to kick over the traces. No, you have got to keep the reins firmly in your own hands . . . Suppose you allow them to acquire or to extort one right after another, and in the end to achieve complete equality with men, do you think that you will find them bearable? Nonsense. Once they have achieved equality, they will be your masters . . .[45]

Cato's speech failed. The Senate voted to overturn the Oppian Laws. But the same basic argument has been used ever since to deny women everything from the vote to access to birth control. Cato states it with startling clarity: give women freedom in one sphere, and the floodgates of immorality will open in all the others.

Within a decade of the repeal of the Oppian Laws, an extraordinary scandal rocked Rome, which Livy, writing at a later, more 'decadent' period, uses as proof that Cato was right. It led to a ferocious crackdown on unorthodox religious practices, foreshadowing the witch-hunts of the Middle Ages.

Roman state religion was a very masculine affair. It involved the appeasement of dominant gods through prescribed ritual and sacrifice. Cults were divided along class lines; practices that allowed patricians and plebeians to mix socially were frowned upon. Several cults were in the care of women: the goddess Fortuna, for example, was meant to bring women luck in their sex lives. There was an altar dedicated to Plebeian Chastity, which Livy laments was much neglected. The most famous women's cult was that of the Vestal Virgins. Vesta was the goddess of the hearth. She guarded the sacred eternal flame of Rome that burned in the deepest recesses of her temple, one of the most beautiful in the Forum. Six Vestals, selected from the noblest families, tended the flame. According to an ancient and deeply rooted belief, should it go out, Rome would fall. Any Vestal who allowed this to occur was scourged; any who lost her virginity during her tenure (which lasted 30 years), was buried alive. Freud has suggested that women were entrusted to protect the eternal flame because, given their anatomy, they were less likely to urinate on it to extinguish it![46] Whether or not this was the case, by 186 BC the traditional Roman cults were tempting fewer women. Increasingly, Eastern mystery religions and such cults as that of Bacchus, were attracting devotees and becoming especially appealing to women, offering an emotional release from the stifling moral regime under which they lived.

As recounted by Livy, in 186 BC a former slave girl confessed to the authorities that she had been involved in the cult of Bacchus, the wine god, whose worship had spread to Rome from Greece. Prompted by fears for her lover, who was under pressure from his mother to join the cult, the freedwoman painted a lurid picture of Roman matrons gathering by night to indulge in wine binges and orgiastic sex. 'Unnatural' sex acts had become normal and, she claimed, were part of the initiation rites. Anyone who resisted the cult's sexual demands was killed, and their bodies secretly buried. Women from the most distinguished families, dressed up in animal skins as devotees of Bacchus, got drunk, became possessed, and with loose hair flowing wildly behind them, went racing through the night, crying and screaming gibberish. The cult followers came from all social classes, including slaves. For the Romans, always on the look-out for slave rebellion, such a gathering would have seemed socially as well as sexually subversive, a threat to the prevailing order.

The former slave's frightening tale strikingly resembles the accusations of sexual abandonment and promiscuity brought against medieval women thought to be witches. The female Bacchae, like the later women accused of witchcraft, were accused of murdering anyone who defied them, including their children. Some were said to perform black magic. We see the portrait of the medieval witch taking shape: women, young and beautiful, or hags with serpents entwined in their hair, abandoning themselves in drunken orgies, making hellish concoctions at the dead of night out of the blood of frogs, bones and the remains of children they have murdered. This misogynistic portrait of female wickedness was born some twelve centuries before the first witch was burned in Europe. The Roman authorities arrested and executed the men and handed over the women cultists to their families where the *pater familias* administered the death penalty. As many as 7,000 people were arrested and executed.

The association of upper-class women with plots and conspiracies preoccupied another Roman historian Sallust (86–35 BC). In 63 BC a gang of reckless patricians, driven to desperation by debt, conspired to overthrow the state and seize power. At their head was Lucius Catiline a man whom Sallust in his account of the plot describes as being of 'powerful intellect and great physical strength', but having a vicious and depraved nature.[47] Sallust, himself a failed revolutionary, singled out one aspect of the conspiracy as especially worrying:

> About this time, Catiline is said to have gained many adherents of every condition, including a number of women who in their earlier days had lived extravagantly on money by prostituting themselves, and then, when advancing age reduced their incomes without changing their luxurious tastes, had run headlong into debt. These women, he thought, would do good service by acting as agitators among the city slaves and organizing acts of incendiarism; their husbands, too, could be either induced to join his cause, or murdered.[48]

Only one of these upper-class prostitutes turned revolutionaries is named – Sempronia. Descended from one of the most renowned families in Rome she was:

a woman who had committed many crimes that showed her to
have the reckless daring of a man. Fortune had favoured her
abundantly, not only with birth and beauty, but with a good
husband and children. Well educated in Greek and Latin
literature, she had greater skill in lyre-playing and dancing
than there is any need for a respectable woman to acquire . . .
There was nothing that she set a smaller value on than
seemliness and chastity . . . Her passions were so ardent that
she more often made advances to men than they did to her.
Many times already she had broken a solemn promise, repu-
diated a debt by perjury, and been an accessory to murder . . .
Yet, her abilities were not to be despised. She could write
poetry, crack a joke, and converse at will with decorum, tender
feeling, or wantonness; she was in fact a woman of ready wit
and considerable charm.[19]

Sempronia was for a time Julius Caesar's mistress, and one
of her children, Decimus Brutus, was widely rumoured to be
Caesar's. (Brutus was more successful as a conspirator than his
mother, being one of the group of assassins who murdered
Caesar in 44 BC).

Catiline's plot was betrayed, and the conspirators executed.
However, Sempronia escaped unscathed, and later historians
have questioned Sallust's allegations of her complicity. What is
not in doubt is the mixture of disapproval and powerful
fascination with which the historian rendered Sempronia's
portrait. Dancing, writing poetry, having affairs, plotting with
revolutionaries, stirring up slaves; it is certain that had there
been marijuana in Rome, Sempronia would have smoked it.
She is the prototype of the bohemian intellectual woman
against whom in all her many manifestations moralists for
centuries will rant and rail. In Sallust's eyes, her real fault was
that she was a 'modern' woman. His account is meant to be a

warning of what happens when women pursue pleasure as openly as do men. Women's taste for extravagance leads them into sexual misbehaviour which in turn transforms them into desperate revolutionaries, prepared even to consort with slaves. No more anxious and worrisome association was imaginable for Roman rulers than that between rebellious women and restless slaves.

In the years following the failed conspiracy, Rome was convulsed by the horrors of a civil war which finally brought down the republican form of government and replaced it with the one-family rule of the Caesars. As a handful of powerful families began to struggle for dominance over the growing Empire, and political action in the public arena became more dangerous, women were forced back into a more familiar area of competition. Access to power meant access to the ruler or a likely prospect; it meant the struggle to promote the prospects of their offspring, especially the males. The closer to the source of power they were, the deadlier the struggle became, providing the moralizing misogynists of imperial Rome with an entire gallery of female rogues who defied the standards of modesty, restraint and passivity expected of the traditional matron.

The most notable of these women who cast a long shadow over the twilight years of the Republic could not be expected to be an icon of matronly values. Indeed, Cleopatra (69–30 BC) was not even a Roman, but an Egyptian pharaoh who was a direct descendant of one of Alexander the Great's Macedonian generals. Romans seized on her as dramatic proof of the evils of allowing women to have an influence on matters of state and of public policy. They helped make Cleopatra one of perhaps the two women from the ancient world – the other being Helen of Troy – whose name is still recognizable to ordinary people today. The deep impression that Cleopatra made on Roman and Greek historians, poets and chroniclers was passed on to Shakespeare, Bernard Shaw and Hollywood, where as portrayed by Elizabeth Taylor she was the subject of one of the biggest flops in the history of film-making.

Cleopatra was the descendant of Ptolemy, one of the Macedonian generals who inherited parts of the vast empire of Alexander the Great upon his death in 323 BC. She was the product of the Hellenistic period, which begins with Alexander's death and ends in 30 BC with her suicide and the absorption of Egypt into the Roman Empire. During the intervening three centuries, Greek women had escaped from many of the suffocating restrictions of the Classical period and enjoyed improvements in their status, including more liberal marriage contracts and educational opportunities. They also took a more prominent role in political affairs. Cleopatra was the last and most famous of a line of Hellenistic queens who took part in the dynastic battles which raged for control of the remains of Alexander's empire.

Her affairs with Julius Caesar and, after his assassination, with his lieutenant Mark Antony, have become the stuff of tragedy, high romance and Hollywood kitsch. Both men were charmed more by her wit and intelligence than by her beauty. According to the biographer Plutarch, she could speak ten languages, converse with Caesar into the small hours of the morning, and respond in kind to the bawdy banter of Antony. She was the only one of the long line of Ptolemies who could speak the native language of Egypt. Her lively intellect extended into many spheres – she even penned a treatise on hairdressing and cosmetics.[50] But to her contemporaries in Rome, she was a devious, bewitching, and overweeningly ambitious seductress, who had to be stopped at all costs. In the contest between Octavian and Antony for absolute imperial power, his enemies portrayed the latter as a gormless soldier. The accusation that she was using Antony to gain control of the Empire became a vital part of Octavian's propaganda. As with Sempronia, Cleopatra's enemies linked her intellectual independence to her wanton sexuality. It was typical of the age-old campaign to prove that women who are smart enough to think for themselves have no morals; or if they have, will surely lose them. So Horace and other Roman poets of the period directed their invective at her alleged promiscuity. She was nicknamed in Greek 'Meriochane', which means, 'she who parts for a thousand men'. In a pornographic fantasy that eclipses *Debbie Does Dallas*, her detractors have her performing fellatio on a hundred Roman nobles in one day.

Antony was clearly comfortable with accomplished and intelligent women. His wife Fulvia was the daughter of Sempronia, and has been described by one modern historian as an 'Amazon'.[51] His political enemies used this as proof that he had been 'unmanned' by such women and therefore was not fit to rule the Empire. After Antony's defeat in 31 BC, Cleopatra tried to seduce Octavian, but he stayed away from her. Rather than be dragged to Rome in chains to grace his triumph, she committed suicide.

However, Cleopatra lives on, while the obscenities intended to insult her are seen now for what they were and instead demean the men who made them. It is her wit and charm that triumphed in the end, as celebrated by Shakespeare in some of the most famous lines ever written about a woman:

> Age cannot wither her, nor custom stale
> Her infinite variety. Other women cloy
> The appetite they feed, but she makes hungry
> Where most she satisfies. For vilest things
> Become themselves in her, that the holy priests
> Bless her for when she is riggish.[52]

As the Roman Republic passed into history, a few women made their voices heard publicly as speakers and advocates, much to the outrage of the historian Valerius Maximus. 'We must be silent no longer about these women whom neither the condition of their nature nor the cloak of modesty could keep silent in the Forum and the courts,' he wrote.[53] Thanks to his determination to register his disapproval, we know they existed. Most notable among them was Hortensia, the daughter of one of Rome's greatest orators Quintus Hortensius. In an incident that has gone into the history books as a mere footnote, she used her eloquence to directly intervene in political affairs. By 42 BC in Rome, the powerful triumvirate of Mark Antony, Octavian (later to become the emperor Augustus), and Marcus Lepidus ruled as a three-man dictatorship, mercilessly purging their political opponents, 2,300 of whom were arrested and executed. Starved for cash, the triumvirate imposed a heavy tax on 1,400 upper-class women. The women marched in protest, and tried to speak to the womenfolk of the three rulers, hoping for a sympathetic hearing. They were only partially successful, but managed to force their way into the Forum to the speaker's rostrum.

According to Valerius Maximus, 'no man dared take their case.' Hortensia stepped forward and 'pleaded their case before the triumvirs, both firmly and successfully.' Something remarkable then happened, both in the history of misogyny and in the history of women (which to a large extent is the story of the struggle against misogyny). For the first time the question of franchise was raised, if only by implication. During her powerful speech, which focuses on the sufferings of women during war, Hortensia asks, 'Why should we pay taxes when we have no part in the honours, the commands, the statecraft, for which you contend against each other with such harmful results?'[54]

Though there is no outright demand for extending the vote to women, Hortensia's words come very close to the demand the American revolutionaries voiced many centuries later: no taxation without representation.[55]

The women's protest of 42 BC is the high point of their public activism in Rome and the last such demonstration they ever undertook in this era. It is also the last public protest by women aimed at political change that we know about in the history of Western civilization until the nineteenth century. Then the rise of the suffragette movement made the demand for the vote central to the campaign for women's rights.

Out of the turmoil that destroyed the Republic and replaced it with one-family rule came the conservative backlash against women. Fretting at women's freedoms, moralists took up the refrain, 'less lust and bigger families'. No sooner had Octavian become the Emperor Augustus in 27 BC than the historian Livy began to write his history of Rome (as seen from the winner's point of view) and expressed clearly the new regime's moral intentions:

> I hope everyone will pay keen attention to the moral life of earlier times . . . and will appreciate the subsequent decline in discipline and in moral standards, the collapse and disintegration of morality down to the present day. For we have now reached a point where our degeneracy is intolerable – and so are the measures by which alone it can be reformed.[56]

As in the 1960s and 1970s, the problem was that women were having fewer children but more sex. The resurgence of the 'family values' movement was an attempt to reverse that trend. The Roman state, however, had more coercive power than the moral majoritarians of 1980s America.

The old strict form of marriage, which had placed a wife

under the absolute authority of her husband, lapsed with the centuries, and was replaced by more informal arrangements. Clearly, husbands were no longer made of the stern stuff of Rome's founding fathers and had grown too tolerant over the years. Some were refusing to divorce their wives when they caught them in adultery. A few husbands were accused of even profiting by it. Liberalism of this sort was judged to be the cause of the rot which moralists saw all around them. Augustus drafted a series of laws, known as the Lex Julia, aimed at encouraging men and women to marry and at restoring the traditional Roman family. Augustus imposed penalties on those who had not married by a certain age, and rewarded those who did and fathered children. He revived the ancient law allowing fathers to kill their daughters, and husbands their wives, if caught in the sexual act; husbands were again obliged to divorce their adulterous wives or face severe penalties. Augustus took the jurisdiction of adultery cases away from the family and handed it over to a public court. Divorce was not enough. Augustus wanted erring wives dragged through the courts and punished. The wronged husband was given sixty days after the divorce to prosecute his former wife. If he proved too soft-hearted, she could still be prosecuted by any member of the public who was above the age of 25 – surely one of the greatest encouragements ever codified for self-righteous busybodies who enjoyed the spectacle of a woman being publicly disgraced. Although the new law allowed a woman to divorce her husband for adultery, it did not oblige her to do so; and she was barred from bringing a criminal prosecution against him. That is, adultery was a public offence only for women.[57]

The new laws also made it an offence for a man to have sexual relations with any woman outside of marriage, except a prostitute. Applied to upper-class women, it meant they were not permitted to have any form of sexual liaison at all, unless they were married. In protest, some women put their names on the registry of prostitutes kept by the Roman authorities who oversaw the city's 35 official brothels. This desperate dodge was eliminated later when Tiberius, Augustus' successor, barred any woman who came from a respectable family (that is middle-class or senatorial) from registering as a prostitute.

Augustus proclaimed this new legislation from the ancient rostrum, the speaker's platform in the Forum, which he redecorated with marble and bronze ships' prows. They are the only laws passed in his long reign to which he gave his name (Julia, named in honour of his family, the Julian, into which Julius Caesar had adopted him), an indication of the importance he attached to them. It was one of his proudest moments as ruler. Augustus, it was declared, had refounded Rome. Shortly thereafter, in 2 BC, the Senate proclaimed him Father of his Country, the first Roman ever to receive this honour. But the Lex Julia was deeply unpopular. Given the moral freedoms Roman men and women enjoyed, a backlash against them was inevitable. For the proud emperor, it came in the most humiliating form imaginable.

Within weeks, perhaps days, of the Senate's proclamation, Julia, the thirty-seven-year-old daughter of the 'Father of his Country', made an incredible mockery of his laws and shook the foundations of the new moral order he had attempted to impose. Had there been a tabloid newspaper, its front page would doubtless have screamed: 'Julia in Orgy Shock: Sex Romp on Rostrum'.

According to the Stoic philosopher and imperial adviser Seneca: 'She had received lovers in droves. She had roamed the city in nocturnal revels, choosing for her pleasures the Forum, and the very Rostrum from which her father had proposed the adultery law.' She was accused of seeking every kind of gratification from casual lovers.[58] She was even alleged to have hired herself out as a prostitute. (The same allegations would later be made against Messalina, the wife of the Emperor Claudius.)

The anecdotes that survive about Julia, Augustus' only child, depict a witty, strong-willed young woman. Once, her father commented unfavourably on the immodesty of her dress. The next day when she appeared in proper attire, he complimented her, to which she replied: 'Today I dressed for my father's eyes, yesterday for a man's.'[59]

Daughters' talents or ambitions, however, were of little importance compared to their ability to produce sons. Between the ages of fourteen when Julia was first married and twenty-eight, she had three husbands, all chosen for her by her father who was desperate to have a male heir. She must at times have felt like the imperial incubator. She dutifully produced three boys and two daughters, all with her second husband, Agrippa, her father's right-hand man, who was over twice her age when they married. But none of her sons survived to fulfil her father's dreams of finding a male heir of his own direct lineage. It was one of her two daughters, Agrippina, who would go on to produce a male heir to the throne – the emperor Caligula.

Julia's behaviour was more than just a wild fling. The orgy on the rostrum was timed (as well as placed) for maximum effect. The very year that Augustus was declared Father of his Country, his daughter demonstrated his complete failure as a father to his own family. She knew how a daughter can most keenly wound her father. Her promiscuity was the revenge of a daughter who rebelled in the only way that was open to her – to seek her own personal gratification, as Seneca notes with horror. She was playing sexual politics, forced to do so because her body had become a political commodity. Paradoxically, by giving it away she was reclaiming it as her own. But Julia's acts were acts of political defiance as well as of personal protest. Augustus' laws were deeply unpopular (as Livy noted), nowhere more so than within the intellectual coterie in which Julia moved and from which evolved a counter-cultural rebellion. Something similar happened in America and other Western democracies with the sexual revolution of the 1960s against the conservative, family-oriented moral code of the previous decades.

Augustus, enraged, did not try to keep the scandal secret. He dragged his daughter and her friends before the courts, accusing her of promiscuity, adultery, and prostituting herself. The court heard the full, lurid story. She was condemned. He banished her forever. She died 16 years later without ever seeing him or Rome again.

The stage was now set for one of the great creations of misogyny. Cato the Elder had warned his fellow Romans long ago, when women were demanding the right to wear gorgeous clothes, that 'woman is a violent and uncontrolled animal' to whom any concession of freedom will lead to complete abandonment and the collapse of all moral standards. That fear was embodied in Messalina, the wife of the emperor Claudius (10 BC–AD 54).

Messalina was the great-granddaughter of Augustus' sister Octavia, who married Mark Antony after Fulvia died. She married Claudius in AD 37, when she was probably still a teenager (though the year of her birth is not known for certain) and he was almost 47. Four years later, after the assassination of Caligula, Claudius succeeded him to become emperor. He would last for 13 years. Perhaps the most unlikely of Rome's rulers, he is portrayed as a rather scholarly eccentric, maladroit, and consumed with the pursuit of arcane history. In dramatic contrast, his young wife has become identified with a psycho-sexual disorder: 'Excessive heterosexuality (promiscuity) or what is known as the Messalina complex . . .'[60]

According to Havelock Ellis, one of the twentieth century's most famous sex experts: 'Sex is no real pleasure to the Messalina type. It's only an attempt to find relief from deeper unhappiness. You might call it a flight into sex.'[61]

In modern times, various theories have been expounded to explain 'the Messalina type', from frigidity to thwarted maternal instincts to latent lesbianism; more recently, the whole notion of such a thing as nymphomania has been questioned.[62] But the Messalina of history is more than a psychological category. Among other things, she is one of the outstanding examples of how prejudice works as a kind of reductionism.

Messalina's historical importance stems from the fact that she was only the second woman to become a Roman empress. Her sole role model was Livia, the austere wife of Augustus whose private life was as impeccable as any matron's. In but one thing Messalina seems to have imitated her: her determination to get rid of anyone suspected of hostility to her or to her husband, or of harbouring ambitions to supplant her son Britannicus as Claudius' heir. In this, she was brutally efficient, eliminating potential rivals to Julio-Claudian dominance before they could act. But the Messalina that has come down to us is not the ruthless politician but the nymphomaniac, largely thanks to the poet Juvenal's portrait of her in his *Sixth Satire*. In it he accuses her of sneaking through the dark streets as soon as Claudius was asleep, her black hair disguised by a blonde wig, to enter a brothel:

> Look at those peers of the gods, and hear what Claudius
>   suffered.
> Soon as his august wife was sure that her husband was sleeping,
> This imperial whore preferred, to a bed in the palace,
> Some low mattress, put on the hood she wore in the nighttime,
> Sneaked through the streets alone, or with only a single
>   companion,

Hid her black hair in a blonde wig, and entered a brothel.
Reek of old sheets, still warm – her cell was reserved for her,
    empty,
Held in the name of Lycisca. There she took off her dress,
Showed her golden tits, and the parts where Britannicus came
    from,
Took the customers on, with gestures more than inviting,
Asked and received her price and had a wonderful evening,
Then, when the pimp let the girls go home, she sadly departed,
Last of them all to leave, still hot, with a woman's erection,
Tired by her men, but unsatisfied still, her cheeks all
    discoloured,
Rank with the smell of the lamps, filthy, completely disgusting,
Perfumed with the aroma of whore-house, and home, at last, to
    her pillow.[63]

This portrait by Juvenal (AD 50–127) of rampant female sexuality has, like the myths of Pandora and Eve, become proverbial, reducing woman to a voracious vagina, forever unsatisfied. He also uses Messalina to generalize about women:

Their appetites all are the same, no matter what class they come
    from;
High or low, their lusts are all alike . . .[64]

But is his portrait also a myth? Juvenal was writing about sixty years after the reign of Claudius, and the new dynasty under which he lived was still very anti-Julio-Claudian. The virtuous Roman matron had made a comeback in the form of the wives of the emperors Trajan (AD 98–117) and Hadrian (117–138). Besides, Juvenal was a satirist, holding up to ridicule the vices of mankind and society. The satiric method involves taking vices to extremes for comic as well as moral effect. Moralists in any age, whether it is second-century Rome, or twenty-first century America, enjoy nothing so much as horrifying their audiences by playing on their deepest fears and prejudices. How much of a misogynist Juvenal himself was is open to debate, but he was certainly playing to the misogyny of his audience. He did so with remarkable eloquence, as have many misogynists before and since. Juvenal's *Sixth Satire* is yet another instance of what may at first appear to be a paradox about misogyny: it has inspired more great writing than any other prejudice. One cannot imagine anti-Semitism or any other type of bigotry for that matter, producing good poetry. The paradox goes to the very heart of misogyny and its deepest contradiction. Juvenal's portrait of the woman of whom he so strongly disapproves is coloured by fascination and desire. And it is his desire and fascination as much as his indignation that make him eloquent.

Messalina lasted seven years at Claudius' side, during which time it appears he had no knowledge of her sexual adventures. The incident that precipitated her fall from power has perplexed historians. In AD 48 when the emperor was out of Rome, she married the lover who was her current favourite, a handsome aristocrat named Caius Silius, during a bacchanalian festival. The theory that the marriage was part of a plot to replace Claudius as emperor flies in the face of Messalina's record of defending the interests of her son as future ruler. Why would she entrust Britannicus to the care of a stepfather, who already had sons of his own? Her interests and his were best protected by ensuring Claudius survived. The historian Cornelius Tacitus has a more reasonable, less complicated explanation: 'Messalina's adultery was going so smoothly that she was drifting, through boredom, into unfamiliar vices . . . the idea of being called [Silius'] wife appealed to her owing to its sheer outrageousness – a sensualist's ultimate satisfaction.'[65]

Messalina's marriage was the moral equivalent of Julia's sex romp on the rostrum from which her father had pronounced his anti-adultery laws – a defiant act of sexual theatre. But it lacked Julia's political motivation. Messalina was quickly found out and the list of her outrageous sexual misdemeanours handed over to Claudius by the emperor's staff, who were growing concerned at her increasing license. She was ordered to commit suicide. But the young woman's nerve failed her, and an officer of the Praetorian guard stabbed her to death.

For a more contemporary account of Rome's first-century dynastic battles, we must turn to the dark, ironic genius of Tacitus, who broods over the years when the Julio-Claudian family was tightening its blood-stained grip on the administrative machinery that ran the vast Empire. He provides us with extraordinary portraits of the early Caesars and their women. There is none more evocative than that of the woman who succeeded Messalina as empress, Julia Agrippina, the mother of Nero. Agrippina came closer to power than any Roman woman before or after her.

Conservatives and misogynists used Agrippina's extraordinary rise to power as proof that Cato the Elder had been right, when over 200 years earlier he had warned of the dangers of women's emancipation and the fear of their taking political power: 'Once they have achieved equality, they will be your masters . . .'

Agrippina was one of nine children of Germanicus, the emperor Tiberius' popular nephew, and Agrippina the Elder, one of the children of the first Julia, Augustus' doomed daughter. Six children, three boys and three girls, survived into adulthood. Only one, Agrippina's younger sister Drusilla, died of natural causes. All the others were to die violently, victims of the dynastic struggles that shaped the early Empire. Agrippina would live to be the sister, wife and mother of emperors. Malicious gossip has it that she was the lover of all three.

As the great-great-great granddaughter of Julius Caesar's sister, Agrippina inherited an imperious tradition, one as fully realized in her ambitious character as it was in her mother's. Agrippina the Elder, while accompanying her husband on a campaign in Germany, had stopped a panicky legion from abandoning its post by effectively seizing command, and holding an important Rhine crossing until Germanicus and his army returned from a dangerous expedition into the interior. Germanicus was the JFK of Rome, one of the great 'What Ifs' of history, cheated of absolute power by an untimely (and suspicious) death. Agrippina's mother enjoyed the support of a powerful faction within Rome called by Tacitus 'the party of Agrippina', which sought to advance her and her children's claims to supreme power. She had commanded troops, now she commanded a party; she earned herself the opprobrium of being called a 'masculine' woman. But more than that – her 'masculine' ambition inspired fear. Tiberius asked her, 'My girl, do you think you are badly done by if you do not rule?' It finally drove him to exiling her. She starved herself to death in protest and died in AD 33. Her daughter Julia Agrippina was almost 18. She would live to provoke the same name-calling and inspire the same fears.

The younger Agrippina married Claudius, her uncle and third husband, in AD 49, after a special law was passed making marriage between niece and uncle legal. 'From this moment the country was transformed,' wrote Tacitus. 'Complete obedience was accorded to a woman – and not a woman like Messalina who toyed with national affairs to satisfy her appetites. This was a vigorous, almost masculine despotism.'[66]

Within a year, the new wife appeared on official coins alongside Claudius, with the title Augusta, marking the first occasion on which the wife of a living emperor enjoyed this honour. 'The significance of Agrippina's elevation cannot be exaggerated,' wrote one historian. 'Perhaps more than anything else, it conveyed the notion of empress, not, of course, in the technical sense of a person having the formal authority to make legally binding decisions, but as someone who could lay equal claim to the majesty that the office of emperor conveyed.'[67]

In AD 51, after a long war in the new province of Britain, the Celtic rebel Caratacus was brought to Rome in chains. Agrippina appeared with the emperor to meet the triumphant legions and their prisoners, some of whom were freed. Tacitus noted:

> Released from their chains, they offered to Agrippina, conspicuously seated on another dais nearby, the same homage and gratitude as they had given to the emperor. That a woman should sit before Roman standards was an unprecedented novelty. She was asserting her partnership in the empire her ancestors had won.[68]

Her privileges continued to accrue, including the right to receive the supplications of the courtiers and clients who paid homage to Claudius each morning. The sculpted heads of Agrippina from this period show her wearing a diadem, an unheard of honour. At the same time as she was consolidating her power, she was advancing the interests of her son. Claudius formally adopted Nero as his own, thus placing him in front of his own son Britannicus, who was several years younger, in the line of succession. Agrippina's rise to power, however, began to provoke fierce criticism and hostility. Eventually Claudius began to take note. But Agrippina pounced first. In AD 54, Claudius died suddenly, almost certainly poisoned, and Nero was emperor, just two months short of his seventeenth birthday. When the head of the palace guard asked the new emperor for a new password, he replied at once: 'Optima mater' – the Best of Mothers – a grimly ironic beginning for a reign that would be darkened by matricide.

At first Agrippina's political position seemed stronger than ever. Early on in her son's reign, imperial coins were issued in Rome, depicting mother and son facing one another, conveying the impression of joint rule, for which no precedent existed in Roman law. More shocking still to Roman custom, a contemporary relief of the two shows Agrippina placing a laurel wreath, the symbol of military victory, on her son's head. Romans of course suspected that Nero was emperor thanks to his mother, but were appalled that it was so boldly acknowledged. Equally revolutionary was the decision to allow Agrippina to hear the proceedings of the Senate from behind a veiled enclosure specially constructed for the purpose. She had achieved 'the unthinkable'.[69] Public opposition to her was dangerous, but privately the muttering grew louder about her 'female arrogance'.

Agrippina's success in having her role publicly celebrated showed a character unable to accept the 'power behind the throne' destiny reserved for women. Nor did she conceal her rage at aspects of Nero's private life. She no doubt hoped that he would be more like his grandfather Germanicus than his father Domitius, Agrippina's first husband, who had been notorious for his coarseness and brutality. But Nero disappointed her and she made it known. Then he began to fear her. He murdered Britannicus (by poison) in front of her eyes to forestall any attempt she might make to follow through on her foolish threats to install Claudius' son on the throne. Driven by dread, Nero concocted a series of elaborate plots to get rid of her. Mixing comedy with tragedy, he had a collapsible boat built which precipitated her into the Bay of Naples. Agrippina was injured but she swam ashore. Terrified that the people would rally to her support, he dispatched one of his most reliable thugs. In one of the great dramatic scenes from history, Tacitus describes how the murderer and his helpers surrounded Agrippina in her bedroom, under the flickering lamp light. As the assassin raised his sword, she bared her belly and cried: 'Strike here,' pointing to the womb that bore Nero.[70]

The tragedy of Agrippina was in a sense unavoidable. Roman women could become doctors, run shops, practise law and even fight in the arena, but they could not take an overtly political role. Looking back, it seems as foolish and destructive a custom as those the Taliban enforced in Afghanistan in 1999 to exclude women from any sphere of activity outside the home. In both cases, misogyny wasted a potential source of talent. Who could now doubt that Agrippina and her mother would have made competent rulers? But it was unthinkable then, as it still is in many places today, that women should rule. As a result, the insistence on male heirs threw the Roman state into one series of destructive crises after another which drained men and resources.

There would be other powerful women during the four centuries that the Empire endured after Agrippina's death, but none would ever dare directly challenge as she had the political constraints that bound them or the misogyny upon which they were based.

Increasingly, as the Empire first waxed and then waned, sensation-seeking became the key to the Roman imagination and its most misogynistic manifestations. Central to that sensation-seeking was the spectacle of slaughter provided on a regular basis by the gladiatorial games. Begun as private displays of valour and skill held at funerals in honour of the deceased, by the imperial period these displays had been transformed into vast, expensive public spectacles of carnage and cruelty. The most famous venue for these contests was the Coliseum in Rome, which could hold up to 90,000 spectators. At its opening in AD 80, 5,000 wild animals were slaughtered during 100 days of hunts and gladiatorial combats. Women occasionally took part in the gladiatorial contests – one relief shows two women combatants, who fought under the names Amazonia and Achillia, confronting each other; they are not wearing helmets because the spectators wanted to see their faces. A whole section of Juvenal's *Sixth Satire* expresses the usual mixture of outrage and fascination at the spectacle of women training to fight:

> How can a woman be decent
> Sticking her head in a helmet, denying the sex she was born
>   with? [. . .]
> These are the women who sweat in the thinnest, most flimsy of
>   garments;
> Even the sheerest silks are too hot for their delicate bodies
> Hear her grunt and groan as she works at it, parrying,
>   thrusting . . .[71]

What is supposed to be an expression of disapproval conveys instead the lust for the woman who transgresses. But more often women in the arena were there as victims, not protagonists. Because of this, the Coliseum, while not known as a monument to misogyny, can lay claim to having played a role in the history of that hatred, however accidentally.

Convicted criminals were fed to wild animals in the arena during interludes between the more interesting gladiatorial contests. Special horrors were reserved for women convicted of murder. From the second century AD comes one fictional account that seems to be based on real events. A woman convicted of murdering her husband and children was tied spread-eagled to a luxurious bed in the middle of the arena, ready to be raped by a jackass. Hungry lions waited in the wings to finish her off. This spectacle was put on by popular demand.[72] Some women were raped to death in the arena during the recreation of mythological scenes, usually enacting one of Zeus' numerous assaults in animal form on a mortal female.

Sexual fantasies about animals mating with women are common throughout human history. A battery of social, psychological and moral mechanisms usually keeps our fantasies, the unusual and the mundane, separate from our ability to realize them. But in Rome the border between even the most violent fantasy and reality was breached on such a regular basis that it became commonplace to enjoy the most sadistic spectacles imaginable. The immediate impact of this on the male psyche is well documented, at least anecdotally: prostitutes are said to have done a roaring trade under the arches of the Coliseum after the bloody games had concluded.

While the Roman mob satiated itself, the late Empire staggered from crisis to crisis. In the turmoil, a new religious movement was gathering strength. Christianity would dramatically change first the Empire, then the world and the lives of its inhabitants forever. In a corner of the ruined Coliseum, now one of the most popular tourist attractions in the world, stands a black cross, which millions of visitors gaze at each year. It is a memorial to the Christian martyrs who died there. Many, if not a majority of these, were women – ironically, the religion they were devoted to was to play a crucial role, unparalleled to this day, in the history of misogyny.

3

DIVINE INTERVENTION: MISOGYNY AND THE RISE OF CHRISTIANITY

The rise of Christianity from an obscure sect to the world's dominant religion is a phenomenon unprecedented in human history. So too is the power and complexity of its misogynistic vision, which derives, essentially, from three sources.

From the Jews, the early Christians took the Fall of Man myth, as well as the notion of sin and a profound sense of shame. Later, from the Greeks, they borrowed aspects of Plato's dualistic philosophy and Aristotle's 'scientific' proofs of women's inherent inferiority. To this potent brew, Christianity itself contributed its central and unique tenet, that God has intervened in human history in the person of Jesus Christ to save mankind from death, sin and suffering, the evil effects of the fall from grace brought about by woman.

The Christians had inherited the Jewish attitude to history as a preordained unfolding of God's plan: the chosen Church replaced the chosen people, just as centuries later Karl Marx would pass the mantle of historical determinism on to the shoulders of the chosen class. But no other religion before or since has been so audacious as to claim that God was a historical person as real as Julius Caesar or Marilyn Monroe, and that salvation would come only to those who recognized him. It endowed Christian teaching with the power of Divine Revelation. When backed by an aggressive, crusading, and omnipotent institution, it proved a lethal combination, especially to heretics and women. The bitterest irony in this is that during Christianity's first three centuries, women were a key to its remarkable success, thanks to the fact that it gave them a kind of liberation unheard of in the ancient world.

The strain of Jewish misogyny already had a long history by the time it was absorbed into Christian teaching. But it would have remained largely irrelevant to the rest of the world had it not been for the events of the mid-first century AD concerning an obscure prophet named Jesus. What seemed like just another split within the always contentious ranks of Judaism attracted little attention at the time. Had there been headlines, they would have been claimed instead by the bloody fall of Sejanus, the Emperor Tiberius' favourite, and the resulting turmoil within the Roman ruling elite; what took place in Judaea would not have been worth even a sound bite. However, thanks to Christianity's extraordinary triumph over the ensuing centuries, a handful of proverbs and practices belonging to a small and politically insignificant nation have achieved almost universal status. The myth of creation as told in Genesis is now central to the belief of two billion Christians in 260 countries – that is, one-third of the world's population have inherited a myth that blames woman for the ills and sufferings of mankind.

Unlike Greek misogyny, the Jewish version remained, as did Jewish religion, at the level of proverb, parable and practice. Instead of philosophy, the Jews had extensive commentary and interpretation of the sacred texts. But the similarities in both the creation and Fall of Man myths are clear. As in the Greek myth, in the Jewish tradition God creates the first man, Adam, as an autonomous being who lives a happy, contented existence in the Garden of Eden. His only communion is with the divine. Eve, like Pandora, is an afterthought. She is created from Adam's rib because God thought he required 'an help'. And, as with her Greek equivalent Pandora, Eve is disobedient, ignoring God's instruction not to eat the fruit from the Tree of Knowledge. 'The serpent did beguile me and I did eat,' Eve confesses rather nonchalantly (Genesis, 3.13).

The God of the Old Testament proves every bit as vindictive as Zeus. He tells Eve:

'And I will greatly multiply thy sorrow and thy conception; and in sorrow shalt thou bring forth children and thy desire shall be for thy husband and he shall rule over thee' (Genesis, 3:16).

The message for Adam is clear. 'And I shall put enmity between thee and the woman,' God tells him in what turns out to be a self-fulfilling prophecy (Genesis, 3:15).

The moral universe of Judaism differed profoundly from that of the Classical world in ways which, through Christianity, would deeply affect the development of misogyny. It was dominated by a sense of sin, a concept unknown to the neighbouring Greeks and Romans. Zeus and his fellow divinities held gripes and grudges against individual mortals, but with the exception of the punishment inflicted on mankind for Prometheus' overweening ambition (see Chapter 1), rarely do they threaten to punish the world because of this or that violation. But Jehovah took offence easily, saw sin everywhere and throughout much of the Old Testament sits in heaven with his finger, metaphorically, on the nuclear button.

> And the Lord said, I will destroy man whom I have created from the face of the earth; both man, and beast, and the creeping thing, and the fowls of the air; for it repenteth me that I have made them.' (Genesis, 6:7)

He was as good as his word on at least one occasion, flooding the world and drowning the whole human race, save for Noah and his family, intending them to repopulate the world.

Along with sin came a sense of shame of the human body, something completely alien to the world of the Greeks and Romans. Shame strikes as the very first consequence of Eve's transgression: 'And the eyes of them both were opened, and they knew that they were naked; and they sewed fig leaves together and made themselves aprons' (Genesis, 3:7). Passing from the Jewish tradition into Christianity, shame took a firm grip on human sexuality. To a surprising extent, it has not yet relinquished this hold. It gave misogyny a new and destructive dimension.

Linked to shame was the Jewish belief, which the Christians inherited as well, that sex was for procreation, not recreation. Among the Romans, moral reformers, no doubt reflecting on the futility of their own efforts to get Roman men and women to behave themselves, admired the moral strictness of Jewish family life. Adultery was punished severely, with both the adulterer and the adulteress being stoned to death. As we also learn in Deuteronomy (22:20–21), loss of virginity incurred the death penalty for unmarried women:

> But if this thing be true and the tokens of virginity be not found, for the damsel: Then they shall bring out the damsel to the door

of her father's house, and the men of her city shall stone her with stones that she die: because she hath wrought folly in Israel to play the whore in her father's house: so shall thou put evil away from among you.

Homosexuality was forbidden, as was any wasteful spilling of man's seed, including sodomy, masturbation and oral sex. Not a drop could be spared from the business of begetting.

Apart from the magnificent poetry of the Song of Solomon, the Old Testament is harsh and bleak in its attitude to human sexuality, and almost always hostile towards women. The God of the Old Testament sits gloomily aloft and alone, a brooder whose emotional range is usually restricted to jealousy and anger. The beauty of the beings he has created does not usually fill him with pride, and never with desire. Unlike the divinities of Mount Olympus, he is devoid of love or even lust. He is a master of the psychology of revenge, forever eager to chastise and punish his chosen people for breaking one of the 613 laws that governed all aspects of their daily life; or ready to smite their enemies and prepare the way for the Day of Judgement when the righteous Jews will be saved and the rest of humankind cast down into the flames of perdition.

The Jews shared with their pagan neighbours the premise that the moral health of the nation depended to a large extent on the virtue of its women. The most bitter outbursts from the Jewish God against women come when they indulge in a fondness for finery. This is deemed an act of rebellion against God.

Moreover the Lord saith, Because the daughters of Zion are haughty, and walk with stretched forth necks and wanton eyes, walking and mincing as they go, and making a tinkling with their feet:

Therefore the Lord will smite with a scab the crown of the head of the daughters of Zion, and the Lord will discover their secret parts.

In that day the Lord will take away the bravery of their tinkling ornaments about their feet, and their cauls, and their round tires like the moon.

The chains, and the bracelets, and the mufflers.

The bonnets, and the ornaments of the legs, and the head-bands, and the tablets, and the earrings.

The rings and nose jewels.

The changeable suits of apparel, and the mantles, and the wimples, and the crisping pins.

The glasses and the fine linens, and the hoods and the vails.

And it shall come to pass, that instead of sweet smell there shall be stink; and instead of a girdle a rent; and instead of well set hair baldness; and instead of stomacher a girding of sack-cloth; and burning instead of beauty. (Isaiah, 3:16–24)

The God of the Old Testament was remarkable, if not unique, among divinities, in being both grandiose and extra-ordinarily petty, one minute creating the universe, the next making women's hair fall out.

In Ezekiel God goes even further than threatening to give women a bad hair day. Women accused of idolatry, as well as adultery and harlotry with Assyrians and Egyptians whom they allow to press and fondle their bosoms shall 'drink a cup of horror and desolation . . .'

And I will set my jealousy against thee, and they shall deal furiously with thee; they shall take away thy nose and thine ears . . . And the host shall stone them and dispatch them with their swords; they shall slay their sons and their daughters, and burn up their houses. Thus shall I cause lewdness to cease in the land, that all women may be taught not to do after your lewdness. (Ezekiel, 23:25, 48–9.)

Ecclesiastes sums up the misogyny of the Old Testament succinctly when he states: 'From a garment cometh a moth, and from woman wickedness.'[73]

The misogynists of Greece and Rome were constantly berating women for moral failings. But divine disapproval was a new and powerful addition to the history of misogyny. It lent it cosmic significance. The God of the Old Testament is not, one would think, a good model from which to create a religion of forgiveness and love. Yet, it is one of the many paradoxes of history that it was on this stock that the vine of Christianity would first grow.

The Jehovah – or God the Father – we encounter in the New Testament has mellowed considerably from the thundering sky-god of the Old. Indeed, some early Christians like Marcion found the contrast so incredible that they advocated ditching the Old Testament's entire corpus altogether.[74] What is most striking about the parables and proverbs attributed to Jesus, as recounted in the Gospels, is the absence of both misogyny and vengefulness. Women were among his first followers. We are told by Matthew: 'Many women were there beholding afar off, which followed Jesus from Galilee, ministering unto him.' They had good reason to do so. Matthew also tells us (9:20–22) of a woman 'which was diseased with an issue of blood' who touched the hem of his garment. Jewish law had strict taboos on menstruating women as 'unclean', forbidding them contact with the male and entrance into the Temple, among others. In contrast, Jesus does not rebuke the bleeding woman but tells her, 'Daughter, be of good comfort; thy faith hath made thee whole.' (28:55).

In the Gospel according to St John, Jesus' disciples are said to have 'marvelled that he was talking with a woman'. (John:

4:57) In that Jesus was unique. None of the great Classical teachers/philosophers, nor the Jewish prophets who preceded him such as John the Baptist, gathered women followers about them to any significant extent.[75] When Jesus is invited to dine at the house of Simon, he defends a woman whom the host accuses of being extravagant when she uses an expensive oil to anoint him: 'And Jesus said, Let her alone; why trouble ye her? she hath wrought a good work on me.' (Mark 14:6)

The story is repeated in Matthew and Luke. Luke gives the most detail, including the fact that she is a sinner. When Simon points this out to Jesus, he waves it aside: 'Wherefore I say unto thee, Her sins, which are many, are forgiven; for she loveth much.' (7:47). Jesus judges women not according to some rigid code but in terms that acknowledge and understand women's experience. In a society where women risked being stoned to death for loving too much, it was a liberating alternative that accounts for the strong following he had among them, one that Christianity later inherited. Luke (1:24–80) describes woman's experience of conception and the wonder of the baby moving in the womb – the first time in ancient literature that this experience is given any sort of attention. The radical nature of Jesus' morality is made explicit when the woman 'taken in adultery, in the very act', is dragged before him. The Pharisees ask what should be done, knowing full well that the penalty for such an act is death by stoning. Jesus seems to ignore their questions at first and disdainfully bends down to write in the sand:

> So when they continued asking him, he lifted up himself, and said unto them, He that is without sin, first cast a stone at her. None who had accused her dared accept his challenge, but turned and melted away, and Jesus resumed his writing. Then he looked up and finding the women alone said: Neither do I condemn thee: go, and sin no more. (John, 8: 4–11)

Jesus' sympathy for the woman is in startling contrast to the attitude prevalent in the Old Testament, which is too often a case of (in Bertrand Russell's words) 'the infliction of cruelty with a good conscience'.[76]

Mark notes that at the crucifixion there were 'many women' (15:40). The male disciples flee from the scene, but the women remain to pray. Significantly, after his resurrection, Jesus appears first to a woman, Mary Magdalene (Mark: 16: 9). When she reports the event to the apostles, they do not believe her. The resurrection is the central doctrine of Christianity, promising salvation. That it was revealed to a woman, and one who was the first to accept it, gave women in general a powerful basis to play a dramatic role in the new religion.

Jesus' whole attitude to women was revolutionary. They became crucial to early Christianity's spread. Three centuries later, when the Church had triumphed, St Augustine admonished: 'O you men, who all fear the burdens imposed by baptism, you are easily beaten by your women. Chaste and devoted to the faith, it is their presence in great numbers that causes the Church to grow.'[77]

Women flocked to the new faith right from the start. In the mid-first century AD St Paul in his epistle to the Romans mentions 36 believers, 16 of whom are women. Most remarkably, one of the very first people we know of thought to be a Christian was Pomponia Graecina, the wife of Aulius Plautus, the commander of the Roman invasion of Britain in AD 43 when Claudius was emperor (AD 41–54). The historian Tacitus describes her as a 'distinguished lady' who was accused of adhering to a 'foreign superstition', a phrase usually employed when referring to Christianity.[78]

This and other hints suggest that at a very early stage, the new faith found adherents among women of the very highest rank. It penetrated even into the imperial family by the end of the first century AD[79] Dissatisfied middle- and upper-class women have frequently been a fertile ground for those seeking converts to new cults and religions, as the experience in the United States has shown, especially from the mid-twentieth century onwards. Other Eastern religions with a strong appeal to women, including those devoted to the great goddesses Bona Dea and Isis, had spread through the empire. But aspects of Christianity's moral code gave women an advantage unlike any found in the competition.

Because Christians held that every member of the faithful carries the spark of the divine in his or her soul, infanticide was forbidden, as was abortion.[80] Since a majority of exposed infants were girls, this meant that gradually the proportion of females who were Christians began to rise. Women's numbers were further augmented in this new faith by its ban on abortion, which due to the dangers of the operation, killed many women and often rendered those who survived it infertile.[81] In the ancient world, both in Greece and Rome, it was the man who, as head of the household, had the legal power to order a woman to have an abortion. Aristotle advocated it as a form of birth control. Evidence also shows that Christian women married later than their pagan contemporaries, so had better chances of surviving their first pregnancy. Nor were widows compelled to remarry, as was the common practice as enforced by the Lex Julia (see Chapter 2). Christians were expected to marry for life, and infidelity was regarded as being as much of a sin for a man as for a woman. In this, Christianity levelled the moral playing field for women. Christian women were also less likely to be forced to marry, as Christians valued virginity. Traditionally, in the world of Classical Antiquity, men had been called on to resist the wiles of women. Now, for the first time, women were being told that they could reject men. Women were being offered a choice whether to marry or not. Since marriage was a perilous state, quite a few exercised that choice and opted for celibacy. It offers interesting parallels and contrasts with what happened in the West during the sexual revolution of the 1960s, when for the first time women could control their own fertility, thanks to the contraceptive pill. Though the early Christian revolution was in many ways anti-sexual, it was like the 1960s in one important aspect: it offered women the right to choose whether or not they wanted to reproduce.

The phenomenon of women choosing celibacy was undoubtedly one of the factors that attracted them to the new faith and so conspired to increase the ratio of Christian women to men. The lists of those who died during the occasional persecutions against Christians bear this out. In Lyons, Gaul, in AD 177, 24 men and 23 women were martyred; at Scilli, in Italy, three years later, it was seven men and five women who died. According to Rodney Stark: 'The ancient sources and modern historians agree that primary conversion to Christianity was far more prevalent among females than among males.'[82] The result was that with a shortage of women in the larger, surrounding pagan culture, pagan men often married Christian women; and a significant number of these men then underwent secondary conversion. In his studies of modern religious movements, Stark has invariably found the same pattern of conversion. Its impact on the rapid growth of Christianity can be seen when the numbers are considered. The best guess is that by AD 40 – seven years after the crucifixion of Jesus – there were approximately 1,000 Christians in an empire with an estimated population of 60,000,000. Surveying the best available evidence, Stark estimates that the most probable growth rate of the new faith was 40 per cent per decade. By the beginning of the second century, there were over 200,000 Christians, and by AD 300,

6,299,832. Just over a decade later, weight of numbers was one of the factors that led the emperor Constantine to recognize Christianity, ending the sporadic persecutions that had been launched against those who practised it. By AD 350 Christians represented over 50 per cent of the empire's population.

Evidence gathered by Guttentag and Secord on the relationship between the status of women in any society and the proportion of males to females, links high ratios of females to males to higher status for women. Stark believes that in early Christianity, women enjoyed higher status than they did in the pagan world around them.[83] St Paul's references to women as deaconesses are cited to support this contention. According to St Paul, deacons were important in the early Church, assisting in liturgical functions and administering the Church's charitable activities. And it is clear that Paul regarded it as entirely proper for women to be deaconesses.[84]

Several later sources also reference the prevalence of women deacons in the early Church. The most compelling evidence of all, of course, of the high regard for women in the early Church, is St Paul's statement in his epistle to the Galatians :

> For as many of you as have been baptized into Christ have put on Christ.
> There is neither Jew nor Greek, there is neither bond nor free, there is neither male nor female: for ye are all one in Christ Jesus. (3:27–8)

Whatever its other implications, it is the most radical statement of equality – of a kind – between men and women since Plato's championship of women guardians in his ideal state 400 years before (see Chapter 1). But in fact St Paul is merely making explicit the implications of Jesus' attitude towards

women. He was to Christianity what Lenin was to Marxism –
bent on spreading the new faith and preparing Christians to be
ready for the coming of the kingdom of heaven where men and
women would be united in Christ, and all worldly distinctions
would vanish.

But how often did this spiritual equality for women translate
into social reality? It is relatively easy to claim that men and
women are equal in the eyes of the Lord, but did early
Christianity encourage them to see themselves as equals in
each other's eyes? St Paul is cited frequently by both those who
argue that it did, and those who hold that it did not. Like Plato,
he is hailed by some as a misogynist and by others as a
feminist. What remains undeniable is that the moral teachings
on adultery, the banning of abortion and infanticide, and the
easing of pressure on women to marry would have directly
raised the status of women by eradicating some of the practices
that were prejudicial to them. But it was not equality as
understood in a modern liberal democracy.

There is a further similarity between St Paul and Plato. The
equality they offered men and women could only come about
through the eradication of the sexual differences between
them. Plato's female guardians must become honorary men,
so that their sexuality is obliterated. In the Kingdom of
Heaven, according to St Paul, sexual differences disappear.
Both thinkers see the sacrifice of a vital aspect of our human
nature as the necessary cost of equality between the sexes. In
the meantime, however, certain patriarchal traditions must
continue. In 1 Corinthians, 11:3–16, the Apostle sets down a
series of formulations concerning the relationship between
men and women and the Church. He reiterates the Biblical
tradition of male dominance for 'the head of the woman is the
man' and restates the creation myth of the primacy of man:
'For the man is not of the woman; but the woman of the man.

Neither was the man created for the woman; but the woman for the man.' It is also here that he ordains that women must cover their hair when in church. However, he goes on to recognize our mutual interdependence: 'Nevertheless neither is the man without the woman, neither the woman without the man, in the Lord. For as the woman is of the man, even so is the man also by the woman; but all things of God.'

One could parse this, as does the Jewish feminist Pamela Eisenbaum, as a simple recognition that man depends on woman as much as woman depends on man.[85] If one accepts this interpretation, St Paul here rules out that hoary old misogynist fantasy, beloved of the Greeks and of the Old Testament, the myth of autonomous man. That surely is progress. However, while undermining one of misogyny's pretensions, St Paul went on to supply it with one of its most powerful weapons, one that would change forever how a whole civilization would think about the body.

At first sight, apparently, St Paul was an unimpressive and unattractive little man, with a 'big bold head', crooked legs, dark thick eyebrows that grew together and a large nose; hardly, one would think, a man to foment one of the great upheavals in the human psyche.[86] But the letters of St Paul represent the beginning of a revolution in human sensibility of seismic proportions. In Romans (7:18 –25) he writes about his body:

> For I know that in me (that is, in my flesh,) dwelleth no good thing: for to will is present with me; but how to perform that which is good I find not . . . For I delight in the law of God after the inward man:
>
> But I see another law in my members, warring against the law of my mind, and bringing me into captivity to the law of sin which is in my members.

O wretched man that I am! who shall deliver me from this body of death?

I thank God through Jesus Christ Our lord. So then with the mind I myself serve the law of God; but with the flesh the law of sin.

This is a declaration of war on the human body. And when a man declares war on himself, the first casualty is woman. It is a war that is still being fought.

Many thinkers in Classical Antiquity, such as Plato, were dualists, aspiring to greater knowledge of the world by attempting to apprehend what they believed was the perfection of its underlying principles. As a result, they rejected everyday reality, including that of the body and its needs and desires, as woefully inadequate, indeed a hindrance. But they did not reject it as inherently evil as does St Paul. His anguished cry of near despair at his rebellious body had not been heard before. Plato may have regarded the body as an unfortunate inconvenience that a philosopher somehow had to by-pass on his road to the truth. But to St Paul the body represented a rejection of the Divine, an insurrection against the supreme truth for which the Son of God had died on the cross. Inevitably, women would carry the cross as the chief instigators of this rebellion of the flesh.

In the epistle to the Corinthians, written to advise Christians who were debating whether or not to become celibate, St Paul tells them (7:1–9):

It is good for a man not to touch a woman.

Nevertheless, to avoid fornication, let every man have his own wife, and let every woman have her own husband . . . I say therefore to the unmarried and the widows, It is good for them if they abide as I.

But if they cannot contain, let them marry: for it is better to marry than to burn.

Thus marriage became a 'defence against desire'.[87] Though St Paul did not advocate that all Christians remain celibate, realizing that such a condition would have been incompatible with his ambitions to broaden the new faith's appeal, his bleak view of human sexuality as a necessary evil provided one justification for the Church's increasingly misogynistic vision. Sanctity was identified more and more with virginity. The rebellious body had to be put down, and like an enemy citadel, it was laid siege to with fasts, deprivations, and other punishments including, most importantly, abstinence from sex. The Greeks and Romans were taught it was necessary to master passions. But according to the Christian teacher Clement of Alexandria (circa AD 150–215) 'our ideal is not to experience desire at all.'[88] By the end of the second century AD, one of the most powerful and influential figures in the early Church, Quintus Septimius Florens Tertullianus, better known as Tertullian (AD 160–220), could write: 'Think of how a man feels in himself when he abstains from a woman. He thinks spiritual thoughts. If he prays to the Lord, he is next door to heaven; if he turns to the Scriptures, he is all of him present to them . . .'[89]

In theory at least, it is easier for a man to abstain from having thoughts about having sex with a woman if she dresses modestly. According to Tertullian, 'salvation – and not the salvation of women only, but of men – consists in the exhibition principally of modesty.'[90] Women were already expected to wear veils while attending Christian services. It was Tertullian who had women barred from holding ministries in the Church because of their power to distract the pious. In the Christian male's war with his body, an attractively dressed woman was his rebellious member's greatest ally. So Tertullian devotes a whole treatise 'On Female Dress' to neutralizing this powerful force. In it, he asserts that women originally learned the art of decorating their bodies and wearing make-up from the angels expelled from heaven with whom they coupled. The fallen angels conferred 'peculiarly upon women that instrumental means of ostentation, the radiance of jewels wherewith necklaces are variegated, and the circlets of gold wherewith the arms are compressed, and the medicaments of orchid with which wools are coloured, and that black powder itself wherewith the eyelids and eyelashes are made prominent.' St Paul had introduced the notion of the body as 'the temple of the living God'.[91] Women's love of ostentation and make-up pollutes that temple, forcing God to forsake it.

> For they who rub their skin with medicaments, stain their cheeks with rouge, make their eyes prominent with antimony, sin against Him. To them, I suppose the plastic skill of God is displeasing. In their persons, I suppose, they convict, they censure, the Artificer of all things! For censure they do when they amend, when they add to, His work; taking these their additions, of course, from the adversary artificer. That adversary artificer is the devil. For who would show the way to change the body, but he who by wickedness transfigured man's spirit.[92]

The misogynists of Greece and Rome similarly censured women for beautifying themselves. To a Cato or a Juvenal, however, a woman's love of decoration was merely a sign of human vanity. Though it was an admittedly powerful distraction for those high-minded men who strove towards the virtues of self-control and discipline, it was also an opportunity to show how foolish women were for aspiring to possess such a transient bauble as beauty. But with Tertullian we are in a different world, one where the border between the natural and the supernatural has been blurred, where God and Satan now struggle for dominance on the battlefield of the human body, and where sexual desire has been deployed on the side of the forces of darkness as one of their most potent weapons. The Divine has intervened on the side of those who strive to suppress human sexuality, which means first and foremost suppressing women's sexuality. To avoid becoming the devil's ally, women, writes Tertullian, should 'go about in humble garb . . . and affect meanness of appearance, walking about as Eve mourning and repentant, in order that by every garb of penitence she might the more fully expiate that which she derives from Eve – the ignominy, I mean, of the first sin, and the odium attaching to her as the cause of human perdition.'

To the suggestion of allowing an unveiled girl into church, Tertullian responds with an example of how moralists can enjoy masturbatory fantasies in the guise of condemning them: 'There she is patted all over by the roving eyes of total strangers, is tickled by the fingers of those who point her out, and the darling of us all, she warms to it amid assiduous hugs and kisses.'[93]

In a passage that has become notorious since Simone de Beauvoir's citation of it in *The Second Sex*, Tertullian proclaims the link between women and the devil.

The sentence of God on this sex of yours lives in this age: the guilt must of necessity live too. You are the devil's gateway: you are the unsealer of that forbidden tree: you are the first deserter of the divine law: you are she who persuaded him whom the devil was not valiant enough to attack. You destroyed so easily God's image, man. On account of your desert – that is, death – even the Son of God had to die. And do you think about adorning yourself over and above your tunics of skins?[94]

Tertullian thunders at women in the manner of the God of the Old Testament who once threatened to make their hair fall out. But his tone and his words are altogether more menacing. Not only are women held responsible for the Fall of Man, but it is they – not the Jews, not the Roman authorities – who are blamed for the suffering and death of Jesus, man's Redeemer. It is through their flesh that the devil comes into the world. Indeed, apparently oblivious to Jesus' own attitudes to women, Clement of Alexandria asserted that Jesus' mission had been specifically 'to undo the works of women', by which he meant sexual desire, birth and death. His words echoed those of Ecclesiastes (3:19): 'And marriage followed the woman, and reproduction followed marriage, and death followed reproduction.'

With Christianity there was a new concept in the world – the concept of salvation. Increasingly, as their faith struggled to define itself, Christians believed that salvation could only be achieved by rejecting sex. This feeling intensified to unheard of levels during the third century. It was accompanied by a radical misogyny of a ferocity never before seen.

The background to these developments was a crisis that struck about 200 years after the death of Jesus, when Western civilization was almost extinguished. Its impact on the way people thought and felt about themselves and the world was even more unsettling than the impact the Peloponnesian War had on the Athenians of the fifth century BC (see Chapter 1). A series of wars of succession weakened Rome internally: twenty emperors took power between AD 235 and 284[95] and uncontrolled inflation threatened the empire with economic collapse. Barbarian hordes burst across the borders and thrust deep inside the empire's hitherto tranquil provinces. For the first time in 700 years, Rome had to be ringed with massive walls.[96] A Roman emperor bowed the knee to a Persian king.[97] Two

major epidemics of what is now thought to have been the first
outbreaks of smallpox and measles struck the major cities and
their rural hinterlands, carrying off between a quarter and a
third of the people and deepening an already profound population crisis.[98] Rarely had the world seemed more mutable
and transient. And it was during these decades of disaster and
despair that Christianity enjoyed the period of its most rapid
growth; by the end of it there were over 6,000,000 members of
the faith, making it a force to be reckoned with.[99]

Since St Paul, there always had been a powerful feeling of
ambivalence about sexuality within Christianity. But the early
Christians experienced the joy of believing that the return of
Jesus was imminent, when all such problems would be resolved. The mood changed as time passed. Origen (AD 185–
254), the first real philosopher of the early Church, decided
not to wait for the Kingdom of Heaven and resolved the
conflict between body and soul by having himself castrated.[100]
During the third and fourth centuries, the desire to avoid the
temptations of the flesh became radicalized into an outright
rejection of the body. Edward Gibbon observed in his *Decline
and Fall of the Roman Empire* that Christians felt a 'contempt
for their present existence', which they believed was a merely
passing phase that had to be endured. Some declared 'a
boycott of the womb'. A young wife turned Christian rejects
her husband when he comes to her bed with these words:
'There is no place for thee beside me because my Lord Jesus
with whom I am united is better than thee.'[101] Another young
woman signals her rebellion against marriage and reproduction by informing her parents she is refusing to wash. St
Jerome (AD 342–420) would later sing the praises of Paula
'squalid with dirt' as the ideal of Christian womanhood.[102]
According to Brown: 'To break the spell of the bed was to
break the spell of the world'.[103] The effect of this and similar

sentiments was to make early Christianity – with its hostility to sex, disparagement of the married state and obsession with virginity – one of the most profoundly anti-family movements ever to come into existence.

In the eastern half of the empire this anti-family sentiment expressed itself most radically in the rise of militant asceticism. It is not surprising that the eastern Mediterranean, which was the original cradle of misogyny, also gave birth to its most profound and disturbing manifestation. John the Baptist had set a Biblical precedent by living in the desert, surviving on locusts and wild honey. Jesus himself had spent forty days and forty nights in the wilderness. During the third and fourth centuries, thousands of monks known collectively as 'the desert fathers' took refuge from the world in the deserts of Syria and Egypt, living in caves or primitive huts, even on top of pillars, sometimes alone, sometimes in small communities. Running from society was a lot easier than running from the body – it has a habit of coming along with you with its bundle of desires and needs, especially those related to women.

'Torture your senses, for without torture there is no martyr-dom,' advised an old monk to a neophyte.[104] The spell of the bed was transfigured into a nightmare of self-loathing, as misogynistic tendencies intensified to psychopathic levels, creating scenes like those from a grade-B horror movie. One ascetic monk, driven crazy with lust, dug up the rotting corpse of a woman, dipped his cloak in her putrefying flesh, smelled it and then buried his face in it. He hoped – undoubt-edly with some justification – that this would turn him off women for life.[105]

In the West, meanwhile, Christianity was undergoing other profound transformations that would affect the history of misogyny. As a religion and a cultural force, Christianity had become so powerful that the authorities were compelled to recognize it. In AD 313 the emperor Constantine (306–337) issued the Edict of Milan, proclaiming religious tolerance. In the form of Catholicism, the universal Church, dominated by the bishop of Rome, Christianity began to assume the mantle of the established religion, run by a clerical class determined more than ever to restrict the role of women. A few years earlier, the Church Council of Elvira had passed a series of rulings that imposed strict controls on women both sexually and socially. Clerics could remain married but were forbidden to have sex with their wives. Christians were forbidden to have sex with Jews. Of the eighty-one rulings enacted, thirty-four were codes applying greater restrictions on marriage and women's behaviour, especially in relation to their role in the Church. It is as if the Council clerics forbade themselves sex and then took out their anger on women.[106]

Seven years after the Edict of Milan, Constantine, as the first Christian emperor, revealed the stern hand of the new, increasingly absolutist morality. He passed a law that meted out the death sentence to any virgin and her suitor for the crime of eloping together. The penalty for any female slave held to have collaborated in the enterprise (and they were always suspected of such collaboration) was death by having molten lead poured down her throat. The young woman's consent to the elopement was ruled irrelevant 'by reason of the invalidity associated with the flightiness and inconsequentiality of the female sex'.[107] We find here echoes of the old misogyny of Solon and Cato, but enforced with a horrifying brutality.

The increasing intolerance manifested itself in other ways. During the reign of the pious Catholic emperor Theodosius 1 (AD 379–395), Christian mobs ran amok, knocking the heads off the statues of Vestal Virgins in the Roman Forum (where the results of their vandalism can be seen to this day), attacking pagan temples, and burning down a synagogue.[108] The revolution against the body brought the Olympic games to an end in AD 393, because the athletes competed naked. As a subject for art, the body disappears from view in the West for about 1,000 years. Another hint of what lay in the future as the Church strengthened its grip on sexual behaviour came in AD 390 when raids were conducted on homosexual brothels (which had thrived in Rome for centuries). Prostitutes found there were publicly burned alive. They had been condemned for playing the woman's role in sexual acts, a crime against the new orthodoxy which ruled that the differences between the sexes were irrevocably ordained by God and thus everlasting. Earlier Christianity had tolerated a more fluid notion of male and female. But fluidity, or flexibility, in thought and behaviour was coming to an end. Catholic orthodoxy began defining all the fixed spheres – social, moral, religious, intellectual and sexual – in which men and women were destined to be set forever as fixed as the spheres of the starry heavens above.

However, if Christianity's profound dualities between soul and body, man and God, man and woman, the world of the spirit and the world of the senses were to be given a philosophical dimension, there was intellectual work still to be completed.

Early Christianity was as innocent of philosophy as modern American Protestantism. Its evangelism bypassed rational thought in favour of faith-based revelation. Tertullian dismissed with contempt any suggestion that 'the Greeks' (as he called philosophers) could be of any use to Christians. The one important exception was the fourth gospel of St John, with its pronounced strain of Platonic thought: 'In the beginning was the Word, and the Word was with God, and the Word was God' (1:1). The Word is identified with Plato's Perfect Form, existing in a state of timeless perfection beyond the realm of the senses, the Absolute Reality that the Christians equated with the one true God: 'And the Word was made flesh, and dwelt among us, (and we beheld his glory, the glory as of the only begotten of the Father) full of grace and truth' (1:14).

In this way, John declares that the perfection of the everlasting divine presence entered the stage of history in the person of Jesus. Plato's Perfect Form had become human, the ideal merged with the real, declaring an end to dualism. So it is one of the profound ironies of Christianity that when it began to systematically absorb Platonism (to become Catholicism), it was as a philosophical justification for the set of dualities on which Christian thinking about the world rested.

There are two reasons why Catholicism took so readily to Platonism. Plato's appeal was made on both intellectual and social grounds. His Theory of Forms fitted in very well with a religion that stressed the importance of the next world and expressed contempt for this one. His theory of society, as recounted in *The Republic*, appealed directly to a Church developing an increasingly elaborate hierarchical structure, with a ruling cast of clerics who, like Plato's guardians, have comprehended the Absolute Truth and are there to interpret it for the faithful and protect it from heretics. According to Bertrand Russell, Origen was the first to begin the synthesis of Platonic thought and the Jewish scriptures. But it was left to St Augustine (AD 354–430), the greatest thinker since Plato, to establish the philosophical edifice that intellectually propped up the Christian view of the world, including its misogynistic vision.

Born of humble parents in what is now eastern Algeria, Aurelius Augustinius was of a family that typified the pattern already seen with the rise of Christianity: his mother, Monica, was a Christian and his father, Patrick, a pagan who converted before he died. As intellectually and emotionally complex as he was sexually driven, Augustine began living with a concubine from Carthage at age 17. Monica was deeply upset, and devoutly wished her son would become a Catholic and devote himself to higher things – rather the way, later on, Irish mothers would pray ardently for their sons to become priests. First a student, and then a teacher, of grammar and literature, Augustine moved to Carthage, then to Rome and Milan. He dallied with Manichaeism for years, finally rejecting it because of the incoherence of its cosmology.[109] It was in Milan in AD 386 under the influence of St Ambrose's sermons, that Augustine converted to Catholicism. But before he found the Lord, he had found Plato.

Augustine is one of the watershed personalities of history. He stands at the great division between the world of Classical Antiquity (which had endured for about 1,000 years) and that of Christian civilization. He is the first person from Antiquity who revealed to us the turmoil of his interior world as recorded in his remarkable work *Confessions*. It is like tuning into a television talk show where the guest is revealing his deepest shame, his greatest love, his worst sin, and his highest goal, one broadcast 1,700 years ago, but still with the immediacy of an Oprah Winfrey interview. At the centre of the turmoil of Augustine's search for God is the struggle between the desire of the flesh and striving of the will, the profound dualism that Augustine will incorporate into the very heart of Catholicism using Plato's philosophical apparatus. His cry of anguish echoes that of St Paul, but with a power and complexity the Apostle could not match:

> I came to Carthage and all around me hissed a cauldron of illicit loves. I therefore polluted the spring water of friendship with the filth of concupiscence. I muddied the clear stream by the hell of lust, and yet, though foul and immoral in my

excessive vanity, I used to carry on in the manner of an elegant man about town.[110]

His bodily desires have condemned him to be a prisoner: 'fettered by the flesh's morbid impulse and lethal sweetness, I dragged my chain, but was afraid to be free of it.' He was 'stuck fast in the glue of pleasure'. Such is his disgust at the physicality of the human condition that he compares us to pigs: 'We roll in the mud of flesh and blood,' he proclaims.

In a later work, *The City of God*, he returns to this theme compulsively. Referring to the Fall of Man, he writes:

> From this moment, then, the flesh began to lust against the spirit. With this rebellion we are born, just as we are doomed to die and because of the first sin, to bear, in our members and vitiated nature, either the battle with or defeat by the flesh.'[111]

The Hell of lust has been with us ever since. For Augustine, the struggle could only be resolved on a higher plane. He read the works of the Platonists which had been translated into Latin and found that in all the Platonic books God and his Word keep slipping in. The Idea, the Pure Form, eternal and unchanging, he could equate with God. The Platonic vision of a higher intellectual reality corresponded to a certain extent to Augustine's desperate endeavours to break the 'fetters' of bodily desire. But the intellectual 'heaven' of Plato was too abstract and remote; most crucially, it did not promise salvation and everlasting life: that is why today there are so many millions of Christians and so few Platonists. And it was to Christianity that Augustine was converted in AD 386.

Augustine's relevance to misogyny can be summed up in the sentence from Book Two of his *Confessions*:

I had no motive for my wickedness except wickedness itself. It was foul, and I loved it. I loved the self-destruction, I loved my fall, not the object for which I had fallen but the fall itself. My depraved soul leaped down from your firmament to ruin. I was seeking not to gain anything by shameful means, but shame for its own sake.

The idea of 'fall' had been inherited from the Jewish myth of the expulsion of man from the garden of Eden. To this Fall of Man, Augustine adds another, even more terrible dimension: the Platonic fall. This is a fall from the Pure Form, to Christians, the timeless perfection of union with God, into the mutable world full of life, lust, suffering and death. It comes about through conception. From that moment we are in a state of sin – Original Sin. As Augustine says, quoting the Psalms, we are 'conceived in iniquity and in sin' in our mother's womb. The instrument of this fall from grace is woman: both in the sense that it was Eve's disobedience that led to our expulsion from paradise, and in the Platonic sense – she represents the wilfulness of the flesh to reproduce itself. We are thus carried away from God into temporal life in which we (thanks to our bodies) are in a state of rebellion against him. We will this fall upon ourselves, and our rebelliousness expresses itself most directly through sexual desire. Because of Original Sin 'man, that might have been spiritual in body, became carnal in mind'.[112]

Augustine, like other Christians, believed that the only way to break this cycle of rebellion was to subdue the body. It was his own inability to do so that had delayed for so long his conversion:

Vain trifles and the triviality of the empty-headed, my old loves, held me back. They tugged at the garment of my flesh and

whispered: 'Are you getting rid of us?' And 'from this moment
we shall never be with you again, not for ever and ever.' And
'from this moment this and that are forbidden to you for ever
and ever.'[113]

In spite of the misogynistic interpretation of his doctrine,
which became enshrined in the Doctrine of Original Sin, St
Augustine's attitudes to women were more complex. He did
not see women as inherently evil. In *The City of God* he
stresses that 'the sex of woman is not a vice but nature.' But the
terrible anguish of his struggle with desire, which he records
with such power, reveals clearly that it is man's battle with
himself that is at the root of misogyny. However, for St
Augustine, ultimately it is our will that is the source of evil.
Ego, not libido, is the problem that made us defy God in the
first place. As a punishment, God gave us sexual desire,
something over which our will has no control. Just as we
defied God, so our desires defy us. Sex became the battleground, both as a pleasure and a punishment, in a way
unheard of before in Western culture. Woman was bound
to suffer because of our nasty habit of blaming that which we
desire for making us desire it.

In a frightening glimpse of what lay ahead for women in the
coming centuries of Christian domination, consider the terrible fate of the last pagan woman philosopher: Hypatia of
Alexandria. There are but a few women philosophers from
ancient times who are known by name.[114] Hypatia is the most
renowned, thanks to Christian fanaticism and intolerance.

She was born in Alexandria towards the end of the fourth
century, the daughter of the mathematician Theon, who
commentators say she excelled in ability and intelligence to
'far surpass all the philosophers of her own time'.[115] She wrote
commentaries on the geometry of Apollonius and Diophantus,

played music, taught Platonic and Aristotelian philosophy at Athens and Alexandria, where she opened an academy, and published a work on astronomy. Hypatia was something of an ascetic, and though described as 'beautiful and shapely', remained chaste and virginal. From one source we learn that when one of her students fell so madly in love with her that he exposed himself to her, in order to cure him of his infatuation she handed him her undergarments stained with menstrual blood.[116] It is a novel way of discouraging a suitor and proves that it was not only Christians who were affected by the revolt against the body that characterizes this epoch. But Hypatia's virtues (however Christian-like) did not mollify the local Christians' hostility towards her.

Alexandria, one of the greatest cities of Antiquity and famous as a seat of learning, nevertheless also had a reputation for sectarian violence often accompanied by the lynching of political and ideological opponents. (One of the earliest instances of rioting against Jews in the ancient world took place there in AD 38.) In AD 412, Cyril, a Christian fanatic, became bishop of Alexandria. Cyril had punished himself for several years as a desert monk, but as was often the case, the tribulations of the flesh served merely to deepen his fanaticism and fire his intolerance: imagine him as a kind of fundamentalist mullah. Certainly, his desert years had done nothing to dampen the fires of ambition. As bishop, he challenged the rule of the Imperial Prefect Orestes, who ruled Egypt on behalf of Rome. In these, the twilight years of Antiquity, the growing power of the Church was absorbing that of the civil authority, a precursor of the theocracy of the Middle Ages. Cyril was a heretic hunter, and Jew hater. Around Easter AD 415, he roused a Christian mob to attack the local Jews, sacking their homes, and seizing their synagogues to purify them and turn them into churches. He drove this ancient community from the city. When Orestes objected, a Christian mob assaulted him.

Christians began muttering that Hypatia had bewitched the Imperial Prefect and was responsible for the breakdown in understanding between him and the bishop. In a sinister premonition of what was to come, a Christian writer accused her of being 'devoted at all times to magic, astrolabes and instruments of music, and she beguiled many people through her Satanic wiles.'[117] For a woman to be learned and accomplished was not only a novelty but a sign that she was a witch, in league with the Devil. Cyril was happy to use Hypatia as a scapegoat for his troubles with the civil powers. After a fiery sermon, one of Cyril's followers, Peter ('a perfect believer in all respects in Jesus Christ,' according to John, Bishop of Nikiu) led an excited mob to attack her academy.

The mob 'found her seated on a lofty chair; and having made her descend they dragged her along till they brought her to the great church, named Caesarion.'[118] There, she was stripped naked. Holding her down, the Christians used oyster shells to skin her alive.[119] Then, 'her quivering limbs were delivered to the flames,' in the words of an outraged Gibbon.[120]

Bribes blocked all attempts to prosecute the murderers of Hypatia. Cyril's career in the Catholic Church blossomed. He was canonized a saint. Apparently, miracles, not murders, are what count on a saint's curriculum vitae.

From being martyrs, Christians had quickly become inquisitors. In the coming centuries, the perfume of church incense would all too often mingle with the smell of a woman's burning flesh.

4

FROM QUEEN OF HEAVEN
TO DEVIL WOMAN

The thousand years or so separating the end of the Classical world and the rise of the modern witnessed the development of two seemingly contradictory processes: the beatification of woman and her demonization. The Middle Ages would begin by elevating women towards heaven and end by consigning many thousands of them to hell. In the latter case, however, the process was more than mystical or metaphorical. The flames were all too real. It marked an extraordinary period when the human imagination soared with the great spires of the Gothic cathedrals of France that seem to scrape the very floors of heaven. It was a period too when the human spirit was convulsed by outbreaks of mass hysteria, pogroms, and witch hunts that plunged it into some of the most hellish regions it has ever visited.

In AD 431 the highest council of the Catholic Church

declared that Mary, a Jewish peasant girl from Palestine, was the Mother of God. The girl, about whom, historically speaking, almost nothing was known apart from her name, was not just the mother of a god – and in the Classical world gods were as plentiful as celebrities are in modern times – she was the mother of the only God, the creator of the entire universe. The other gods had been banished or transformed by St Augustine into demons, leaving the Christian God to loom over the cosmos in solitary majesty. Mary was his mother – or Theotokos (the god-bearer). Because of this unique claim, Mary would play not only an unprecedented role in the history of religion, but a vital and determining part in the history of misogyny.

The proclamation by the gathering of bishops came after a heated debate, in which crowds (pro-and-anti Mary's elevation to Theotokos) demonstrated on the streets of Ephesus where the council met – the ancient city on the eastern coast of what is now Turkey. It was renowned for being the centre of the worship of the virgin goddess Diana whose temple there had been one of the seven wonders of the ancient world before an army of Goths destroyed it in the upheavals of the third century. One of those most actively involved in the controversy was St Cyril of Alexandria, something of an expert at exciting mobs – his fiery sermon sixteen years earlier had provoked a Christian mob to skin alive the woman pagan philosopher Hypatia. This time, however, St Cyril was ardently in favour of promoting woman, in the form of Mary, to the highest elevation imaginable, and excommunicated Nestorius, the bishop of Constantinople who had pointed out that since God had existed forever, it was impossible for Mary or any woman, however virtuous and miraculous, to have been his mother. Nestorius was concerned that declaring Mary Theotokos elevated her to the status of a goddess and smacked of paganism: perhaps on his way to the council meetings, held in the church of the Virgin Mary, he had glanced up at the remains of Diana's temple, and worried that the Catholic Church was in danger of replacing one virgin goddess with another. Some fifty years before, another learned mustering of ecclesiastics had already declared Mary a perpetual virgin. In any case, Cyril's victory was popular with the masses, who held a candlelit procession through the ancient streets to celebrate Mary, the Mother of God. The persistence of their devotion to Mary has proven to be one of the most remarkable and enduring features of Catholicism. In 1950, 1,431 years after the Council of Ephesus, enormous crowds of the faithful, said to be a million strong, would gather in St Peter's Square in Rome, to greet Pope Pius XII's proclamation of the dogma of Mary's Assumption into Heaven with outbursts of hymn singing, tears, and joyous prayers. In the meantime, the Jewish peasant girl from Palestine, would find her name on twenty-eight churches in Rome and many thousands more elsewhere, as well as being the inspiration of some of the greatest works of architecture and art (including poetry and song) the world has produced.

The debate over Mary's status was originally a by-product of the rancorous controversies surrounding the status of her son, Jesus. The bishops were trying to settle questions about his nature – should it be defined as human, divine, or some combination of both? The Orthodox Church eventually rejected the two extremes of the argument, that Jesus was either human or divine, in favour of a complex compromise under the term consubstantiation. That is, Jesus as the Son of God was 'consubstantial' with his Father, sharing his divine nature, and at the same time was 'consubstantial with the flesh', that is partaking fully of human nature. The status of Mary, like that of any mother, rose with that of her son. The gospels had already described her as a virgin. By the fifth century, the Church decided she was a virgin before, during and after her son's birth. Once Jesus' 'consubstantial' nature with God was established, it was only fitting that Mary should be declared God's mother.

After that, her progress up the mythological ladder was unstoppable, at least until the Reformation of the sixteenth century. By that time, the cult of Mary had in all its complex manifestations replaced the Incarnation and the Resurrection as the focus of belief for the vast majority of Catholics. The thousand years between the Christianity of the Church Fathers and the climax of Mary's cult saw a shift away from the expectancy of the Second Coming and hopes for immediate redemption that had animated the faith's early followers. Though tremors of millenarianism shook the Middle Ages, especially as they drew to a close, the vast majority of the faithful did not expect redemption in this life and looked to Mary to console them for the arduous and painful passage through it to the next world.

It was deemed unsuitable that the Mother of God should meet the fate of other mortals upon death. From AD 600 onwards the Church celebrated the Feast of the Assumption on 15 August, when it was believed Mary was assumed bodily into Heaven. She shares the almost unique privilege of defying human fate and existing in bodily form in Paradise with Jesus.[121] Once installed among the angels alongside her son, it was not long before Mary was to find herself crowned Queen of Heaven. Later, the question arose as to her own conception. It became unthinkable for some theologians of the Church that the Perpetual Virgin, Mother of God and Queen of Heaven, should have been tainted with Original Sin, sharing our fall from divine grace which is a direct consequence of our sexual lusts. Anxiety about the purity of the Mother of God being blotted by this aspect of the human condition troubled

Duns Scotus back in the fourteenth century. But a firm decision on the matter had to wait another 500 years. In 1854, Pope Pius IX proclaimed the doctrine of Mary's Immaculate Conception, making her the only human being (aside from Jesus) to have escaped the taint of Original Sin. This meant that Mary was the only human being (again apart from Jesus) to have been conceived in perfection, with no in-built tendency to sin. That is, she lived a life completely free of temptation, thus exceeding the state of perfection Adam and Eve had enjoyed in the Garden of Eden before the Fall.

It was indeed remarkable progress for a Jewish peasant girl from Palestine, especially considering the paucity of references to her in the Bible. The earliest source for our knowledge of Jesus, the Apostle Paul, does not even mention her by name, merely noting that Jesus was 'made of a woman' (Galatians, 4:4). Mark refers to her once by name, and once in the context of a rather dismissive exchange between Jesus and 'his brethren and his mother'. Their pleas for his attention because they are family are swept aside.

'Who is my mother, or my brethren?' Jesus replies (3:33). He answers his own question by declaring that all those who followed him are his real family.

John contains two references to Jesus' mother. She is more present in Matthew and Luke who provide the narrative of Christ's nativity and infancy upon which Christianity's rich tradition of Christmas is based. Even here, she is far from being centre stage. But the lack of detail did not prevent Christianity over the centuries, and the Catholic Church in particular, from placing on her shoulders the enormous weight of its most important dogmas. In fact, the very absence of scriptural tradition allowed for the proliferation of myths and legends about Mary that helped turn her into the most venerated woman in human history.

The very core belief of Christianity, the Incarnation, rests on the claim that Mary was a virgin when she conceived. Claims of virgin births as a result of some divine intervention were, of course, not unusual in the ancient world as a way of establishing the exceptional nature of the person for whom the claim is made – Alexander the Great is one example, and Plato is another. But thanks to their profound rejection of the body as the Devil's gateway into the world, the Christians had to protect the Mother of God from any suggestion that the experience leading to the miraculous event was in any way physical, that is, pleasurable. Therefore, sex could not be involved. The Redeemer cannot come into the world as a result of an act of filthy lust. As the seventeenth-century theologian Francisco Suarez put it:

'The Blessed Virgin in conceiving a son neither lost her virginity nor experienced any venereal pleasure . . . it did not befit the Holy Spirit . . . to produce such an effect, or to excite any unbecoming movement of passion . . . On the contrary, the effect of his overshadowing is to quench the fire of original sin.'[122]

The most venerated woman in the world could only be venerated on the grounds that she did not share with other women something so fundamental to their nature as the experience of sex. A woman was being exalted yet at the cost of holding in contempt her sexuality. Mary as Mother of God was exempted from the pains, as well as the pleasures, of motherhood, and learned theologians of the early Church debated how she might have produced Jesus without breaking her hymen; the alternative opinion that it did break but was miraculously made whole again was rejected. Thus began a long process that would make Mary increasingly abstract and distant from the experience of the women who looked up to her for some relief from the male-dominated Christian pantheon. The Word became flesh in the form of her son Jesus, but the flesh of the woman who gave birth to him became an abstraction. In a sense, the abstraction of Mary through her elevation into a sexless, saccharin goddess-like being, far beyond human nature, acted as a counterpoint to the Incarnation. The old dualism of body and spirit, threatened by the belief in the Incarnation, reasserted itself with the cult of the Virgin Mary. The 'Word became flesh' signalled the end of dualism but the cult of the Virgin Mary meant that the old contempt for matter was perpetuated.

Even today, stepping into the marble-cool and dimly lit interiors of the great basilicas dedicated to Mary leaves the visitor with the overwhelming sense of the other-worldliness of the Virgin Mother turned Heavenly Queen. In Santa Maria Maggiore, which legend says was founded between 352 and 366 by Pope Liberius I, the Queen of Heaven gorgeously arrayed in cloth of gold and pearls, sits on a luxuriously cushioned couch as, with hands slightly raised and an almost expressionless face, she accepts the crown from Jesus. Across the Tiber, in the even earlier basilica of Santa Maria in Trastevere, the Queen of Heaven is portrayed in an icon over six feet high. She sits on imperial cushions, her son Jesus next to her, a protective arm extended around her shoulder. A great diadem crowns her head and a faint nimbus glows around her. Her long, narrow face carries an expression, impassive, remote, and otherworldly, as she stares down from a plane of being far above that of mortal flesh and blood.

The icons send out a complex if not contradictory message. They are, of course, intended to convey messages other than those relating to women. In an age when Rome was asserting its primacy over the other episcopates, the depictions conveyed a very clear signal that its status as capital of the Catholic Church was divinely sanctioned. But if we look at what they tell us about the status of women we find that while a woman is exulted, like no human being has ever been before, reigning over the very pope, crowned by the king of Heaven, she is not the agent of her own exaltation. And the cause of her elevation to the highest is her very passivity ('Behold the handmaid of the Lord, be it unto me according to thy word' Luke, 1:38) and asexuality.

As a role model for women, Mary set contradictory (if not downright impossible) standards for them to meet – representing as she did the apotheosis of passivity, obedience, motherhood and virginity. Indeed, she served as a constant reminder that women were inadequate because of their own, very human, nature. Her sexlessness was a rebuke to their sexuality, her obedience an encouragement to believe that the norms of social relationships had divine sanction, her virgin motherhood a miraculous state beyond the reach of merely human females. That is, she is a specific rebuke to women in a way that Jesus is not to men. Jesus' suffering and death rebuke all of humankind, and are not aimed specifically at men the way the Church used Mary's elevation to target the rest of the female sex for denigration. In Catholic imagery to this day, her foot remains firmly planted on the serpent's head, a call to Catholic girls and women to repress desire in themselves and deny its fulfilment in their men folk.

The only way that women could hope to emulate her was by foreswearing their sexuality.

In the early years of Christianity, thousands of women did so by taking up the ascetic life, usually by converting a private house or villa into a retreat. By AD 800, some 400 years after the proclamation that Mary was the mother of God the movement had become institutionalized, and convents, monasteries and priories were a common feature throughout

Europe. Women's energy and commitment that had contributed so much to the rise of Christianity were not rewarded through the granting of any role in the power structures of the Church. Instead, they were now channelled into the great monastic institutions, which, for the first time in history, offered large numbers of women an alternative to marriage and childbearing – albeit at the price of accepting life-long chastity and other restrictions, part of an often harsh way of life. But it was a price many thousands of women were prepared to pay. By the eleventh century, convents had become a major educational resource for women where they learned to read and write, and where they could become acquainted with learning and the classics. As of 1250 in Germany alone there were some 500 nunneries, holding between 25,000 and 30,000 women.[123] They spent their time praying, meditating and working in wool and linen. It was the nuns of Normandy who sewed the beautiful Bayeux tapestry, commemorating the Norman victory over the Anglo-Saxon King Harold at the battle of Hastings in England in 1066. They also embroidered the garments for the priests and bishops (a task many nuns still perform). During this period, women were also able to oversee the institutions as abbesses, and a few rose to powerful positions. Abbesses could find themselves ruling over men in joint communities such as that founded by St Fara in Brie in northern France. She and others even heard confessions. Nuns in the abbey of Las Huelgas in Spain appointed their own confessors.[124]

However, by the beginning of the thirteenth century such freedom and independence were in decline. Many of the abbeys lost their lands, and control became increasingly centralized. Pope Innocent III (1198–1216), who launched the crusade against the Cathars in Languedoc, imposed prohibitions on women's role in the Church. Joint communities were

abolished, a move welcomed in misogynistic fashion by one
abbot who wrote:

> We and our whole community of canons, recognizing that the
> wickedness of women is greater than all the other wickedness
> of the world, and that there is no anger like that of women, and
> that the poison of asps and dragons is more curable and less
> dangerous to men than the familiarity of women, have unan-
> imously decreed for the safety of our souls, no less than that of
> our bodies and goods, that we will on no account receive any
> more sisters to the increase of our perdition, but will avoid
> them like poisonous animals.[125]

Although women were never ordained priests, the priest-
hood was not officially closed to them until the thirteenth
century. St Thomas Aquinas issued his opinion that women
cannot be in authority over men and that 'the superior male
essence' was necessary to become a priest for 'Adam was
beguiled by Eve, not she by him'. It was necessary for the
priest therefore to be male 'so that he did not fall a second time
through her female levity'.[126] In future, only priests could hear
confessions, and since only men could be priests women would
be forced to confess any sexual transgressions to often lascivious and frustrated males who frequently exploited their
power.

By the beginning of the following century, the world of the
great abbesses was a thing of the past. But the early Middle
Ages allowed other outlets for women of energy, talent and
status. Eleanor of Aquitaine (1122–1204), wife of Louis VII of
France and later Henry II (Plantagenet), the future king of
England, was 'the richest heiress of western Christendom' and
'the presiding genius . . . of courtly culture'.[127] The women of
southwestern France enjoyed some of the benefits of Roman

law, which persisted in what had been the Roman province of Aquitania, including the right to inherit property. Eleanor's inheritance, comprising of most of southern France, stretched south from the Loire Valley to the Mediterranean Sea and west to the Atlantic coast of Bordeaux. It was there, during her reign, that the culture of courtly love, celebrated in the work of the troubadour poets, reached its peak. Between 1150 and 1250, some two hundred troubadour poets whom we know by name flourished, twenty of them women. They were poets from noble families, who introduced to their aristocratic patrons the refinements of wit and elegant verse; most importantly, they celebrated a new code of chivalrous conduct in the relationship between high-ranking men and women.

The courtly love tradition was an attack upon the clerical misogyny that dominated the Church's attitude towards women, with its unrelenting and obsessive denigration of the female as 'filthy matter'. It did so by exalting love between man and woman. Woman was seen as man's saviour. In terms of Western civilization, this was completely novel. Classical poets had sung the praises of their mistresses, but there was no tradition of elevating woman to the status of the universal beloved object. The worship of Mary as Queen of Heaven had established a precedent. But the courtly love poets celebrated illicit love, mocked marriage and defied prevailing Christian morality. They came close to heresy. The troubadour Renaut de Beaujeu in *Le Bel Inconnu* refutes the Bible by claiming that man was created to serve woman, from whom all good flows.

Speaking of Eleanor's court, the historian Friedrich Heer wrote:

> The essence of love, as taught at Poitiers, was not the indulgence of uncontrollable passion, but the moulding of passion by a man's lady, his 'mistress'.[128]

According to Heer, a revolution in romantic relationships was not all that was achieved in the south of France. He believes that there is some evidence to suggest that women may also have had the right to vote and took part in the elections to the local government.[129]

The elevation of love between man and woman to a sacrament anticipates the work of Dante Alighieri (1265–1321). Dante's meeting with Beatrice Portanari transfigures his life. In her he sees the apotheosis of goodness and beauty. The encounter inspired his first work, *La Vita Nuova*. In his masterpiece, *The Divine Comedy*, written after Beatrice had married a Florentine merchant and died at the early age of 24, he tells of the journey the poet takes through the three kingdoms of Hell, Purgatory and Paradise. It is Beatrice who escorts him from Purgatory to Paradise. As she comes to him in a green mantle, a garland of olives on her head, he remembers his love for her: '*d'antico amor senti la gran potenza*' ('I felt the great power of the old love').

But this is not the adulterous love of the troubadours. Dante's love for Beatrice is chaste, and his salvation depends upon it. However, what is remarkable about his vision is that it implies no disregard of or contempt for what is human, no triumph of spirit over matter: Beatrice is both. Though exalted, she remains a very human figure. In the words of Marina Warner, Dante '. . . was too profound and noble a thinker to fall into dualism and use the perfection of Beatrice to denigrate the human race or the rest of the female sex . . .'[130]

Such a vision of woman as both human and an expression of beauty with the power to transfigure others could not counter the misogynistic currents running through Christianity. By the time Dante had completed his work, those currents were beginning to run more strongly. They would become a raging torrent.

The Church, always disapproving of the courtly love tradition, discovered that the land of the troubadours was home not
only to seditious and disturbing ideas about women, but to a
major heresy – Catharism. A large section of the population
had abandoned the Catholic Church altogether in favour of a
movement that rejected the world as evil and preached that the
Pope and his bishops had forsaken the teachings of Jesus. [131]
The persecution of the Cathars linked heresy to ideas about
women in a way that would facilitate the witch-hunts of later
centuries.

The Cathar movement had originated in the East, cradle of
many such dualistic faiths going back to before Christianity.
Like earlier heresies, and indeed, like early Christianity itself, it
had shocked the orthodox because of the prominent role
women played in it. The Cathars allowed women to preach
and to become part of the movement's spiritual elite, the
Perfects. Wealthy women of Languedoc were among the most
prominent of the patrons of Cathar preachers as they were of
troubadour poets.

Pope Innocent III declared a crusade against Catharism in
1208. It was conducted savagely. Over a period of thirty years,
hundreds of thousands were butchered, burned and hanged,
with Cathar women being singled out for special humiliation
and abuse as the fate of Lady Geralda, one of the most
renowned of the Cathar women, grimly illustrates. After being
taken prisoner, she was thrown down a well and stoned to
death. 'Even by the standards of the day, the act was shocking,'
commented one historian of the heresy.[132]

The crusade against the Cathars effectively wiped out the
culture that had nourished the tradition of courtly love.
Troubadours continued to write love poetry – but it was
chastened and thoroughly Christianized. The purge against
heresy became a purge against expressing certain ideas about

the relationship between men and women. Poets now sang that the purity of love was defined by the denial of its own goal: the possession of the beloved. According to Warner, this was a concept which 'would have been nonsense' to the early troubadours.[133] The Mother of God and Queen of Heaven now emerges as part of the ideological struggle and acquires the title Notre Dame – Our Lady. The poets substitute love for one lady – Mary – for the ladies of the court. Gautier d'Arras, who came from Northern France, and wrote in disapproval of the spirit of Eleanor's court, proclaims 'Let us marry the Virgin Mary; no one can make a bad marriage with her,' and casts disdain on the love of real women.[134]

Deification dehumanizes women as much as its polar opposite, demonization. Both deny women their ordinary humanity. However, that humanity is the theme of one of the greatest portraits of women ever written which appeared around 1387 to light the gathering gloom of the waning of the Middle Ages. It gave voice, perhaps for the first time since the comedies of Aristophanes over 1,700 years earlier, to woman not as goddess or temptress but as a human being with vices and virtues like any other. As portrayed in *The Canterbury Tales* of Geoffrey Chaucer (1342–1400), Alison, the Wife of Bath, is certainly no Beatrice – no man will find salvation through love for her. Nor is she an embodiment of the virtues of Mary. She does not try to be. Her vices, like her virtues, are rooted in the demands made upon her by the exigencies of everyday life. For Alison, men are a management problem, but one that she is confident can be solved by women who use their wits. More importantly, she protests against the history of misogyny and its injustice. In doing so she denounces every misogynist from 'Old Rome' to the Bible, including Metellus, 'that filthy lout' who beat his wife to death for drinking wine, and Gaius Sulpicius Gallus, who divorced his wife because she went out with her head uncovered (see Chapter 2); she is especially scathing on the Church's tradition of defaming women. In 'The Wife of Bath's Prologue', she speaks out:

> For take my word for it, there is no libel
> On women that the clergy will not paint,
> Except when writing of a woman-saint,
> But never good of other women, though.
> Who called the lion savage? Do you know?
> By God, if women had but written stories
> Like those the clergy keep in oratories,
> More had been written of man's wickedness
> Than all the sons of Adam could redress.[135]

Her husband (the fifth) infuriates her, constantly reading from his collection of misogynistic homilies. After a furious row, she persuades him to fling his book in the fire and to submit to her rule.

'The Wife Of Bath's Tale', which follows, is about an attempt to answer the question, made famous many centuries later by Sigmund Freud, 'What do women want?' The hapless knight who is set the task of finding an answer fails until the solution is given to him by an old woman:

> A woman wants the self-same sovereignty
> Over her husband as over her lover,
> And master him; he must not be above her.[136]

But for Alison, there was no real puzzle. Sovereignty meant freedom to be herself, in all her womanly nature.

The Wife of Bath's indignation about the misogyny of the Church came just a few decades before it would take on its most deadly, indeed, nightmarish form. This was also prefigured in the misogynistic disdain for human sexuality expressed by Pope Innocent III, who exterminated the Cathars and the culture of courtly love. He proclaimed 'man was formed from the itch of the flesh in the heat of passion and the stench of lust, and worse yet, with the stain of sin.'[137] The Pope saw the world as beset with evil. In 1215 at the Fourth Lateran Council, confession was made compulsory for all adult Catholics. This way, the Church could police the souls of the faithful more effectively. He ruled that women's role in the religious life be severely reduced. They were permanently barred from hearing confessions and preaching; even their role in singing during service was to be restricted. In everyday life, women too were to be confined to the role of – in the words of St Thomas Aquinas – 'man's helpmate'. He advocated that men should make use of 'a necessary object, woman, who is needed to preserve the species or to provide food and drink'. Brutal force employed by an absolutist Church was the ultimate means of deterrence. Not until the totalitarian states of the twentieth century was there an institution which could wield such power. Yet, underlying it was a terrible insecurity. Cathars were not the only threat. The Church ruled that Jews must wear a distinctive form of clothing – a yellow patch and a horned cap to mark them as the murderers of Christ. In the outbreaks of religious hysteria that became more common during this period, mobs turned upon Jewish communities in vicious pogroms. According to Heer, 'every abortion, animal or human, every fatal accident to a child, every famine and epidemic, was presumed to be the work of an evil doer. Until they had been eliminated the Jews were obvious culprits; afterwards, it was women, witches.'

The witch craze which ran from the late fourteenth to the late seventeenth centuries and resulted in the deaths of unknown thousands of women retains the ability to shock us largely because it is the only known instance in the history of persecution in which to be a woman was to be a chief suspect in a vast conspiracy and the grounds for imprisonment, torture and execution. It is the most deadly event in the history of misogyny, and still, after the lapse of many centuries, the most disturbing and perplexing.

Throughout much of human history, right up until the present, people have believed in witches, both male and female, and saw their magic as capable of being exercised for benign as well as malign purposes. Periodically, witches were punished.[138] But the early Church believed that the Incarnation had effectively vanquished Satan and he was not seen as exercising a powerful influence over witches or anybody else. For the first millennium and more of Christianity, belief in witches was generally treated as a superstition of the ignorant, and the Church warned against it. Usually, when witches were killed it was at the hands of enraged or frightened peasants. The official position of the Church remained that magic did exist, and some women – and men – could use it, in particular to bring about impotence and cause abortions. But it condemned as a sin the belief that witches could ride through the air at night, turn love for a person into hatred, transform themselves or others into animals, and have sex with demons.[139]

By the late thirteenth century the mood had changed. A darker, more pessimistic attitude replaced this healthy caution and theologians began reconsidering the status of the Devil, his demons and their human servants. Why?

Heresies had already shaken the once sturdy edifice of Catholicism. They were followed by the pandemic of the Black Death (1347–50) – one of the greatest disasters ever to strike Europe. An estimated 20,000,000 died. The world that emerged in its wake was one more full of dread and uncertainty. 'At the close of the Middle Ages, a sombre melancholy weighs on people's souls.'[140]

The late Medieval mood of pessimism, mixed with doubt and fear, expressed itself in a way that would have a direct impact on the fate of women: the growth in interest in demons, a need to prove that they were real, and therefore that the Devil and his demons were abroad in the world. As the historian Walter Stephens summed it up, 'Without proof of a devil, there can be no proof of God.'[141]

The most convincing proof of the reality of demons would be their ability to interact with human beings. There is no more powerful and corporal form of interaction than sex. But to have sex, demons needed bodies. Many learned monks bent over ancient texts in bare cells burned the midnight oil pondering the corporality of demons; the great authorities St Augustine and St Thomas Aquinas (1225–74) were invoked for those who were in favour of devilish embodiment. Augustine had pointed to the pagan gods, who he believed were demons, and their fondness for raping and impregnating women as proof they could interact with humans. St Thomas Aquinas believed demons were the supreme, supernatural gender-benders. They could appear as females – succubi – and go about extracting semen from men.[142] Then they would transform themselves into male demons or incubi, and impregnate women. The sceptics argued that demons were illusionary.

To a modern reader, the whole debate over demon bodies and what demons could or could not do with them may seem remote from concerns about the status of women. But the lives of many thousands of women would depend on its outcome. Abstract arguments often have concrete consequences, sometimes of the most horrifying kind.

By the fourteenth century the arguments for the reality of demons had won crucial support at the highest levels of the

Church. Pope John XXII (1316–34) was obsessed with witch-craft and heresy; and he was a true believer in demons. It was during his long reign that for the first time in history a woman was accused of having sex with the Devil. In 1324, Lady Alice Kyteler of Kilkenny in Ireland earned that dubious distinction. The Pope had appointed Richard Ledrede as Bishop of Ossory in southeastern Ireland, a man who shared his obsessions.[143] Lady Kyteler was on her fourth husband when she was brought to the bishop's attention. Bishop Ledrede listened eagerly to accusations from the children of Lady Kyteler's three dead husbands that she had used witchcraft to dispose of their fathers. She was also accused of running a sect that forswore Christianity, using the swaddling clothes of dead unbaptized babies to concoct evil potions and poisons with which to harm good Catholics. Most sensationally of all, under torture her maid Petronilla told the bishop how she acted as a go-between for the Devil and her mistress. When the Devil as lover first appears in history he does so in the form of three big, handsome black men. Petronilla said she saw with her own eyes (and apparently she looked on frequently) Lady Alice making love with them, sometimes in broad daylight. 'After this disgraceful act, with her own hand [Petronilla] wiped clean the disgusting place with sheets from her own bed.'[144]

Lady Kyteler was also accused of being the leader of an anti-Christian sect, thus linking witchcraft, demonic sex and heresy. No longer would witches be seen as lonely women mixing potions in village cabins. They were becoming part of a vast conspiracy.

Lady Kyteler escaped to England and avoided punishment. But the unlucky Petronilla was burned alive. She was one of only two people, and the only woman, to be burned as a witch in Ireland.[145]

Accusations of witchcraft and demonic sex began to occur more frequently in the fifteenth century. They were a feature of the first wide-ranging witch-hunt in the Rhone Valley in southern France in 1428, during which between one and two hundred witches were burned.[146] Less than sixty years later, a landmark text in the history of misogyny appeared to explain why it was that more and more women were apparently leaving the Church and throwing themselves into the arms of Satan and his demons. It is not that *Malleus Maleficarum*, or 'Hammer of The Witches'(1487), has anything original to say about misogyny – it has not; it merely repeats all the abuse heaped upon women in the Bible and the Classical authors. But what it does do for the first time is explicitly link the supposed weaknesses of women's nature to their propensity to fall for the Devil, and thus become witches. Its influence was hugely augmented by a new invention – the printing press. There is more than a little irony in the fact that the invention that would revolutionize people's access to information should be so instrumental in spreading one of the most lethal forms of ignorance, fear and prejudice ever to manifest itself.

Malleus was the work of two Dominican Inquisitors, James Sprenger and Henry Kramer (though Kramer is thought to have been chiefly responsible for writing it). Sprenger had spent time as an Inquisitor in Germany. But his main claim to fame was that, before he occupied himself with burning women, he established in 1475 the Confraternity of the Holy Rosary, a form of devotion to the Virgin Mary, which even to this day good Catholic schoolchildren are expected to join. The terrible polarity of Christian misogyny has found no more powerful expression than Sprenger's devotion both to the Virgin Mary and to torturing and burning innocent women for supposedly having sex with the Devil.

Of Kramer less is known. He seems to have become interested in demons thanks to a chance encounter in Rome in 1460, when he met a priest who was possessed by the Devil.[147] It convinced him that it might be possible to find physical evidence of demons and so prove beyond all doubt that they were real.

Kramer and Sprenger had a powerful accomplice in their campaign to prove that women were having sex with Satan. Pope Innocent VIII (1484–92) had a reputation of being not so innocent. He was born Giovanni Battista Cibo, and contemporary chroniclers depict him as one given to 'unbridled licentiousness', who fathered several illegitimate children. He would spend the last weeks of his life unable to digest any food except woman's milk, an ironic fate for a man who in effect consigned untold thousands of innocent women to the flames. Kramer and Sprenger convinced the Pope with their tales of women copulating with demons, eating children, making men impotent, aborting foetuses, and killing cattle, that witchcraft was a serious threat to civilization and the Church.

In 1484, the Pope issued a Papal Bull, which gave dogmatic force to the claims that witches were engaging in sex with demons. It declared:

> It has indeed lately come to Our ears, not without afflicting us with bitter sorrow, that in some parts of Northern Germany, as well as in the provinces, townships, territories, districts, and dioceses of Mainz, Cologne, Treves, Salzburg and Bremen, many persons of both sexes, unmindful of their own salvation, and straying from the Catholic Faith, have abandoned themselves to devils, incubi and succubi, and by their incantations, spells, conjurations, and other accursed charms and crafts, enormities and horrid offences, have slain infants yet in the mother's womb, as also the offspring of cattle, have blasted the produce of the earth, the grapes of the vine . . . these wretches

furthermore afflict and torment men and women . . . they hinder men from performing the sexual act and women from conceiving, whence husbands cannot know their wives nor wives receive their husbands . . . and at the instigation of the Enemy of Mankind they do not shrink from committing and perpetrating foulest abominations and filthiest excesses to the deadly peril of their own souls . . .

Wherefore We . . . decree and enjoin that the aforesaid inquisitors [Kramer and Sprenger] be empowered to proceed to the just correction, imprisonment, and punishment of any persons, without let or hindrance, in every way . . .[148]

It was the equivalent of a declaration of war, and *Malleus* became a sort of justification for it. Women would be its chief victims. In the coming centuries, 80 per cent of those executed in the witch-hunts would be women.

The Inquisitors have a simple explanation for why it is that nearly all witches are women: 'All witchcraft comes from carnal lust, which is in women insatiable,' they write, citing Proverb XXX. 'There are three things that are never satisfied, yea, a fourth thing which says not, It is enough; that is, the mouth of the womb . . . Wherefore for the sake of fulfilling their lust they consort even with the Devil.' They allege other faults in women that make them vulnerable to temptation, of course, including vanity, feeble-mindedness, talkativeness and credulity. But in the minds of the Inquisitors, women's greater carnality is the primary cause for witchcraft. Since presumably this fault identified as particular to women is not new, it might be asked why there are almost no reports of women copulating with the Devil before 1400, when the Church decreed making love to demons a capital crime? *Malleus* has no explanation for this, other than to say that in the good old days, 'the Incubus devils used to infest women against their wills'. But modern witches 'willingly embrace this most foul and most miserable servitude'. The claim that neither women nor witches are what they used to be is a grotesque version of the age-old lament uttered by every misogynist from Cato the Elder to the latest TV evangelist about the low morals of modern womanhood. It would have been comic if its consequences had not been so horrific.

There is nothing comic about *Malleus*; it is written with all the deadly seriousness that cold fanaticism can muster, the sort that makes Hitler's *Mein Kampf* such a repulsive read. Nothing can make these two authors crack a smile, not even the tale of the missing penises. Bearing in mind that Sprenger and Kramer fault women for being the credulous sex, consider how they treat the accusation that witches steal penises.[149] It is claimed that some witches collect penises 'in great numbers, as many as twenty or thirty together, and put them in a bird's nest or shut them up in a box, where they move themselves like living members, and eat oats and corn . . .' As proof, they claim that:

> a certain man tells that, when he had lost his member, he approached a certain witch to ask her to restore his health. She told the afflicted man to climb a certain tree, and that he might take whichever member he liked out of a nest in which there were several members. And when he tried to take a big one, the witch said, 'you must not take that one,' adding, 'because it belonged to a parish priest'.

In fact, what the *Malleus* has reproduced – clearly without realizing it – is a standard anti-clerical joke. According to the historian Walter Stephens: 'There are other instances of Kramer's using jokes as if they were transcripts of court proceedings; the impression of insanity radiated by the *Malleus* comes from Kramer's willingness to believe almost anything as evidence that witchcraft and demons are real.'[150]

There is speculation on whether or not others can see the incubi when witches are having sex with them. The Inquisitors are also intrigued to know whether sex with a demon is more enjoyable for the woman than sex with her husband. In *Malleus*, there is evidence that sex with the Devil is just as good, if not better than, sex with a man. This changed over the years. In witches' confessions from the sixteenth century onwards, though the Devil's member gets bigger 'like a mule's . . . long and thick as an arm', and even develops prongs so that she can have oral, anal and vaginal sex all at once, sex with demons becomes much less pleasurable, and even painful.[151]

The speculations of the Inquisitors about sex with demons is almost entirely devoted to women and their incubi. Little is said about men making out with succubi. Kramer and Sprenger are not curious to know how enjoyable it is for a man to make love to a lady demon. That is because, they argue, men are not so prone to lusting after demons: 'And blessed be the Highest Who has so far preserved the male sex from so great a crime,' they exclaim solemnly.

The vocabulary of *Malleus* when it deals with human sexuality and especially with women is one of cold repugnance. It distances the authors from their subject as if the accusers did not belong to the same species as those whom they accuse of performing such acts of 'diabolical filthiness'. Even more repellent is the chilling detachment the inquisitors display when they deal with the remedies for this 'high treason against God's Majesty'. It might be compared to the detachment of a Nazi bureaucrat totting up the daily death rate in a concentration camp.

The institution of the Inquisition into whose hands the

accused fell did indeed resemble the institutions of terror created by the totalitarian states of the twentieth century. The job of the Inquisition was to find out and punish heretics. The person accused was not told by whom he or she had been accused. Legal representation was practically impossible. Anyone crazy enough to come to her legal defence is warned that he too might be condemned as a heretic. 'Those who endeavour to protect witches are their cruellest enemies, subjecting them to eternal flames in place of the transitory suffering of the stake,' warns Peter Binsfield, the Suffragan Bishop of Trier, one of the areas worst affected by the witch-hunts.[152]

The accused was imprisoned before being brought to trial, and while awaiting judgement, often for considerable periods of time, fed on a diet of bread and water. Torture was employed to extract confessions, and there was no appealing the sentence. The Inquisitor was prosecutor, judge and jury. Technically, the Church did not actually carry out the sentence of death, since it is forbidden to take life – it merely 'relaxed' its protection of the accused (if convicted). The victim was handed over to the civil authorities, who administered the punishment. The civil authorities, of course, could be certain to concur with the Inquisitor's findings.[153] Henry Kramer and James Sprenger sum up the Church's role in a chilling phrase when they speak of 'those whom we have caused to be burned'.[154]

The accused may be kept in a state of suspense by 'continually postponing the day of examination', the Inquisitors advise. If this does not make her confess 'let her first be led to the penal cells and there stripped by honest women of good character', in case she is concealing some instruments of witchcraft made 'from the limbs of unbaptized children'. It is then a good idea to shave or burn off all her hair, except in Germany, where shaving 'especially of the secret parts . . . is not generally considered delicate . . . and therefore we Inquisitors do not use it . . .' They are not so squeamish in other countries where 'the Inquisitors order the witch to be shaved all over her body'. In Northern Italy, the *Malleus* reports: '. . . the Inquisitor of Como has informed us that last year, that is, in 1485, he ordered forty-one witches to be burned after they had been shaved all over.' The unmistakable relish Kramer and Sprenger derive from stressing this detail betrays the underlying sadism.

If the squalor of the prison and the humiliation of stripping and shaving, never mind the mounting terror as she awaits the coming torture, do not break her, the judge should 'order the officers to bind her with cords, and apply her to some engine of torture; and then let them obey at once but not joyfully, rather appearing to be disturbed by their duty.' Usually, the first instrument of torture applied was the strappado. Her hands are tied beneath her back. She is roped to a pulley and then yanked violently into the air, where she is jerked up and down until her shoulders are dislocated and her sinews torn. 'And while she is raised above the ground,' the Inquisitors write with the detachment of civil servants, 'if she is being tortured in this way, let the Judge read or cause to be read to her the dispositions of the witnesses with their names, saying: "See! You are convicted by the witnesses."'

If she is still obstinate, other tortures can be used. She might be burned with candles or with hot oil. Flaming balls of pitch might be applied to her genitals or gallons of water forced down her throat until she is bloated and the officers then beat her belly with sticks. She can be forced to sit on the witch's chair – a sort of narrow cage with clamps and a spiked seat. Thumbscrews, and other devices for crushing the legs and feet might be used. Some victims were held in irons so long in filthy conditions that they died of gangrene before coming to trial.[155]

However, the Inquisitors are not without sympathy. They forbid torturing pregnant women. They are to be tortured only after giving birth.

Cheating and lying are also permitted to the judges. A judge may promise the woman that he will spare her life, then, once she has confessed, hand her over for sentencing to another judge. Or a judge may 'come in and promise that he will be merciful, with the mental reservation that he means that he will be merciful to himself or the State; for whatever is done for the safety of the State is merciful.' As in twentieth-century totalitarianism, things become their opposite according to the dictates of the regime. It reminds us of the nightmare world of George Orwell's *Nineteen Eighty four*, with its dominant slogans, 'WAR IS PEACE, FREEDOM IS SLAVERY, IGNORANCE IS STRENGTH'; the authors of *Malleus* might add, 'CRUELTY IS MERCY'. And, as in Nazi Germany and Stalinist Russia, it was held to be acceptable for children and parents to denounce each other. Peter Binsfield tells the story of an eighteen-year-old boy who denounced his mother 'out of filial piety'. She went to the stake, along with three of her children in November 1588.[156]

Once the accused is convicted, the Church decrees she suffers 'relaxation to the secular arm', that is, it hands her over to the civil authorities for punishment, which meant painful death. There is little hope that the secular arm will oppose the Church's will. A French demonologist warns: 'The judge who does not put to death a convicted witch should be put to death himself.'[157] On her way to the stake, the woman was often forced to wear the witch's bridle – a spiked iron gag, jammed and locked in her mouth, to stifle her screams and her protests of innocence.

By such methods, over a period of some two hundred years, an unknown number of women were executed, mostly by being burned alive. Overall, it has been impossible to gauge the number of victims who died as witches – estimates range from several millions to around 60,000.[158] The numbers, and some of the methods, varied from country to country. The witch-hunts raged most violently in Germany, Switzerland, France and Scotland. However, within those countries, the numbers executed varied considerably from area to area. In France, the witch-hunts tended to concentrate in areas such as the south-west where previously heresies such as Catharism had flourished. The same was true of Germany – the major witch-hunts broke out along religious fault lines that produced the upheavals of the Reformation and the religious wars of the 1600s. In the area of southwest Germany, between 1561 and 1670, 3, 229 witches were burned; around the town of Wiesenteig, in one year – 1662 – sixty-three women were burned, that is, at the rate of more than one per week.[159] Near Trier, in 1585, after the Catholics had reclaimed it from the Protestants, two villages were left with only one woman each – all the rest having been burned. Nicholas Remy, a scholar, a Latin poet, author of *Daemonolatreia*, as well as an Inquisitor, burned between 2,000 and 3,000 witches before dying in 1616. Between 1628 and 1631, Philip Adolf von Ehrenberg burned 900 witches, including several children. At this time, also in Germany, children as young as three and four were accused of having sex with devils. Children who had been convicted of attending the witch's Sabbat with their parents were flogged in front of the stake as their mother and father burned.[160] Jean Bodin, the author of the 1580 treatise *De la Démonomanie des sorciers,* writes 'children guilty of witchcraft, if convicted, are not to be spared, though, in consideration of their tender age, they may, if penitent, be strangled before being burnt'.[161] Girls above the age of twelve, and boys over fourteen, were treated as adults.

In England, approximately 1,000 witches were executed during a 200-year period, far fewer than in most other parts of Europe gripped by the craze. Demonic copulation was generally not a feature of the accusations, and the kind of torture that was authorized on the continent was forbidden. Instead, the accused were deprived of sleep for days at a time, until they confessed.[162] English women's sexual embrace of the Devil coincided with the arrival of the Puritan Matthew Hopkins as Witch Finder General during the English Civil War (1642–9). Up until then, they had apparently been content to suckle demonic toads and cats at their breasts. Hopkins hung some two hundred women as witches in fourteen months, including nineteen in one day in the town of Chelmsford, Essex. One of his victims, Rebecca West of Colchester, accused of killing a child by witchcraft, confessed to have married the devil. Hopkins was paid a bounty for each witch he hanged, and legend has it he retired a rich man.

Just north of the border, in Scotland, however, where continental-style torture prevailed, copulation with the Devil was as common as it was in France, Switzerland, Northern Italy and Germany. Scottish witches also confessed regularly to eating their children. Four thousand were burned during the years of the witch-hunts, a horrific level given Scotland's sparse population.

The English Puritans brought the fear of witchcraft with them to the New World. They brought with them too something of the Old World misogyny that was its inspiration. But the witch craze never caught on with the same ferocity in the colonies as it did in Europe. There were only two intense outbreaks – the first in Hartford, Connecticut (1662–3) and the second and more infamous, in Salem, Massachusetts, for a few months beginning in December in 1691. In Hartford, thirteen were accused and four hanged, and in Salem, two hundred were accused and nineteen hanged. As in Europe, four-fifths of the victims were women; a half of the males who were accused were husbands or sons of witches. The conviction rate was far lower than that of the European witch-hunts. A more democratic system of justice prevailed, allowing those convicted to appeal to higher courts; the outbreaks endured for a far shorter period. The majority of the cases concerned acts of possession. There was only one instance, in 1651, of a woman accused of going to bed with the Devil, and she only did so when he appeared to her in the form of her lost child. At an official level, scepticism prevailed very rapidly. Within a generation of the Salem trials, a man and wife who accused one Sarah Spenser of witchcraft were sent to see a doctor in order to establish whether or not they were sane.[163]

Undoubtedly, one of the reasons that the persecution of witches in North America lasted for so short a time was the fact that Old World misogyny did not enjoy a completely successful transplant to the New World. The Puritan tradition shared something of the early Christians' belief in equality before the Lord. Women enjoyed a higher status in the colonies. Two centuries after the witch craze had passed, Alexis de Tocqueville (1805–59) observed that in America 'while they have allowed the social inferiority of woman to continue, they have done all they could to raise her morally and intellectually to the level of man; and in this respect they appear to me to have excellently understood the true principle of democratic improvement'[164] (see Chapter 6). That great democratic experiment that had its roots in the seventeenth century's social and religious radicalism, helped protect women from the worst excesses of the witch craze.

The last woman to be legally executed as a witch was burned in Switzerland in 1787. In 1793, a woman in Poland was burned, but illegally. By then the craze had long ago run its course. The threat from the Devil and his legions of female devotees had vanished. We now read the writings of Kramer and Sprenger, and the other demonologists and Inquisitors, with utter incredulity, mixed with horror and disgust.

The question remains: How is it that women came to be demonized for close to 300 years in a society where learning and the arts were entering one of their most fruitful periods, and the scientific, philosophical and social revolutions in Europe would soon transform forever how people viewed themselves and the world? Another way of looking at this question is to ask why it was that misogyny, so long a fundamental element in Christian thinking, took on its most lethal form at a time otherwise associated with great human progress?

The historian Walter Stephens argues that doubt not misogyny lay at the root of the witch-hunt craze. The profound intellectual, social and moral changes that were shaking society challenged people's faith, and they sought ways to vindicate their traditional beliefs in the old divine order. In his detailed analysis of *Malleus*, Stephens argues that the preoccupation with women having sex with demons was mainly a concern with finding evidence that demons existed; the more detail they could get from women's alleged experiences, the better. The inquisitors' sexual obsessions about women that to the modern sensibility resemble pornographic fantasies, are really a desperate quest for proof that will ward off uncertainty. 'The expert testimony of witches themselves has made all these things credible,' the *Malleus* asserts. That is, Inquisitors tortured women in a search for evidence that the Devil really existed. They sought to transform their metaphysics into physics. The witch-hunt was a hideous experiment to make unobservable entities real. Confirming their existence confirmed that the whole world of the spirit was actual, and not just a fantasy. Stephens agrees that there was a misogynistic dimension, and that Christianity's long history of contempt of and hostility towards women led to many more of them being arrested and tortured than men. But it was the search for proof that was the primary motivation for the horrors of those years.

Even if we accept the argument that misogyny was a secondary motive for the witch-hunt, it does nothing to mitigate the appalling picture that it presents. It merely means that many thousands of women perished in the flames and at the end of a rope in order to assuage men's doubts. The flames affirmed the dualism of Christianity, inherited from Plato, which saw the everyday world as contemptible, and the world of the spirit as the true reality. For women, dualism could not have had a more horrific consequence.

At least three conditions conspired to create the emotional, moral and social context for the witch-hunts. First, the fourteenth century, which ushered them in, was, like the fifth century BC in Greece and the third century AD in the Roman Empire, a period of terrible calamities. Plague and war threatened to unhinge society. Fear and doubt caused people to view the world in a darker and more sinister light. Secondly, heretics real and imagined threatened a once seemingly all-powerful institution, the Church, and its claims to embody the absolute truth. Finally, Christian society's deep-seated misogyny provided the needed scapegoat in the form of woman. Just as centuries of Christian anti-Semitism provided the ideological grounds for the Nazi holocaust, so the long tradition of contempt for and dehumanization of women made the witch-hunts possible.

The crises of the fourteenth century passed, but the crises confronting the Catholic Church did not. With the Reformation, the great edifice that had endured for more than a thousand years cracked apart. The new Protestant churches proved themselves every bit as fanatical about witch-hunting as the Catholics they reviled. But there was a deeper crisis gathering that would one day threaten the whole Christian world-view. The first tremor came in 1543, with the publication of *On the Revolutions*, by Nicolaus Copernicus, a quiet, cautious priest, who knowing the import of what he wrote ensured that it would only be made public after he was dead and safely out of the reach of the Inquisition. Copernicus set the earth in motion around the sun. The ground moved under the very intellectual foundations of Christianity. We were no longer at the centre of a fixed, unchanging cosmos, as ordained by God – and Aristotle. It was a queasy feeling from which Christianity would never recover.

Witchcraft retains its fascination in modern times. The success of the many movies and books about witches and witchcraft – most recently, the Harry Potter novels – indicate their still powerful fascination. But what is astonishing is not that witchcraft should retain (at some level) its appeal in modern times, but that misogyny should. This is typified by the Rev. Montague Summers, the only English translator of *Malleus Maleficarum*, who it seemed welcomed the misogyny of Sprenger and Kramer. Though feminists and scholars have often quoted from his text, his introduction is generally ignored. In it, Rev. Summers thoroughly approves of the job undertaken by Sprenger and Kramer, and wishes they were still around to deal with the rise of socialism, of which he sees witchcraft as a forerunner. He notes 'the misogynistic trend of various passages', but he writes they are a 'wholesome and needful antidote in this feministic age, when the sexes seem confounded, and it appears to be the chief object of many females to ape the man . . .' This extraordinary condoning of the demonization and mass murder of women was written in

1928 – nine or ten years after women received the vote in the United States and Britain.

In recent years, many crimes perpetrated by states and other organizations – including those against women – have been acknowledged, and those responsible for them have in some cases apologized to the descendants of their victims. For example, in 1431, a nineteen-year-old French peasant girl called Joan, who had heard God's voice instructing her to lead the armies of France against the English, which she did with remarkable success, was condemned and burned as a heretic. To her English captors, the voice she had heard was not God's but Satan's. She was also condemned as an 'enchantress' – that is, a witch. Joan of Arc is the only witch that the Church has rehabilitated and made into a saint.[165] The Church has since apologized, through the Pope, to the Jews, for its anti-Semitism, and just a few years ago, to Galileo the astronomer for persecuting him because of his assertion that Copernicus was right in arguing that it is the sun, not the earth, which is at the centre of the solar system.

'Great evils form the groundwork of history,' wrote the medievalist Huizinga.[166] Is it not time for the Pope to set an example for other Christians and acknowledge the great evil of the witch-hunts, the awful wrongs inflicted upon thousands of innocent women, recognize their innocence and apologize for their horrendous deaths?

5

O BRAVE NEW WORLD: LITERATURE, MISOGYNY AND THE RISE OF MODERNITY

Even as the pall of smoke still hung over Europe from the raging fires of the witch-hunts, a new world began to emerge in the sixteenth and seventeenth centuries, dimly perceived at first. It would not be a world free from misogyny. In fact, the term itself would be first used in 1656.[167] But it was a world that challenged the authorities on whose dogmas and doctrines misogyny rested.

Between 1500 and 1800 occurred a series of revolutions, intellectual, social, economic and political, that would transform not only Europe but eventually the entire world. Never before had authority come under such scrutiny. What was regarded as sacred was challenged. Many of the old certainties collapsed. Out of the rubble emerged the modern world.

This was neither a straightforward nor a consistent process.

Nor at times did it seem to have anything to do with the status of women. When Galileo Galilei (1564–1642) climbed the steep stone stairs of the campanile in the Piazza San Marco in Venice in 1609 and pointed a crude optical instrument called a telescope at the night sky, how would what he saw challenge a civilization's view of women? What he saw through his telescope was a universe on the move, not the fixed, unchanging spheres of an earth-centred cosmos, as had been taught for more than 2,000 years. His observations (which, he believed, supported the theory of the sun-centred solar system of Copernicus) challenged the teachings of the Church, the Bible and Aristotle, the main pillars of authority on which the medieval view of the world and women had rested. If Galileo's discoveries showed that the ancient authorities, including even the Bible, could get the nature of the cosmos wrong, how reliable were they on other matters, including the nature and status of women? But it would prove easier to gain credence that the earth moves round the sun than it would to shift traditional misogynistic prejudices and practices.

As of 1600, in England, socially and intellectually among the more progressive countries in Europe, legally a woman had no rights at all, other than those recognized by local custom. Her father had charge of her until she was married, when she came under the authority of her husband, who took absolute control of all her personal property. As the law of the time stated: 'That which a man hath is his own. That which the wife hath is the husband's.'[168] Women could become queens in the sixteenth century, and like Elizabeth I command and inspire fear and respect, but by the beginning of the seventeenth century their status had if anything declined. Contemporary Platonists debated whether or not women had souls.[169] At the level of dress, always an indication of women's status, their suffering was taken for granted. The late seventeenth century fashion was to encase women's bodies in tight corsets. At the autopsy of one young woman who died at age 20 it was found that 'her ribs had grown into her liver, and that her other entrails were much hurt by being crushed together with her stays, which her mother had ordered to be twitched so straight that it often brought tears into her eyes whilst the maid was dressing her'.[170] Young women were also constantly subjected to purges and enemas to 'maintain a fashionably pallid complexion'.[171] Men who murdered their wives were hanged, but women who murdered their husbands suffered the same terrible fate as traitors and were burned at the stake. By the end of the eighteenth century, by which time most educated people accepted the theory of a sun-centred solar system, the struggle for legal reforms to marriage in favour of women was as yet in its infancy. Marriage still 'suspended' a woman's legal existence, incorporating it into that of her husband 'under whose wing, protection and cover, she performs everything'.[172]

However, changes as a result of the religious, social and political revolutions beginning with the Reformation, would challenge misogyny as never before. While the legal situation of women within marriage remained oppressive, the Reformation caused the status of marriage itself to undergo a dramatic change, affecting the relationship between husband and wife. It also cast the issue of women's education into a new light.

The reformers' rejection of priestly celibacy was at the heart of their revolt against the Catholic Church. By allowing clergy to marry, they raised the status of marriage, which the Catholic Church had viewed as very much an inferior state. This put husbands and wives on a more equal footing than was common before.

Women had taken a prominent role in the religious upheavals following Martin Luther's declaration of the ninety-five articles, which provoked an irreparable break with Catholicism in 1517. However, the convulsions that pitched women into active and public roles, even allowing a few of them to command the pulpit, inevitably created great unease. As the new Protestant faith stabilized, and the revolutionary fervour abated, so did the willingness of the reformers to grant women equality. In 1558, the founder of Scottish Protestantism John Knox published a pamphlet entitled 'The First Blast Against the Monstrous Regiment of Women', attacking the more prominent role women were taking in the new faith. The patriarchal family was if anything reinforced: now father not only knew best, but he knew better than the priest, whose role he adopted, to the extent of leading the family in daily prayers and in conducting readings from the Bible. Woman's subordinate role was reaffirmed, as summed up in the words of the great English Puritan poet John Milton (1608–74): 'He for God only, she for God in him.'

According to Lawrence Stone:

> The ideal woman in the sixteenth and seventeenth centuries was weak, submissive, charitable, virtuous and modest, like the wife of the Massachusetts minister in the 1630s, whom he publicly praised for her 'incomparable meekness of spirit, towards myself especially'.[173]

But it was not that simple! Relations within marriage had been set on a course towards greater conjugal intimacy from which they would not be deflected until they produced the nuclear family.

Just as, with the astronomical revolution started by Copernicus, the wrecking ball of science was delivering its first major blow against the authority of the Bible, the Reformation was declaring Biblical authority as essential to faith. Ironically, however, that declaration was good for women because reliance

on Scripture implied that it was important for all Protestants –
male and female – to be able to read, thus raising the vital matter
of women's education. There had been earlier advocates of
education for women. In the fifteenth century, the poet and
scholar Christine de Pisa had written: 'If it were customary to
send little girls to school and to teach them the same subjects as
are taught boys, they would learn just as fully and would
understand the subtleties of all arts and sciences.'[174]

In 1552, a pamphlet published in England argued that
women's disabilities were a result not of nature but of 'the
bringing up and training of women's life'.[175] There was something of a movement in favour of the education of women,
among whose exponents was the philosopher St Thomas
More, the author of *Utopia*, the most influential vision of
an ideal society since Plato's *The Republic*. 'I do not see why
learning . . . may not equally agree with both sexes,' he
wrote.[176] But the following century, the idea was still deeply
opposed, often at the highest levels. King James I denounced
the notion. 'To make women learned and foxes tame had the
same effect: to make them more cunning,' he said, expressing
the misogynistic prejudice of the centuries – though it is
worthwhile to note that it was a slight against the character
of women not their intelligence.[177]

King James' opinion prevailed – for a time. It is estimated
that as of 1600 in London – the London of Shakespeare – only
10 per cent of women could read. Within forty years, it had
risen to 20 per cent. [178] Outside of the city, the situation was
worse. As of 1754 only one woman out of three in England
could sign her name in the registry of marriages, compared to
slightly less than two-thirds of men.[179] By that date the total
population of England was around 6,000,000. Ironically,
considering his opposition to women's education, it was under
King James that the first great translation of the Bible into

English was undertaken, creating an incentive for English Protestants to teach their daughters to read in order to acquaint them first hand with the word of God, a vital defence against the blandishments of the still powerful Catholic Church.

'In Nature we have as clear an understanding as men, if we were bred in schools to mature our brains,' wrote Margaret, Duchess of Newcastle.[180] But upper-class and well-educated women like the Duchess of Newcastle were mercilessly derided and satirized on the stage for their ability to read Greek and Latin. The 'Plato in petticoats' became a standard figure of fun, for daring to defy male notions of women's intellectual capacities. However, the broader benefits of educating women were gradually gaining acceptance.

With the rise of the middle class from the mid-seventeenth century onwards, another important incentive to educate women came into play – the development of the notion of marriage as companionship and the subsequent need for a wife to be a fitting companion for her husband, someone with whom he might hold an intelligent conversation. By 1697, Daniel Defoe (1660–1731), one of the most influential writers of his time, was a strong advocate for women's education. Defoe had good cause to champion the education of women – as one of the first novelists, he knew that women were a growing part of his readership. These developments were the manifestation of a much deeper social transformation that would have a major impact on women's status.

According to Bertrand Russell: 'The modern world, so far as mental outlook is concerned, begins in the seventeenth century.'[181] An essential part of that outlook took root in Holland, England and the North American colonies. It was defined by revolutionary notions concerning the importance of the individual, stressing equality and the pursuit of happiness. The concept of individual autonomy as it emerged in the early modern period involved a redefinition of the relationship between men, their government and society, and the responsibilities that each bore to each.[182] Making the individual, not God, central to the scheme of things was a shift of emphasis that would have revolutionary consequences for the status of women.

All these ideas were central to the thinking of the English philosopher John Locke (1632–1704), who laid the foundations for the philosophy of liberalism. Locke attacked the notion that the structure of the family must reflect the patriarchal structure of society, where the king as the head of state was a model for the rule of the father over his household. He offered a more fluid theory of family, state, and the individual's relationship to the state. Linked to his concept of autonomy were ideas of equality, and the right of the individual to pursue happiness. Locke declared that 'all men by nature are born equal,' and that 'the necessity of pursuing true happiness is the foundation of all liberty.'[183]

Perhaps as importantly, Locke was an empiricist who argued that all human beings are at birth a blank slate on which circumstances, especially upbringing and education, inscribe the thing we call 'human nature'. The blank-slate hypothesis located the causes of human behaviour not in the brain but primarily in the world outside. Eventually, the blank-slate hypothesis would replace that of Original Sin as the primal state of being for us all. For women the implications of this were profound. If, like a man, a woman was a blank slate at birth, then her 'inferiority' was not inherent to her nature or predetermined by it but was a product of her upbringing and education.[184]

It called into question one of the foundation stones of misogyny. Genesis had decreed that the subjection of women to their husbands and their suffering in childbirth were punishments for Eve's part in the Fall of Man. In *Two Treatises of Government* Locke adopted a common-sense approach and declared: '. . . there is no more law to oblige a woman to such subjection, if the circumstances either of her condition or contract with her husband should exempt her from it, than there is that she should bring forth her children in sorrow and pain if there could be found a remedy for it, which is also part of the same curse upon her . . .' Since Locke equated good with pleasure and evil with pain, it made no sense to endure suffering if it could be avoided. He was among the first to protest against the fashion of encasing women's bodies in tight corsets.

It is not hard to imagine how much of a challenge this was to the prevailing order where subordination of women was part of the divine plan, and a model of the very structure of the cosmos. The idea that women could escape what is deemed their biological fate remains for some an affront to what they believe is God or Allah's grand design and has been fiercely opposed over the centuries. The churches would cry out against the use of chloroform to ease the pangs of childbirth in the nineteenth century (see Chapter 6); conservative Catholics and fundamentalist Protestants would campaign sometimes with violence against contraception and abortion in the twentieth.

The implications of liberalism were impossible to avoid almost as soon as the principles from which they derived were formulated. English women did not need to wait for Locke to formulate the new philosophy with all its ramifications. In 1642, for the first time since the late Roman Republic, women took to the streets in political protest. Some 400 assembled outside the English parliament to protest their financial hardships. During the English Civil War (1642–9) women belonging to one of the more radical sects chanted:

We shall not be wives
And tie up our lives
In villainous slavery[185]

Within two years of Locke's death, Mary Astell (1668–1731), often described as the first English feminist writer and the author of *A Serious Proposal to the Ladies* (1694–7) and *Some Reflections Upon Marriage* (1700), posed the inevitable question: 'If all men are born free, how is it that all women are born slaves?'

The application of liberal notions about the rights of the individual had already led to improvements in women's status in the colonies of North America. In 1647, Massachusetts passed a law forbidding husbands to beat their wives. But the influence of liberalism went much further. It helped create a whole new notion of the family as a unit based on affection as well as on authority. Locke envisioned the family as a power-sharing unit 'in which the mother too has her share with the father'.[186] This in turn revolutionized the rules regarding the role of sex between husband and wife. It also undermined the parents' control over their children's choice of whom to marry. As Stone has pointed out: 'How could paternal control over the choice of marriage partner be maintained, if the pair were now to be bound by ties of love and affection?'[187]

The idea that husbands and wives might have intercourse for 'mutual comfort' as well as for procreation signalled a loosening of control of the churches and other authorities over sexual behaviour. The traditional misogyny of Christianity had tolerated sex between men and women as, regrettably, the only means that was available to human beings to reproduce. (This, fundamentally, remains the attitude of the Catholic Church to this day.) From St Paul onwards, the basic attitude of Christianity towards sex was that it was a shameful act –

more shameful if enjoyed. However, as society became more secular, so did sex. This process did not by any means move inexorably forward. Periods of sexual liberation have always been countered by periods of conservative backlash. But the development of more liberal attitudes to sex was accelerated after the failure of the Puritan Revolution in England (1647–60) when there was a moral revolt against the religious zealots who during the rule of Oliver Cromwell had shut down theatres, banned cock-fighting and closed taverns. The Puritans may have won the Civil War, but in their war against pleasure they were decisively defeated.

Prising apart sex from the Divine Plan inevitably led to an increasing emphasis on its recreative rather than its procreative function. This was made easier by the invention of the condom, which first became available in London and Paris in the seventeenth century. Though initially used as a prophylactic against venereal infection, the condom was soon functioning as a contraceptive device. The condom represented the first major step towards the transformation of sexual activity into a pursuit that was mainly, not just occasionally, recreational.[188] The ability of women to protect themselves, and avoid pregnancy, challenged the biological determinism that lies behind so much misogyny. The anxiety that this creates, today as in the seventeenth century, is often disguised in moralizing that such protection makes women even more vulnerable to men's lusts. But it cannot hide the essential fear of women controlling their reproductive fate, thus achieving the autonomy that all misogynists dread.

As the possibility of one form of autonomy began glimmering into view, science laid to rest the fantasy of another – that of the autonomous male, that lies behind the Greek myth of creation and Aristotle's 'scientific' exposition of the lesser, even dispensable role women play in reproduction (see Chapter 1). For millennia both reduced the role of women to that of a pouch to nurture the all-life-giving seed. However, with the invention of the microscope a miniature world was opened up that was as fascinating as anything that the telescope had revealed. In 1672, the ovaries were discovered. It was gradually realized that a woman's role in conception was not that of the passive incubator, with the male seed carrying all the essentials of life, including the soul, as had been propounded since Aristotle. Her eggs were shown to be essential to the creation as well as the sustenance of life. Athena might one day spring from a petri dish, but never from her father Zeus' head.

The rise of science, the advancement of reason, the birth of democratic ideas, and the development of a philosophy centred on the individual, did not however banish misogyny, no more than the intellectual triumphs of the Greeks did 2,000 years earlier. Misogyny, like all prejudices, is often most powerfully felt as a reaction to changes that threaten its underlying assumptions. It must be remembered that the most lethal form of misogyny in history, witch-hunting, reached its peak in the seventeenth century, even as Locke was elucidating the rights of the individual and protesting against tight corsets. Every age, as the poet T. S. Eliot remarked, is an age of transition.[189] But the seventeenth century was one of the most turbulent in human history, riven by moral, intellectual, social and political conflicts that have left their mark on the subsequent centuries.

In literature misogyny never went out of fashion in Europe during the period that we identify as the birth of the modern world. The sixteenth century and early seventeenth produced a rich crop of misogynistic writing. It ranged from scurrilous pamphlets, most notoriously Joseph Swetman's 'The Arraignment of Lewd, Idle, Forward and Unconstant Woman', which went through ten editions between 1616 and 1634, to the morbid and bitter denunciations in the work of the finest of the Elizabethan and Jacobean poets and dramatists. Misogyny did not want for exponents.

It was not the first time that alongside lyric poetry, devoted to praising women for their beauty, there should run the sewer of misogyny, often issuing from the pen of the same poet. The French poet Clement Marot composed a poem in praise of women's breasts that created a literary fashion:

> A little ball of ivory
> In the middle of which sits
> A strawberry or cherry
> When one sees you, many men feel
> The desire within their hands
> To touch you and to hold you.

Later, he composed its opposite:

> Breast that is nothing but skin,
> Flaccid breast, flaglike breast
> Like that of a funnel,
> Breast with a big, ugly black lip
> Breast that's good for nursing
> Lucifer's children in Hell.[190]

Many of these attacks on women are part of a rhetorical convention, and consist mostly of hoary clichés that go back to the Greek and Roman misogynistic tradition. In English, it persisted through the eighteenth century as a major literary tradition. In *Epicoene: or, The Silent Woman* by Ben Jonson (1573?–1637), a husband, Captain Otter, describes his wife in a manner that would have been understood – excepting the contemporary references – by the Roman poet Juvenal:

O most vile face! And yet she spends me forty pound a year in
mercury and hogs-bones. All her teeth were made in Black-
friars, both her eyebrows in the Strand, and her hair in
Silverstreet. Every part of the town owns a piece of her . . .
She takes herself asunder still when she goes to bed, into some
twenty boxes; and about the next day noon, is put together
again, like a great German clock.[191]

Misogynists deploy anti-make-up propaganda in every age,
with more or less the same tedious lament. But a more
psychologically disturbing anxiety arises that focuses on the
independence of women. *Epicoene* features a coterie of independent women known as the Collegiates, who spend their
time discussing poetry, politics and philosophy. Their independence is underscored by the fact that they can afford to ride
around London in their own coaches. Their masculine traits
stand in contrast to the male characters, who like Captain
Otter are effeminized through their failure to control their
wives. Gender roles are switched, as the independent women
become masculine and the weak men become effeminate. The
Collegiates are accused of pursuing sex for pure pleasure, like
men, and of sleeping with each other. The result is moral and
social chaos and disorder.

Such women were the target of scathing satire by Jonson
and his contemporaries. Of one woman called Morilla, who
like the Collegiate women, dared to ride around in her own
coach – one supposes it was the Elizabethan equivalent of a
woman roaring around on a motorbike – the satirist William
Goddard wrote:

> Speak: could you judge her less than be some man?
> If less then this I'm sure you'd judge at least,
> She was part man, part woman; part a beast.[192]

In *The Taming of the Shrew*, William Shakespeare (1564–1616), then an up-and-coming young playwright, dealt with the prevailing anxiety over women's domestic rebellion. The play is a perennially popular comedy, which is both raucous and erotic. It deals with the issue of sex and power, and its ending, while ostensibly representing an outright male triumph, is framed somewhat ambiguously.

No man will marry the heroine Katherine Minola of Padua, because she is in a state of permanent insurrection about the prospect of being subservient to a husband. Petruchio, desperately needing to get married for economic reasons, proves her match. Katherine's concession speech in Act 5, Scene 2, is a plea to women to surrender and abandon their struggle with men for dominance:

> Fie, fie, unknit that threat'ning, unkind brow,
> And dart not scornful glances from those eyes
> To wound thy lord, thy king, thy governor.
> It blots thy beauty as frosts do bite the meads,
> Confounds thy fame as whirlwinds shake fair buds . . .
> Thy husband is thy lord, thy life, thy keeper,
> Thy head, thy sovereign, one that cares for thee
> And for thy maintenance; commits his body
> To painful labour both by sea and land . . .
> Whilst thou liest warm at home, secure and safe . . .[193]

To the male audience, it may be gratifying to see a woman hoist the white flag so conspicuously. *The Taming of the Shrew* seems to celebrate a return to the status quo, with woman as subject and man master.

However, in the play appearance and reality are confused. It is often forgotten that this is a play within a play. *The Taming of the Shrew* is an entertainment that two noblemen stage to

dupe a hen-pecked and drunken beggar named Sly into believing that he is a lord. When it ends, they dump him on the street
and he falls into an alcoholic stupor. Sly is reawakened from
his dream of lordship to face the prospect of confronting a wife
angry because he has been gone all night drinking. He declares:
'I know now how to tame a shrew,' then quickly adds, 'I
dreamt upon it all this night till now.' The taming of the shrew
is a drunken man's dream, a mere appearance of reality, which
evaporates when Sly wakes. Shakespeare leaves his audience
with an uncomfortable ambiguity. Is the crushing and domes-
tication of the rebellious woman appearance or reality?

There is much in the work of William Shakespeare that is
uncomfortable and ambiguous when he deals with women and
their relationship to men. But to generalize about any aspect of
Shakespeare is no easy matter, since he explored a bewildering
range of emotions with extraordinary complexity and depth.
In doing so, he produced the greatest body of dramatic
literature since the Athenian dramatists of the fifth century,
and filled it with poetry that ranks with that of Homer, Virgil
and Dante. So it is not surprising that misogyny is among the
feelings with which he deals. In two of his greatest tragedies, it
is expressed with a poetic intensity that is perhaps unrivalled,
raising the question as to whether or not the world's greatest
poet carried a deep-seated contempt for women.

Women play key roles in a majority of his works. In his
comedies, their love affairs are pivotal to the plot, and in these
plays he presents the audience with a wide range of love-sick,
ironic, romantic, rebellious, clever, deceptive, spirited, and
independent women characters, a range unmatched by any
other writer. However, unlike the Athenian tragedians, Shakespeare did not make women the central figures in his greatest dramas – his tragedies, all written in an incredible ten-year
period of poetic achievement between 1599 and 1609. Though

women are crucial to the main action of all the tragedies, the principal focus is on the hero and the weaknesses that undo him. That is, in the tragedies, Shakespeare's chief concern is with the qualities necessary for men to wield power and authority. In them, women do not challenge male authority as they do in the great Athenian tragedies. But their relationship to the hero is frequently the driving force that leads to his tragedy. Most famously, it is Lady Macbeth's ambition for her husband to be king that pushes him to murder and even to regicide, and Antony's infatuation for Cleopatra that inspires him to believe he can be sole ruler of Rome with her as his queen.

In neither of these plays does the doomed hero decry or condemn the woman for the part she played in his downfall. Shakespeare does not use the opportunity (which a misogynist might view as ideal) to replay the Fall of Man theme with Lady Macbeth and Cleopatra in the predictable role of Eve or Pandora, bringing about man's destruction. Macbeth and Antony go to their deaths accepting full responsibility for their fate.

However, in both *Hamlet* and *King Lear*, women are blamed not as individuals only but as a sex in general for helping to bring about the hero's suffering and downfall. Because these are regarded generally as Shakespeare's two greatest works, they have led some to accuse him of being a misogynist or 'at best, somewhat ambivalent about woman's worth and sexuality'.[194]

It is not easy to draw conclusions about Shakespeare's attitude to women and sexuality from *Hamlet*. The play is an enigma, and has been called 'the Mona Lisa of literature'.[195] At the same time as it has been praised as the greatest play ever written, it has been faulted as 'most certainly an artistic failure'.[196] The problem is the difficulty in identifying just what it is that *Hamlet* is actually about. *Macbeth* is about ambition; *Antony and Cleopatra*, passion; *Coriolanus*, pride; *Othello*, jealousy; *King Lear*, ingratitude. But *Hamlet*, which should have been the easiest of all to categorize, since it is on the surface at least a revenge play, eludes any such simple summary. If asked what the play is about, we can say that Hamlet's uncle Claudius has murdered his father the king, married his mother; and thus preempted Hamlet's succession to the throne. Hamlet must revenge his father's death. But we will have not even touched upon the intense, complex and turbulent emotions, which spill out in some of the greatest poetry ever written. However, what makes Hamlet relevant to misogyny is the fact that one of those emotions, perhaps indeed the most powerful in the whole play, is an expression of his anger and disgust at his mother Gertrude for marrying his uncle.

Even before Hamlet is alerted to his uncle's evil deed by the ghost of his father, we see him in a state of deep melancholy, verging on despair, because of Gertrude's hasty remarriage. His anger at her has become generalized into a profound disgust at the world and at the human body itself, which is the subject of the first of the play's great soliloquies, beginning (Act 1, Scene 2):

> O that this too too sullied flesh would melt,
> Thaw and resolve itself into a dew . . .

It is his mother's lust that has 'sullied' the body and, as becomes apparent as the speech goes on, turned the world into:

> . . . an unweeded garden
> That grows to seed; things rank and gross in nature
> Possess it merely. That it should come to this!

But two months dead, nay not so much, not two;
So excellent a king that was to this
Hyperion to a satyr, so loving to my mother,
That he might not beteem the winds of heaven
Visit her face too roughly; heaven and earth,
Must I remember? Why, she would hang on him,
As if increase of appetite had grown
By what it fed on, and yet within a month –
Let me not think on't; frailty, thy name is woman!

Hamlet's first soliloquy reveals that he was angry with his mother even before her hasty remarriage. Gertrude's sexual attachment to his father is regarded with revulsion, even though, given his description of his father as the very paragon of royalty, it should not be a surprise that she found him so attractive. After Gertrude loses her husband, her apparently insatiable appetite has led her into the arms of a man her son compares to a satyr – the half-man, half-goat figure of Greek myth, the very embodiment of animal lust, often represented as possessing an exaggerated penis. Hamlet's denunciation of his mother turns into an attack on women that has become proverbial. Behind the disgust lurks the notion that once aroused, women's sexual desires are uncontrollable.[197]

Later in the play, Hamlet returns to the theme of his mother's sexual appetite as he presents her with a portrait of his father to compare to that of her current husband (Act 3, Scene 4):

You cannot call it love, for at your age
The hey-day in the blood is tame, it's humble,
And waits upon the judgement, and what judgement
Would step from this to this?

Hamlet's angry outburst continues as he nearly makes himself sick conjuring up an image of Gertrude and Claudius in bed together:

> Nay, but to live
> In the rank sweat of an enseamed bed,
> Stewed in corruption, honeying and making love
> Over the nasty sty . . .

He expresses here a horror of human sexuality that belongs firmly to the misogynistic tradition of Christianity, and might have issued from the pen of St Augustine. But Hamlet's anger at his mother is also provoked by her own inadequacy. She is one of the most negative female characters that Shakespeare ever created. She is not particularly wicked, nor especially cunning, nor manipulative; certainly, she is far from daring. Her rapid marriage to her dead husband's brother is not an act of boldness by a woman defying convention, but of weakness. And in spite of what Hamlet says about her, she does not appear as a monster of lust. Indeed, her chief characteristic is her passivity. One suspects that her son has exaggerated her carnality and in doing so has revealed more about his own sexual obsessions than his mother's.[198]

Ophelia, the only other woman character in the play, suffers because of Hamlet's revulsion against female sexuality. Announcing (Act 3, Scene 2), that he no longer loves her, he tells her: 'Get thee to a nunnery: why wouldst thou be a breeder of sinners?'

What follows is one of the most famous outbursts of misogyny in literature: 'I have heard of your paintings well enough; God hath given you one face, but you make yourselves another: you gig and amble; and you lisp, you nickname God's creatures, and make your wantonness your ignorance.'

Among the powerful emotions expressed in his speech, there is genuine bitterness and cruelty regarding Ophelia's desire to be a 'breeder of sinners', which once more suggests a deep-seated anger at women for (according to Christian theology) perpetuating the curse of Original Sin. But we must recall that in the same speech Hamlet is trying to dupe Claudius and Polonius into believing that his unhappiness is caused by his problems with Ophelia, not with his uncle's usurpation of the throne. That is, the most famous outburst of misogyny in literature is in fact a rhetorical exercise on Hamlet's part, more related to his attempts to deceive his enemies than express his true feelings about Ophelia or women in general.

Hamlet's main focus is on the relationship between a mother and her son. *King Lear*, the other play in which misogyny is a main theme, is centred on the relationship between a father and his daughters. It marked a noticeable change in emotional emphasis. According to a recent biographer of Shakespeare 'after about 1606 the father–daughter bond becomes an almost obsessive theme in his work.'[199]

If psychology has a theory of misogyny, it is one that traces its origins to the primal relationship between mother and son. Usually, by the time a man has daughters, his character is set, and even if they are as wicked as Lear's Goneril and Regan, their behaviour will not form their father's feelings about women in general, it will merely confirm it. For this reason, misogyny, however powerfully expressed in *King Lear*, is less central to the play's dynamic than it is in *Hamlet*. The plot merely affords Lear the opportunity to vent. Made homeless by Goneril and Regan, to whom the old king has foolishly given over his kingdom, abandoned to the elements, Lear erupts in one of the most powerful scenes in literature (Act 4, Scene 6):

Behold yon simpering dame,
Whose face between her forks presageth snow,
That minces virtue, and does shake the head
To hear of pleasure's name;
The fitchew nor the soiled horse goes to't
With a more riotous appetite.
Down from the waist they're centaurs,
Though women all above:
But to the girdle to the gods inherit,
Beneath is all the fiends';
There's hell, there's darkness, there's the sulphury pit,
Burning, scalding, stench, consumption; fie, fie,
Fie, pah, pah! Give me an ounce of civet, good
Apothecary, to sweeten my imagination . . .

Again, as in *Hamlet*, what begins as an attack on a particular woman (or a particular kind of woman – in this case, one who parades false modesty) turns into a fierce denunciation of female sexuality. And once again, as with Gertrude and Desdemona in *Othello*, it is woman's 'appetite' for sex that disgusts the hero and sours his imagination. But unlike Hamlet, King Lear is redeemed by a woman – his third daughter Cordelia, who stood up to him at the beginning of the play with a display of honesty that undercuts the play's misogyny. Refusing to flatter him with false praise, she demonstrates the link between truth and love that her father does not fully grasp until the end – and only at the cost of Cordelia's life, which she loses attempting to rescue him. Misogyny does not survive Shakespeare's tragic vision any more than do other follies that bring about human unhappiness. Pity, which springs from a profound sympathy for the human condition, as endured by men and women alike, replaces them as the dominant emotion of his greatest plays. The triumph of Shakespearean tragedy is that through pity it reveals that we share a common humanity, in which all distinctions, including those between men and women, are rendered insignificant.

In the plays that followed, the works of his last years as a dramatist, such as *The Tempest* and *The Winter's Tale* the diatribes against women – whether rhetorical or deeply felt – disappear. The prevailing mood is reconciliation, usually between father and daughter. The conflict between men and women is resolved satisfactorily in the relationship that a father has with his daughter.

Elsewhere, misogyny showed its resilience throughout the seventeenth and eighteenth centuries in the face of social, moral, economic and political developments that would profoundly transform women's status. In England, a dual process can be discerned. As a new model of family developed among the rising middle classes, with increased emphasis on mutual affection between man and wife, a breakdown in traditional sexual morality took place among the wits of the court circles of the post-1660 period, that at times approached nihilism. Along with it appeared some of the most scurrilous poetic attacks on women since Juvenal (see Chapter 2).

John Wilmot, the Earl of Rochester (1647–80), the poet who penned some of the most exquisite love lyrics in the English language, including that beginning, 'An age in her embraces passed/Would seem a winter's day,' could also describe a woman as 'a passive pot for fools to spend in' (that is, a chamber pot) and liken female genitalia to a sewer.[200] The Earl of Rochester belonged to a new phenomenon – the first generation of rakes, young upper-class males who followed a libertine life style, bawdy, open-minded, rebellious, irreligious, often politically progressive, and at the same time, unrelenting satirists, as given to outbursts of misanthropic despair as they were to misogynistic verses. Theirs was a fierce rejection of the official Puritanism that had prevailed in the previous generation; they would set off a series of moral cycles in the West, with periods of sexual conservatism being followed by outbreaks of hedonism followed by conservative reaction, which would last to this day.

The rakes effectively created a subculture around the court of the Restoration period (1660–88) where sex was pursued only for pleasure. On the continent, the same kind of hedonism prevailed at the court of Louis XIV (1643–1713). It constituted a rebellion against Judaeo-Christian sexual morality, inspired by the humanism of Renaissance Italy. In the past, as in the Rome of the late Republic and early Empire, there had been comparable 'breakdowns' of conventional morality among sections of the ruling class. But in general, they were severely punished. In the late seventeenth century, however, with the weakening of the authority of the churches, and an emerging middle-class worldview from which a coherent morality had yet to be derived, no institution had the power to curb the new hedonism.

The women who were part of the rakes' circle ranged in social status from lower-class prostitutes and actresses (then a novel feature on the social scene) to aristocratic ladies, some of whom, in reputation at least, were as promiscuous as the men. For the first time in English history, a few of them left behind their views of the erotic and verbal game in which they were so intensely engaged, crossing poetic swords with some of the sharpest wits of the period. The most famous, Aphra Behn (1640–89), was renowned, and vilified, as a successful playwright and poet, the first Englishwoman to achieve such literary fame. She was denounced as a 'lewd harlot', who dared to describe how a young wife can sexually exhaust her husband, and reduce him to a trembling wreck. She made literary history by giving the woman's version of premature ejaculation, for which male poets too often blamed their 'fair nymphs'. In her poem 'The Disappointment' the 'hapless swain' is accused of trying to prolong his pleasure 'which too much love destroys' and so finds 'his vast pleasure turned to pain'. [201]

For their part, the rakes' attitude to women was at once decorous and coarse, oscillating between adoration and contempt, which was usually born of disappointment or rejection. There was also a strong strain of anxiety about their sexual performance, which is seen in the number of poems about impotence and the court ladies' increasing use of dildos. The fact that the dildo was from the 1660s onwards usually of Italian manufacture, increased the upper-class English male's sexual angst, since Italy was associated with an effeminizing eroticism. For an Englishman, what could be more humiliating than to be superannuated by an Italian dildo? [202] The rakes broke no new ground in the chronicles of misogyny, except that in the explicitness and coarseness of their language they foreshadowed the first of those that we would recognize as pornographers. Indeed, Wilmot was treated as such until relatively recently. In 1926, an edition of his poems was seized in New York by the police and destroyed.[203] However, the rakes were unlike pornographers in several important ways – one was that they dealt with the frustrations of sex as well as its delights, being as frank about their episodes of impotence as about their conquests. There also prevailed a feeling, particularly powerful in Rochester's case, that the pursuit of sexual pleasure is just another one of life's transient absurdities.

By the late seventeenth century, a significant number of people saw sex as an activity independent of procreation and love. Biology, of course, still imposed constraints on the ability of men, and more so women, to act out that view, the condom and the dildo not withstanding. Though it is a view that has been met with more than one conservative moral backlash, it has continued to thrive in Western society, regardless of all attempts to suppress or contain it.

However, it was far from being the dominant morality, nor was it the one that would determine the shape misogyny would take in the coming centuries. By the early eighteenth century, in England and Holland, thanks to the huge expansion in overseas trade, the mercantile middle class had established itself as a political power to be reckoned with. It had forged a moral code to reflect its priorities. It was a moral code that was in some ways conservative, stressing the virtues of frugality, thrift, hard work and sexual restraint. But thanks to its revolutionary emphasis on the needs and importance of the individual, it made it increasingly difficult to deny women their full share of humanity even as misogyny refashioned itself to fit aspects of the new dominant morality.

During the early eighteenth century, a new literary form arose to embody that individualism: the novel. It would play a unique role in women's history. For the first time characters were portrayed as individuals, living their lives in an actual time and an actual place. The novel was true to women's experience in ways no previous literature had attempted. Before, the great poets and dramatists had presented characters and plots that stayed faithful to certain universal types, derived from mythology or history and intended not so much to represent an individual but to embody some general truth about life. These truths were held to be timeless, unchanging Platonic absolutes contrasting with the ephemera of individual experience. In contrast, the novel from its very beginnings, in the work of Daniel Defoe (1660–1731), relies on realistic detail to tell the stories of characters. We get to know Defoe's characters Moll Flanders and Roxana in an intimate way, quite unlike the way we know Medea or King Lear. The novel was an instrument for exploring the personal lives of recognizable people, and as such allowed the presentation of women characters and their relationships in a completely new way. It is no coincidence that the novel was also the first literary form that women's tastes and concerns helped to shape; nor is it a surprise that, though its earliest practitioners were men, it would soon become the genre in which women excelled more than in any other. By the end of the eighteenth century in England there were more women novelists than men.[204]

The prosperity of the middle classes in England had been accompanied by an expansion of the reading public and an information explosion, with printing presses appearing all over London, producing pamphlets, and the first newspapers and magazines. Furthermore, an increasing number of women had more free time on their hands. Because of an enduring Protestant distrust of the theatre as being somewhat disreputable, a large number of those women turned to the novel for entertainment. Its appeal to the middle class, and to women, was evident. You did not need a Classical education, or knowledge of Greek and Roman history, to enjoy *Moll Flanders*. Its author, after all, had been educated in a trade school and had practised a trade (first as a hosiery merchant then as a pamphleteer and journalist). The fact that novels often featured women characters in lead roles was also a powerful attraction to women readers. Two of Defoe's four greatest novels are about women – *Moll Flanders* (1722) and *Roxana* (1724).[205] He was a strong advocate for women's education. Apart from everything else, he was a successful author who realized the importance of women as readers. Defoe also helped influence the growing opinion that opposed parents forcing daughters to marry against their will, which he likened to rape. As a spokesman for the middle classes, he stressed the importance of love in marriage and argued, 'to say love is not essential to a form of marriage is true; but to say that it is not essential to the felicity of the married state . . . is not true.'[206] However, as a God-fearing Protestant, he warned against 'lewdness', or sexual passion, as a reason to marry, claiming in a pamphlet, that it 'brings madness, desperation, ruin of families, self-murders, killing of bastards, etc.'[207]

However, the moral message that his novels convey is not quite so unambiguous. All Defoe's characters are basically like his first and most famous, Robinson Crusoe; they are shipwrecks. Crusoe is shipwrecked by storm at sea; Roxana, on the other hand, is shipwrecked by a foolish, selfish husband who abandons her and her five children to starve. The stories are all tales of survival under difficult circumstances. Roxana survives and prospers by becoming a whore and courtesan to a series of rich men. A predictable enough if not respectable route for a beautiful woman to take, it might be thought, and Defoe tries to reassure the reader with frequent moral asides stressing that he is not recommending that women should follow his heroine's example. But Roxana does not conform to the prevailing stereotypes of women and though Defoe does his best to disapprove of her, it is evident throughout the novel that his admiration for her as an economic success story overcomes his conventional moralizing against how she makes her money. Most importantly, she is not governed by love but by the desire to preserve the autonomy that she has achieved thanks to her economic success. A considerable part of the novel is about how she manages her money. In doing so, she redefines her relationship with men. She rejects marriage when proposed to by a man who loves her because, she says, 'tho' I could give up my Virtue, and expose myself, I could not give up my Money . . .' She explains: 'my heart was bent upon an Independency of Fortune; and I told him, I knew no State of Matrimony, but what was, at best, a State of Inferiority, if not Bondage; that I had no Notion of it; that I lived a Life of absolute Liberty now; was as free as I was born, and having a plentiful Fortune, I did not understand what Coherence the words Honour and Obey had with the Liberty of a Free Woman.'[208]

Even when pregnant, she resists the offer of marriage. Defoe reverses the usual situation. It is the father that is pleading for marriage to the mother on behalf of their unborn child. Roxana rejects him and he is stunned. 'For it was never known,' he responds, 'that any Woman refused to marry a Man that had first lain with her, much less a Man that had gotten her with-child; but you go upon different Notions from all the World, and tho' you reason it so strongly, that a Man knows hardly what to answer, yet I must own, there is something in it shocking to Nature . . .'[209] Roxana's concern about the security of her fortune accurately reflects the legal situation of married women in the eighteenth century, which was still governed by patriarchal notions that went back to Roman times. On marriage a woman's property became her husband's. (This would remain the case until well into the nineteenth century.)

In the end, Roxana does marry – for a title, and only after the strictest measures are in force for preserving the independence of her fortune. The strongest characters in her story are all women, and the most intense relationships are between them. The male characters are passive, insubstantial creatures, who do not even have names, mere rungs on the ladder of Roxana's climb to the top.[210] Just as Robinson Crusoe was the portrait of the autonomous man, forging an independent life for himself against all the odds, Roxana is his female equivalent – the first vision of an autonomous woman that we have. Throughout the novel she is called an 'Amazon' – a member of the legendary tribe of warrior women who lived without men – an indication of the deep-seated and continuing anxiety that the notion of an autonomous woman inspires.

For women the middle-class values that opened up visions of individuality would prove to be fraught with ambiguities. The new morality of the middle class resembled the old in its identification of a woman's worth with her chastity. The middle-class wife and mother of the new model family, while she was expected to be able to 'comfort' her husband sexually, was also being increasingly represented as a person for whom sexual pleasure was not important. Her virtue became propaganda in the moral war the middle class fought against the wastrels and degenerates of the aristocracy. The image of the good middle-class wife of the eighteenth century would prepare the way for the fainting, sexless Victorian maidens of the nineteenth.

The resilience of misogyny can be explained partly by the fact that misogynists have always had it both ways. Perhaps comparable to the way Nazi propaganda portrayed Jews as both Bolshevists and bankers, misogynists have either condemned women for being sexually insatiable or denied they had any sexual desires at all. In this contradictory dualism, women were viewed as either insatiable sexual predators or chaste and virtuous sexual victims.

This dualism clearly manifested itself in the 1740s. The greatest poet of the age, Alexander Pope (1688–1744) in such poems as 'To A Lady' summed up one aspect of traditional misogynistic thinking:

> Some men to business, some to pleasure take,
> But every woman is at heart a rake.[211]

A completely opposite view of women appeared around the same time with the publication of *Pamela: or, Virtue Rewarded*, the first novel by Samuel Richardson. Richardson, a printer and the son of a carpenter, was commissioned by a

publisher to write a volume of letters that would teach the
innocent – or presumed innocent – daughters of the middle
class how to conduct themselves when working as servants in
the homes of the aristocracy. *Pamela* was the tale of how a
virtuous young woman resists the multifarious and determined
attempts of her employer, Mr B, a rake, to seduce her. Pamela
declares that her maxim is 'May I never survive, one moment,
that fatal one in which I shall forfeit my innocence!'[212] Faced
with her impregnable purity, Mr B finally gives up and
proposes marriage. Pamela reconsiders all her previous moral
objections to him and deciding he is not such a bad chap after
all, accepts. By the novel's end, thanks to his wife's sterling
example, the rake has become a Puritan. It was not, of course,
the first tale of a virtuous woman resisting a lustful male, but it
was the first time a servant girl was accorded that heroic role,
proving that while the aristocracy may still be socially superior
to the rising middle class, the middle class were their moral
superiors.

Pamela enjoyed extraordinary success, first in England, where
it went through four editions in a short time, and then in France.
Among its most devoted readers were middle-class women. For
this reason, the novel is a landmark in the history of women as
well as of literature. By making *Pamela* a bestseller, for the first
time women (at least middle-class women) had exercised their
say over what they wanted from writers. And what they chose
was *Pamela*, a parable of middle-class feminine purity pitted
against the desires of the rapacious upper-class male. Its lead
character provided a model for the daughters of merchants,
printers and haberdashers to emulate. But the parable contained
a deep moral ambiguity. Was Pamela being 'pure' for purity's
sake, or merely as a lure to entrap Mr B?[213]

Pamela's purity is clearly for Mr B an irresistible incitement
to lust. The English middle classes were not the first to discover

the powerful sexual allure of the virtuous woman – the original 'good girl', Lucretia, was raped because her virtue was so sexually provocative. As the supreme Puritan Angelo put it in Shakespeare's *Measure for Measure* (Act 2, Scene 3):

> Can it be
> That modesty can more betray our sense
> Than woman's lightness . . . Angelo,
> Dost thou desire to use her foully for those things
> That make her good?

The answer from the Mr Bs of this world is a resounding 'Yes'.

The success of *Pamela* among women raises another, more interesting question. Clearly, it indicates that a sizeable section of women identified with a character who is at best unbelievably naïve and at worst incredibly manipulative. It should not be surprising that women readers should have absorbed these misogynistic stereotypes, but it remains somewhat ironic that exercising their power for the first time as an important part of the reading public they helped make them into a bestseller.

With the growth in power and influence of the middle classes, the ideal of the sexless woman became a standard for society, not only in England, but also in the philosophical and social writings of Jean-Jacques Rousseau in France in the late eighteenth century, and in North America. This standard stressed that the differences between men and women fully explained their different status, the most important of them being the strength of sexual desire in one and its relative absence in the other. Women found themselves dehumanized, this time in the name of purity.

Jean-Jacques Rousseau (1712–78), probably one of the most influential misogynists of all time, took the ideal of the pure woman who uses her virtue as a sexual allure and turned it into an inescapable fact of nature. Dissembling and manipulation were assigned to her as her defining characteristics. 'Whether the woman shares the man's passions or not,' he wrote, in an account of the ideal woman and her education in what became an international bestseller, 'whether she is willing or unwilling to satisfy it, she always repulses him and defends herself, though not always with the same vigour and therefore not always with the same success.'[214] This is merely a roundabout way of asserting that women say 'no' even when they mean 'yes', the same logic that has frequently been used as a defence in rape trials.

Rousseau stood on the brink of the French Revolution. He was a product of the Age of Enlightenment, but the harbinger of the Romantic movement, the intellectual, artistic and moral revolution that would replace it. The old authorities, philosophical and religious, had been overthrown. The universe was now seen to be governed by laws that the human intellect could discover and understand through the use of reason. But it was reason – meant to rid the world of outmoded prejudices – that Rousseau invoked to justify his belief that woman was 'the sex that ought to obey'.[215] He asserted: 'Women do wrong to complain of the inequality of man-made laws; this inequality is not of man's making, or at any rate it is not the result of mere prejudice, but of reason.'[216]

That reason was derived from what he saw as the natural order of things. Since nature has entrusted woman with the care of the children, she 'must hold herself responsible for them to their father'.[217] The keystone of Rousseau's thinking was that man was corrupted the further away he grew from nature. Civilization, and all its iniquities, including selfishness, inequality and greed, is a result of the 'natural man' being uprooted from his original state of existence, which Rousseau equated with innocence. However, one thing had not changed – and should not change – and that was the 'natural' subordination of women to men. The will of nature now replaced the will of God in determining the fate and status of women.

Not surprisingly, in Rousseau's vision of primitive man, men and women lived separate lives, mating when they met, and then moving on, with the women raising their offspring by themselves without any help or concern from the fathers. It was an eighteenth-century version of the old myth of male autonomy. He also returned to the Greeks for a model of how women should be treated, and admired their policy of segregation of the sexes as practised in its most extreme version by the Athenians. He practised the contempt for women that he preached, dumping the five children that he had with his mistress Thérèse le Vasseur in foundling homes. She could neither read nor write. He seems to have enjoyed the feeling of intellectual superiority that he derived from this relationship, for though he taught her to write, she never learned to read, nor count, nor remember the names of the months of the year.[218] Nor is it surprising that Rousseau admired the novels of Richardson, since he too believed that 'chasteness inflames' men's desires, and nothing was quite as sexy as a simpering virgin who knew her place.

However, another view of women, a glimpse of which we caught in Defoe's novel *Roxana*, challenged Rousseau and Richardson's version of misogyny. It might seem something of a paradox that this counter-view, in which women were seen as highly sexual beings, capable of achieving independence and status, found its most dramatic and uncompromising expression in eighteenth-century pornography. But then, the relationship between misogyny, pornography and the status of women is one of the most contentious that can be found.

While it is probably a safe generalization that philosophers and priests have done more harm to women than pornographers, it is not an assertion that most people will today readily accept. But there are many things about pornography that people will not accept, including what exactly it means. To describe something as pornographic is like asserting that such and such an organization is terrorist: it is primarily a value judgement, describing something – acts or things or goals – of which you disapprove. The problem is, values change, and what seemed pornographic to a Victorian lady would not seem so to an American teenage girl who is a fan of rap music.

However, one thing is certain: pornography is inextricably linked to the emergence of modernity. It was not called pornography at the time – in English the word only came to be used in its current sense in the mid-nineteenth century, but many characteristics of the genre were established at the dawn of the modern age which remain typical of it today. The explicit description in words or pictures of sexual acts is still pornography's hallmark. But its satirical and political dimension, which in France especially made it an important vehicle for anticlerical and antigovernment attacks right up to the French Revolution, had disappeared by the late 1790s. Until then, pornography had played a vital propaganda role in the events leading up to the Revolution, and its association with social disorder and political radicalism was one of the reasons it was later suppressed in England.

At first, during the sixteenth and most of the seventeenth century, the distribution of pornography was restricted to upper-class circles. But the invention of the novel did for early pornography what the video recorder did for its twentieth-century descendant. By the early eighteenth century, a popular pornography industry existed in France, and by the middle of the century in England. From there in 1748, came what perhaps was the biggest-selling pornographic book of all time:

Fanny Hill: or, The Memoirs of A Woman of Pleasure, by James Cleland.[219]

One of the most popular forms of pornographic writing in the eighteenth century, the fictional autobiography or 'confessions' of whores and prostitutes, directly challenged the image of the sexless, pure woman, the perennial victim of male lust, that was taking hold among the middle class in England and exalted in the works of Rousseau in France. The memoirs of the 'libertine whore' as she has been called,[220] describe women who are sexually aggressive, self-confident, capable of almost limitless sexual pleasure, financially successful, and usually indifferent or hostile to the ordinary notions that define conventional femininity, such as motherhood and marriage. Sexual differences between men and women in fact are all but erased in the search for pleasure, fulfilment and domination. In the world of the libertine whore, women are as passionate as men, and as willing to fulfil their own desires. The most extreme example is the Marquis de Sade's *The History of Juliette: or, The Fortunes of Vice*.

Sade (1740–1814) remains the most infamous writer of all time, from whose name we derive the word 'sadism'. He spent almost half his life imprisoned, mostly for what would now be regarded as petty or non-crimes, and wrote most of his work behind bars. Three-quarters of that work has been lost or destroyed, and what remains suffered from severe censorship.[221] It presents a picture of sexual excess unrivalled in the history of literature, in which sadistic orgies are as carefully choreographed as the dance steps in Broadway musicals.

It is not surprising that in this work Sade was accused of attacking the very idea of what it is to be human. However, Sade was writing within less than a century of the last woman who was tortured and burned alive as a witch. We, who lie on the other side of the horrors of the twentieth century, are not so shocked by his revelations about the lust for power lurking in the human heart.

Juliette is a new species – a sort of Tyrannosaurus Sex. Though in the tradition of the libertine whore bent on achieving autonomy, Juliette does so regardless of the cost to the other human beings who are her victims (both male and female), whom she tortures and murders for sexual fulfilment. In the world of Juliette, there are no men and no women, there are only the powerful and the weak, the master and the slave, those who are willing and able to use their power to achieve their aims and those who cannot and who become their victims. 'A zealous egalitarian,' she tells a king, 'I have never considered one living creature any better than any other, and as I have no belief in moral virtues, neither do I consider that they are differentiated by any moral worth.'[222] Sade mocks and derides Rousseau's vision of the ideal woman by showing that if as he believed – and history tends to bear him out – the instinct for power is part of human nature, then women can possess it as much as men, and will be every bit as cruel in exercising it. Juliette shows she can sink to the same depths of inhumanity as any man. Her capacity for evil is not moderated by her gender. Through cruelty and violence, therefore, Juliette achieves a kind of equality with men unique for a woman in the history of literature and ideas, but only in a world where absolute contempt for women has been replaced by absolute contempt for the weak.

It was not the kind of equality that women were seeking in the real world. That would emerge as the legacy of the Enlightenment unfolded in the following century, along with its contradictions, to confront misogyny on fresh grounds in both Europe and new, or little known, worlds.

6

VICTORIANS' SECRETS

Misogyny is far from unique to Western civilization. That became clear to Europeans as, from the early sixteenth century onwards, they began expanding into regions of the world with which before they had little or no contact. They encountered complex civilizations at least as old as (and sometimes far older than) their own, and equally (if not in some ways more) sophisticated. Meanwhile, in other, previously unexplored or unknown areas, they discovered cultures that were, at a technological and social level, simpler than anything they had ever seen. But one thing they all shared: Neither the primitive nor the sophisticated societies lacked for prejudices against women.

Sometimes these prejudices took on an almost universal character, as with the taboos relating to menstruation. From the Macusis tribe of South America, who hung pubescent girls in the highest hammocks, then submitted them to a beating

with rods,[223] to the Hindu Brahmins of India, who believed
that a visit to a menstruating woman was one of the seven
things a man might do to forfeit his chance of a happy or a long
life,[224] all over the world men's terror of menstruating women
invested them with extraordinary powers to do harm.

However, it was not the crude superstitions of tribes – who
lived sometimes at the level of Stone Age man – that most
impressed Europeans at the beginning of the modern era, but
the complex and often profoundly contradictory views of
women that they encountered when they began developing
trading relations with the powerful civilizations of the East,
particularly those of India and China. Hinduism and Buddhism had developed in India over 1,000 years between 1500
BC and 500 BC, with Taoism and Confucianism in China
emerging between the seventh and fifth centuries BC. Both
civilizations retained traces of much earlier cultures, with what
some have interpreted as matriarchal elements. In the earliest
Chinese creation myth, for example, it was a goddess Nu Wa
who moulded the human race from clay. Archaeological
investigation of the earliest civilizations in the Indus valley
reveals a plethora of terracotta figurines of naked women, and
the later Hindu pantheon contains several powerful goddesses,
including Parvati, Durga, Sakti and Kali.[225] Whatever conclusions we might draw from this about the status of women in
these early societies, one thing is beyond doubt. Sexual and
religious rituals in both civilizations recognized and at times
exalted the role of women. Yet, alongside this was a profound
contempt, especially noticeable in Confucianism, Hinduism
and Buddhism.

By the middle of the eighteenth century, Britain dominated
the Indian subcontinent both politically and economically, a
rule that would last until 1947 when India became independent. The British and other Europeans were shocked, confused

and fascinated by Indian sexual attitudes and behaviour. Writing about the numerous temple prostitutes found in India, the eighteenth-century missionary Abbé Dubois declared, 'A religion more shameful or indecent has never existed amongst a civilized people.'[226]

Europeans easily found evidence of the low social status of women; it complemented many of their own, Western-based prejudices. But all around them, the newcomers could not ignore the evidence of India's exuberant sensuality. They beheld the extraordinary stone carvings of the vast Hindu temple of Konarak, depicting couples (and sometimes triples) making love with an almost indolent ease, unthinkable to the Western imagination; their entwined bodies with full-breasted women instead of ripe fruit garlanding the sacred place like a voluptuous vine. They read the *Kamasutra*, written between the third and fifth centuries AD, with its unselfconsciously fastidious guide to sexual pleasure – not, as in works such as Ovid's *The Art of Love*, for the joy of the man only – but with the full recognition of the woman's sexual needs to be fulfilled. In this and in other ways, India exalted erotic relations between men and women to a plane unknown in the West. Indeed, in some Hindu and Buddhist sects, rituals of orgiastic intercourse were seen as the principal path to enlightenment, the way of escaping what the Mexican poet Octavio Paz has termed the 'dualistic trap'.[227]

The great religions of the Eastern civilizations are profoundly different from Christianity in that they are not, essentially, philosophically or theologically oriented. Nor do they have a mission – a conviction that they are the holders of an absolute truth regarding the salvation of all mankind with a historical imperative to spread it. Instead their beliefs about the world and the human race's place in it have given rise to complex ethical systems in which ideas are ritualized. They are also completely ahistorical. That is, their beliefs have only personal, not historical consequences; their aim is to allow the individual to achieve happiness in this world (Hinduism, Taoism and Confucianism), or to escape suffering, most radically by extinguishing any sense of self (Buddhism). They do not share the missionary need of Christians and Moslems to convert or exterminate the unbeliever. That means that, unlike Islam and Christianity, their misogyny has largely been internal. But what Taoism, Confucianism, Hinduism and Buddhism do have in common with Christianity and Islam is their profound dualism in which the world is seen as being in a permanent state of tension, if not conflict, between body and spirit, self and nature, the one and the many, life and death, male and female, being and non-being.

Except for Confucianism, which was less a religion than a code of etiquette and ethics, these Eastern religions shared a belief with Christians and Platonists that the world of the senses is fundamentally an illusion that prevents us from achieving a higher state of being. But unlike Christianity, they posited that dualism could be ended in this world through the practices of certain rituals. However, though the body was viewed as an obstacle to this goal, it was not held to be evil, a sign of our falling away from the divine as it is in Christianity. None of the Eastern religions had any concept equivalent to sin, which made the work of the first missionaries who arrived in India and China in the seventeenth centuries extremely frustrating. Even in the most ascetic expressions of these beliefs, and both Buddhism and Hinduism produced traditions of holy men and monks who forswore this world for a life of contemplation and physical deprivation, Puritanism as the West understands it does not exist. Though scholars have linked Eastern asceticism with misogyny in Indian and Chinese societies, the impact this has on women's status remains full of contradictions. Indeed, in Taoism, as in the Tantric versions of Hinduism and Buddhism, the body, and in particular sexual pleasure, were viewed as a path to immortality. Among the practitioners of the Tantric disciplines, it was a release from the cycle of birth, death and reincarnation, a path to Nirvana in which the self is dissolved. In all these rituals, women played an essential role.

Taoism holds that the world is kept in balance between the interaction of two forces yin (female) and yang (male). This interaction gives rise to change, according to the *I-Ching* or *Book of Changes*. There are two keys to a long life. The first lies in the retention of semen – a belief found in many cultures around the world. The second key, held to be just as vital, is the imbibing of vaginal secretions. Taoists believed that while man produced a limited amount of his precious fluid, woman's supply was infinite. In China, it led to elaborate sexual rituals, the aim of which was to rouse the woman to orgasm, but not the man. Not surprisingly, cunnilingus was popular among the Chinese: 'The practice was an excellent method of imbibing the precious fluid,' according to one authority.[228] In a series of texts, known as Bed Treatises, produced between the Sui and Ming dynasties (AD 581–1644), methods of retaining semen whilst absorbing as much of the female fluid as possible are outlined in minute detail. The ultimate aim was to unite the male and female fluids, obliterating sexual dualism, and achieving (it was believed) a kind of immortality.[229] The treatises were eventually suppressed under the conservative Qing dynasty (1644–1912), along with the erotic novels of the Ming years (1368–1644), though some continued to survive on the Chinese black market.

Tantric Buddhism in India was a rebellion against the rigidity of the Hindu caste system and its religious rituals based on the belief in reincarnation (which held that a person's behaviour in this life determines his or her status in the next). Tantrism's sexual rituals were orgiastic, beginning with the banquet, in which food was eaten from the body of a naked woman lying face up; the devotees then had intercourse in public. They believed that through sexual ecstasy they could break free of the cycle of reincarnation and reach the state of Nirvana. One historian has compared Tantrism to the sexual revolution of the 1960s, its sexual permissiveness a challenge to moral, social and political authority.[230] It appalled the Abbé Dubois, on his visit to India in the eighteenth century. He was the first European to describe what he called the 'infamous feast'.

However, one does not have to go to the extremes of Tantric Buddhism to realize that Indian sexual practices differ from those of the West in their recognition of woman as a sexual being. From the *Kamasutra*, to the Tantric rituals, Indian eroticism sees the woman as an active participant, and the aim of both men and women is to give pleasure to each other. Likewise, among the Chinese, sexual relations between men and women were not dominated by a sense of sin or shame but by the need to manage desire and passion. In the Confucian *Book of Rites* husbands are instructed that 'even if a concubine is growing old, as long as she has not yet reached 50, [you] shall have intercourse with her once every five days.'[231] In that sense, a kind of sexual equilibrium is attained, which seems the very opposite to the misogyny that developed in the West and that tried to deny women their sexual nature. Yet, however much the recognition of female sexuality expressed itself both in the Indian and Chinese civilizations, it did not protect women from being treated with contempt in other ways.

In the teachings of Confucius (551–479 BC), which dominated Chinese thinking for at least 2,000 years, a complex ethical system was constructed, along with a precise etiquette to govern social relations. It was a patriarchal system, in which relations within the family reflected both the order of the cosmos, and the structure of the state. China was a polygamous society for much of its history – polygamy was only finally outlawed in 1912 with the collapse of imperial rule. It had a very large middle class, with most men possessing between three and a dozen wives and concubines. There were also luxurious establishments where the rich might visit courtesans. Although, in accordance with Confucian doctrine, which aimed always at balance and order, the husband was expected to look after his wives and concubines' economic and sexual needs, in other ways women were treated with disdain. As the Chinese poet Fu Hsuan expressed it:

> Bitter indeed it is to be born a woman,
> It is difficult to imagine anything so low! . . .
> No one sheds a tear when she is married off . . .
> Her husband's love is as aloof as the Milky Way,
> Yet she must follow him like a sunflower the sun.
> Their hearts are soon as far apart as fire and water.
> She is blamed for all and everything that may go wrong.[232]

Women were completely segregated from males from a very early age. Casual physical contact between men and women was to be avoided because it aroused passions – Confucius did not teach that the body was evil, just that it was dangerous.[233] According to *The Book of Rites*, 'A man and woman shall not give anything directly one to the other from hand to hand. If a man gives something to a woman, she receives it on a bamboo tray.'[234] Women who wanted to attend public festivities had to carry a portable folding screen behind which they placed themselves in order not to be seen.[235] Traditionally, there was no role for women in public affairs. 'They will cause disorder and confusion in the empire,' wrote the statesman

Yang Chen in the second century AD, 'bring shame on the Imperial Court . . . Women should not be allowed to take part in government affairs.'[236]

Most women, it seems, even those belonging to the higher classes, did not receive much if any education, and remained illiterate. As in Ancient Athens, only courtesans were expected to be able to read and write. Women's instruction was usually limited to learning sewing, embroidery and playing a musical instrument. Even those who were educated, such as the woman scholar and historian Ban Zhao (AD 40–120), whose father belonged to the court circle and who advocated that girls should receive at least elementary instruction, were so in order that they should grow up more aware of their subordinate status. Their fate was to be obedient wives, the mothers of sons. A wife who did not produce a son could be displaced by a concubine who did. The prejudice against girl children persists into modern times: It has become common for pregnant women to abort the foetus if it is female, creating a growing imbalance between the numbers of men and women in certain areas. According to researchers, there are 111 males for every 100 females now throughout the country.[237] It has also led to an illegal trade in baby girls, who are sold by poor peasant women who already have one or two children, to supply child-hungry families in the big cities.

Chinese standards of female beauty always emphasized the demure, the delicate and the diminutive, with a special emphasis on small feet. From the tenth century onwards, this predilection took a nasty twist with the rise of foot-binding. From an early age, the outside three toes of the girl's feet were tightly wrapped, bending them back towards the ball of the foot, with the goal of achieving the 'lotus foot'. According to the archaeologist Heinrich Schliemann, who travelled through China and Japan in the late nineteenth century:

A young girl, pockmarked and gap-toothed, or with thinning hair, but with a little foot no longer than three and a half thumbs, is considered a hundred times more beautiful than one who, by European standards, would be considered exceptionally lovely but who has a foot four and a half thumbs long.

He observed that it effectively crippled women, distorting their instep, and made them waddle 'like geese'.[238] Footbinding mainly affected upper-class women and courtesans. It was only with the Chinese Revolution and the establishment of the People's Republic in 1949 that this misogynistic mutilation was banned. Confucianism was also suppressed in the 1950s as counterrevolutionary, though Taoism (or some version of it) survived as a cult.

In India also, the voluptuous eroticism that exalted female sexuality coexisted with a host of discriminatory practices that lowered women's social status. In the Indian epic of the fifth century BC *The Mahabharata* the birth of a daughter is hailed as a misfortune, and it is declared, 'women are the root of evils; for they are held to be light-minded.'[239] Over 2,000 years later, the situation has not changed, except that with the advance of technology it is now easier for parents in India to avoid having daughters at all. Even though they are outlawed, pre-natal sex tests are used to determine the foetus' sex; if it is a girl it is commonly aborted, leading as in China to a growing disproportion in the numbers of men to women. In the 2001 census, it was revealed that in children under age six, there were 927 girls for every 1,000 boys.[240]

Like Chinese women, Indian women did not in general receive an education, unless they were the sacred prostitutes who worked in the Hindu temples. The Abbé Dubois noted:

prostitutes are the only females in India who may learn
sing, to read and to dance. Such accomplishments belong to
them exclusively, and are, for that reason, held by the rest of
the sex in such abhorrence, that every virtuous woman would
consider the mention of them an affront.[241]

The great temple of Rajarajeshvara in Tanjore is said to
have housed some 400 sacred prostitutes.[242] The association
between prostitution and education remained a bar to making
progress for women in that field until the late nineteenth
century. In spite of laws imposed by the British against
soliciting and using premises for the purposes of prostitution,
the custom persisted through to independence, when local
authorities attempted crackdowns.[243]

The Mahabharata makes clear that traditionally Hinduism
was especially fierce in its taboos against menstruating women. In some cases, a woman was whipped if she even touched
a man while she was having her period. A Brahmin could not
eat food that had been looked at by a menstruating woman.[244]
From the medieval period onwards, there was a growth in the
preference for child-brides, which meant an increase in the
fatalities these young wives suffered giving birth. As for the
fate of widows, it was not an enviable one. Usually, they were
not allowed to remarry (though The Mahabharata describes
exceptions), and they were expected to live a life of frugality in
perpetual mourning, sleeping on the ground and eating one
meal a day. As one historian put it, 'the widow was the spectre
at the feast.'[245] The Mahabharata recounts tales of heroic
women leaping into their dead husbands' funeral pyres, choosing to die rather than face life without them, in a custom
known as suttee or sati, which means 'the virtuous woman'.
However, widows who were not so eager were sometimes
forced to burn. In one case, in 1780, the sixty-four wives of the

Raja of Marwar were consumed on his funeral pyre along wi.
his corpse.

Underlying such contempt would appear to dwell the dualism, so well known in the Western and Moslem civilizations,
of woman as nature and man as spirit or soul.

> . . . let man know that women are the continuers of the web of
> the Samsara [the world of the senses]. They are the ploughed
> field of nature, of matter . . . men manifest themselves as the
> soul; therefore let the man before all things leave them behind
> him, one and all. [246]

But while this may seem familiar, resembling a Platonic
divide between form or idea and the mutable world of the
senses, it does not imply a contempt for women because they
are the representatives of matter. The corporality and sensuality of Buddhism is fully realized in men and women, and is
allowed to transfigure them both into a higher state of being.
The body is not rejected but through eroticism it is seen as one
of the paths to enlightenment.

The paradox of India perplexed Europeans, particularly the
English, who had the longest and most intimate engagement
with its culture. They were appalled at the blatant celebration
of women's sensuality, and at the same time, shocked at the
more extreme examples of the contempt and disdain in which
women were held at a social level. By the nineteenth century,
female infanticide had been outlawed, and steps were taken to
try and stop the custom of sati, even when the widow was
willing to enter the flames to follow her husband into death. In
the twelfth century, after the Moslem invasion of India, the
practice had also been outlawed as against the laws of Islam –
to no avail. Under the British, the law did not completely
succeed and the custom did not die out. The last reported

...occurred in August 2002, when a sixty-five-
...w burned to death in the province of Madhya
...n. Nor did the Widow Remarriage Act passed in 1856
uproot the deeply held tradition forbidding remarriage. Education for women did not make much progress either under
British rule: as of 1939, only 2 per cent of Indian women were
attending school.[247]

The traditional Indian view of women, with all its seeming
contradictions, stood in complete contrast to how women
were being viewed in Victorian England and in the United
States. Whereas in India there was a celebration of female
sexuality, coexisting alongside women's social denigration, in
the West the steady improvement in women's social and
political status was accompanied by the increasing denial of
their sexuality. This reached a point in mid-Victorian times
when medical experts could confidently declare that women
had no sexual desires at all. No doubt this would have seemed
preposterous to a Hindu, just as a Victorian gentleman would
have deemed the idea of copulating one's way to salvation as
the very height of impropriety.

In Europe and North America, the Enlightenment and the
revolutions of the eighteenth century had completely transformed political and social relations. Yet, neither the new
republic of the United States nor the National Assembly set
up by the revolution in France extended the rights of man to
women, who were still denied the suffrage that in the following
century was increasingly extended to males regardless of their
economic status. But woman could not be forever regarded as
the eternal exception to the granting of political and social
rights. Thomas Paine (1737–1809), whose *Common Sense*
pamphlet did so much to galvanize the struggle of the colonists
against Britain, had pleaded for women's rights. In 1775, the
year before he wrote *Common Sense*, he lamented:

Even in countries where they may be esteemed the most happy [women are] constrained in their desires in the disposal of their goods; robbed of freedom and will by the laws; slaves of opinion which rules over them with absolute sway and construes the slightest appearances into guilt; surrounded on all sides by judges who are at once tyrants and their seducers . . . for even with the changes in attitudes and laws, deeply engrained and oppressing social prejudices remain which confront women minute by minute, day by day.[248]

In Paris, in 1792, in the National Assembly, of which Paine was a member, he argued for a woman's right to vote, without success. That same year, Mary Wollstonecraft (1759–97) published *A Vindication of the Rights of Woman*, a book that some have hailed as 'the feminist declaration of independence' and 'the first sustained argument for female emancipation based on a cogent ethical system'.[249] When *A Vindication* was published, its author was described as a 'hyena in petticoats' and her support of the French Revolution – Wollstonecraft moved to Paris temporarily in 1792 – was looked on in England with either great suspicion or outright hostility. She was called one of 'the impious amazons of Republican France'[250] Her basic argument was simple: the rights of man imply the rights of woman. Other women in England, such as Mary Astell had, a hundred years earlier, argued for women's emancipation inspired by Enlightenment philosophical thought (see Chapter 5). But the French Revolution took abstract principles of freedom and tried to give them concrete political expression, inspiring many in Wollstonecraft's generation with the hope that their notions of equality and universal brotherhood might now in fact be realized.

Wollstonecraft was one of six children, the daughter of a sometimes tyrannical father who was a farmer, and a mother

179

...ed as 'vague and weak', who doted exceed-
...est son. After working unhappily as a govern-
...e published a treatise *Thoughts on the Education of
Daughters* (1787), and then a novel, *Mary, A Fiction* (1788),
moved to London to pursue a career as a writer, and mixed in
radical circles where she met Thomas Paine, the poet William
Blake, the political philosopher William Godwin and the
chemist Joseph Priestly. Her experience as a governess had
made her fiercely hostile to the life-style of upper-class women,
who spent their days preening themselves, and in what she
regarded as other utterly frivolous pursuits. She took the
opposite course and became, in fact, the archetypal bohemian
feminist, not caring for her appearance, wearing her hair
unkempt and dressing in black worsted stockings, which
disgusted one of her friends who called her a 'philosophical
sloven'.[251]

Wollstonecraft's hostility to women who spent what she
believed was too much time before the mirror is a major theme
of *A Vindication*. It set the tone for a lot of later feminist
writing. Indeed, her contempt for what she saw as female
frivolousness, especially women's devotion to beautification, is
as thoroughgoing as anything ever written by a male misogynist. 'Pleasure,' she writes, 'is the business of women's life,
according to the present modification of society; and while it
continues to be, little can be expected from such weak beings.'
She paraphrases Hamlet's diatribe again women, with approval. Her complaints about women echo those found in
the works of traditional misogynists and she is so vitriolic that
a recent authority upon her work has had to defend her from
being misconstrued 'as unsympathetic to women'.[252] Wollstonecraft, in fact, accepts the dualistic notion that devotion to
the body is a sign of mental and moral inferiority. She asserts
that as long as women are guilty of this, they will be perceived

as inferior – and, according to Wollstonecraft, deservedly so. She warns 'if then, women do not resign the arbitrary power of beauty – they will prove that they have less mind than man.'[253] The old mind/body dualism had taken on a new philosophical force thanks to the work of Rene Descartes (1596–1650), in which the very the proof of existence was contingent upon thinking, as he stated cogently in his renowned maxim: 'I think therefore I am.' Wollstonecraft took this to mean that body is non-rational and therefore inferior to mind – a dichotomy familiar since Plato and a favourite among misogynists who identify women as body. It followed that women who fuss too much over their make-up and dress must be inferior to those who spend their hours reading philosophical works.

Throughout *A Vindication* she stresses the importance of reason. It is reason that makes us human and establishes 'man's pre-eminence over brute creation'. Therefore, she argues, if women are to rise above their lowly status, it is vital that they receive an education that will train them to be rational beings rather than the mere playthings of men and slaves of fashion. Reason will redeem them from their vanities and their sins. A woman of reason will abhor vice, folly and even obscene witticisms. She will be chaste, and modest, avoiding even familiarities with other women, which Wollstonecraft describes as 'gross'. In her priggishness, the woman of reason is beginning to resemble the woman of purity, who would become the female stereotype of the Victorian epoch, except that she will be better educated.

Was then, 'the first major feminist' also a misogynist? While her criticisms of women echo those of traditional misogynists, Wollstonecraft's rationale is different. In the conclusion to *A Vindication*, she asserts: 'There are many follies in some degree peculiar to women – sins against reason of commission as well as of omission – but all flowing from ignorance or prejudice.' These follies 'men have endeavoured, impelled by various

motives, to perpetuate . . .' But unlike misogynists, Wollstonecraft believes such female follies are not based on the inherent
nature of women but on their education, or lack of it. Following Locke, she believes that we are almost entirely the product
of the social forces that shape us. Remove the forces that
inculcate ignorance and prejudice, and you will make women
'rational creatures and free citizens'. Or as Bertrand Russell
put it, 'Men are born ignorant, not stupid; they are made
stupid by education.'[254] The same applies to women.

In the end, most of the ideals Wollstonecraft believed in
failed her, or she failed them. The bloody turn taken by the
French Revolution horrified her. She fell madly in love with an
American, Gilbert Imlay, exactly the kind of man she warned
women against. The passions she despised in *A Vindication* as
proof of women's weakness consumed her, driving her to
attempt suicide when her lover abandoned her and their infant
daughter. Later, she married her old friend William Godwin,
with whom she had a happy and productive relationship. But
tragically, and ironically, she died in agony from septicaemia,
giving birth to a second daughter, also named Mary Wollstonecraft (1797–1851). A clergyman callously commented
that her death was a useful lesson to women because it
'strongly marked the distinction of the sexes by pointing
out the destiny of women, and the diseases to which they
are peculiarly liable'.[255] Her daughter would later marry the
poet and radical Percy Bysshe Shelley and write *Franken-
stein*.[256] She lived to see the first women's rights convention
in 1848, at Seneca Falls, New York, which launched the
campaign for women's suffrage and for many of the reforms
proposed by her mother over fifty years earlier. Within a
century of Mary Shelley's death, women had gained entry
into medical schools and universities in the United States and
to Cambridge University in England.

However, that Mary Wollstonecraft should figure in a history of misogyny at all says something about the paradoxical nature of her legacy. While forcefully proclaiming the need for women's emancipation, she argued that it was incompatible with those things, such as passion and beauty, with which women were traditionally associated. In doing so, she perpetuated the old mind/body dualism that in many ways has been so detrimental to women. Unfortunately, this aspect of her thinking was taken up by later generations of feminists in Britain and the United States, who believed that advocating women's political and social rights meant disdaining or denying altogether the more erotic aspects of women's nature, which they claimed, were male inventions, aimed at manipulating women for their own pleasure. The bra burners of the early 1970s are in this way her direct descendants. Unfortunately, it was a position that alienated a lot of women from the women's movement.

In the eighteenth century, there was a change in the intellectual and political outlook of Western Europe and North America; in the nineteenth, the physical environment of these areas was transformed. The impact on women's lives would be unlike anything experienced before. The conquests of science, especially in biology and chemistry, and the industrial revolution represented considerable intellectual and technical progress. But as the story of misogyny makes plain, progress in other areas of human endeavour does not necessarily mean progress for women.

The industrial revolution sucked the population from rural areas into the expanding cities to feed the factories with cheap labour, destroying the old cottage industries which had employed women's skills in spinning, weaving, brewing, baking, butter-making and other traditional crafts, allowing them to clothe and feed their families. In the overcrowded slums, a new class was created – the working class. It was underpaid and usually underfed. By 1861, in England and Wales – the boiler room of the industrial revolution – almost 3,000,000 women over the age of fifteen, representing 26 per cent of the female population, were working. Of them, only 279 had clerical jobs. The vast majority of the rest were employed in factories or as maids.[257] Like the men, women had become wage-slaves, their subordinate position emphasized by the fact that on average they were paid around half of what men earned for performing the same work. By the middle of the nineteenth century, a male spinner in England earned between 14 and 22 shillings a week, a female around 5; in the United States, a male worker in the cotton industry was paid $1.67 per week, a female employee $1.05. A French male printer's wage was two francs a day, a female's one franc.[258]

Added to the misery of the working conditions was the fact that women workers had to continue to carry the burden of their biological role, enduring multiple pregnancies in horrendous conditions. Working-class women were, in the words of the Irish revolutionary socialist, James Connolly, 'the slaves of the slaves'. Though advances were being made in the manufacture of condoms, the vast majority of working-class women did not have access to them. Contraception was still left in the hands of men, which often meant that even when it was available it was not used.

Rarely, in history, have men and women suffered the kind of degradation that was found in the vast slums of nineteenth-century England's cities and industrial towns. The poor were seen as a separate race, and venturing into their districts was akin to exploring 'darkest Africa'. The novelist Charles Dickens (1812–70) penetrated one slum in 1851 that lay within a few hundred yards of the British Museum and found: 'Ten, twenty, thirty, who can count them! Men, women, children, for the most part naked, heaped upon the floor like maggots in a cheese!'[259] Twenty years later, a French visitor to the London poor reported:

> Three times in ten minutes I saw crowds collect around doorways, attracted by fights, especially between women. One of them, her face covered with blood, tears in her eyes, drunk, was trying to fly at a man while the mob watched and laughed. And as if the uproar were a signal, the population of neighbouring 'lanes' came pouring into the street, children in rags, paupers, street women, as if a human sewer were suddenly clearing itself.[260]

Perhaps poverty does not create misogyny, but experience suggests that it tends to reinforce it. As 'the slaves of the slaves', women bore the brunt of men's anger and frustration when they lashed out because they lost their jobs, or failed to provide for their large families, or suffered some other daily humiliation. Those middle-class observers such as Henry Mayhew, the author of the celebrated *London Labour and the London Poor* (1851–62) who ventured into the slums to see for themselves reported that wife beating and rape were so common as to go unnoticed. These conditions prevailed into the twentieth century. In 1902, the American writer Jack London (1876–1916) penetrated the East End of London, then a vast slum of some 1,000,000 souls, disguised as a working man and reported:

> Wife-beating is the masculine prerogative of matrimony. They wear remarkable boots of brass and iron, and when they have polished off the mother of their children with a black eye or so, they knock her down and proceed to trample her very much as a Western stallion tramples a rattlesnake . . . The men are economically dependent on their masters, and the women are

economically dependent on the men. The result is the women get the beating the man should give the master, and she can do nothing.[261]

Unless murder was involved, such crimes rarely came to the attention of the authorities. In the overcrowded conditions people slept promiscuously, sometimes four or five or six to a bed, sometimes more, usually regardless of sex or age or relationship.

The women of the slums frequently turned to prostitution to make ends meet. In 1841, there were an estimated 50,000 prostitutes in London, out of a population of 2 million. Most were horribly disfigured by venereal disease. One survey in 1866 found that over 76 per cent of those examined were infected, and all suffered from some debilitating disease, most often small pox.[262] The more fortunate women were those who found a place in a brothel, where they could at least expect to be fed and clothed. One madam of a London brothel, known as Mother Willit, boasted that she always 'turned her gals out with a clean arse and a good tog [clothes]; and as she turned 'em out, she didn't care who turned 'em up, 'cause 'em vos as clean as a smelt and as fresh as a daisy.' The law treated such women with the utmost contempt. A visitor to Newgate Prison reported in horror: 'Nearly three hundred women, every gradation of crime, 120 in ward, no matting, nearly naked, all drunk . . . her ears were offended by the most terrible imprecations.'[263]

Middle-class missionaries strove hard to rescue the 'fallen women'. It is estimated that by the time Queen Victoria came to the throne in 1837, the Religious Tract Society had already issued 500,000,000 pamphlets trying to win over prostitutes and convince them to abandon their ways. In the decades that followed, the flood of such tracts increased, but without noticeable effect.[264] Poverty motivated most of the women, and the profound moral dichotomy of Victorianism in relation to sex provided them with a steady clientele of men for whom 'respectable women' – that is, the women who became their wives – were effectively neutered. Sex was for 'fallen women' or the women of the promiscuous poor, who were regarded as somewhat less than human. Sexual desire was an unfortunate urge that mainly afflicted men – one that occasionally their wives were obliged to relieve. This was the age when middle-class wives lay on their backs and thought of England – or the United States, depending on where they were. The misogynistic vision took on its usual dual, and contradictory, aspect, denigrating the women of the slums as less than human because of their sexual promiscuity, while at the same time elevating the middle-class woman to the more-than-human status of 'Angel in the House', thanks to her innate asexuality. According to one of the most prominent medical experts of his day, Dr William Acton, the good wife 'submits to her husband's embraces, but principally to gratify him, and were it not for the desire of maternity, would far rather be relieved of his attentions'. This is because, according to Acton, 'the majority of women (happily for society) are not very much troubled with sexual feelings of any kind.' Taking pleasure in sex led to cancer of the womb or insanity, he warned.[265]

While the majority of medical authorities recognized that women experienced some sexual pleasure during intercourse, they regarded any sign of excitement or loss of control as a worrying indication of moral degeneracy or mental imbalance, which could lead to madness and disease. Both in Britain and the United States at this time, sexual behaviour was coming under 'scientific' study, and being categorized into acceptable and unacceptable types. Science provided an objective way of looking at the world, including the human body and human

behaviour. But behind the new, supposedly scientific categories of 'diseases' there often lurked a familiar morality.
Preferring to make love with a member of your own sex
became a disease called homosexuality. In the area of sexuality, particularly female sexuality, the notion of 'disease' often
carried with it strong moral disapproval. For instance, women
who enjoyed sex too much were liable to be categorized as
nymphomaniacs and listed as 'dangerous, unnatural and
sexually out of control'.[266] In both Classical Greece and
Ancient Rome, women were traditionally believed to have
stronger sexual desires than men, and their carnality had to be
watched as it could easily get out of control. Witness the fate of
Messalina, the emperor Claudius' young wife whose lust for
sex led her to pose as a prostitute in a brothel, according to the
ancient (and hostile) sources (see Chapter 2). But from the late
eighteenth century onwards 'excessive' sexual desire in women
began to be considered primarily as a physical not a moral
disorder. By Victorian times, it had reached the status of full-
blown disease, with various and frequently contradictory
symptoms.

A sure indication of trouble ahead for a girl was masturbation, a Victorian obsession that persisted in the United States
well into the 1950s. Masturbation among males was bad
enough, but female masturbation shook the very foundations
of society if left unchecked. After all, by concentrating on her
clitoris, a woman was ignoring her vagina and in effect
rebelling against her biological and predetermined role as
the bearer of children. It was seen as a disturbing sign of
'masculine' tendencies, which among other baleful consequences, could lead to lesbianism, nymphomania, and a host
of horrific diseases, including uterine haemorrhage, falling of
the womb, spinal irritation, convulsions, haggard features,
emaciation, and functional disorders of the heart. In 1894,

the *New Orleans Medical Journal* concluded that 'neither the plague, nor war, nor smallpox, nor a crowd of similar evils have resulted more disastrously for humanity, than the habit of masturbation: it is the destroying element of civilization.'[267] Clearly, drastic action was often prescribed, and the sooner the better.

As an example of what might be done, the *New Orleans Medical and Surgical Journal* also reported the case of a nine-year-old girl suspected of masturbating by her mother. A gynaecologist, A. J. Block, examined her. He touched her vagina and labia minor, but the child did not respond. He reports: 'As soon as I reached the clitoris the legs were thrown widely open, the face became pale, the breathing short and rapid, the body twitched from excitement, slight groans came from the patient.' The prescription: a clitoridectomy.[268]

In 1867, the *British Medical Journal* described how a Victorian gynaecologist Mr Isaac Baker Brown performed the operation.

Two instruments were used: the pair of hooked forceps which Mr Brown always uses in clitoridectomy, and a cautery iron as he uses in dividing the pedicle in ovariotomy . . . The clitoris was seized by the forceps in the usual manner. The thin edge of the red-hot iron was then passed around its base until the organ was removed, the nymphae on each side were severed in a similar way by a sawing motion of the hot iron. After the clitoris and nymphae were got rid of, the operation was brought to a close by taking the back of the iron and sawing the surfaces of the labia and other parts of the vulva which had escaped the cautery, and the instrument was rubbed down backwards and forwards till the parts were more effectually destroyed than when Mr Brown uses the scissors to effect the same result.

Brown was an enthusiast of clitoridectomy, which he claimed he had used to cure masturbation-induced 'women's diseases' such as melancholia, hysteria, and nymphomania. In December 1866, he received a glowing endorsement from *The Times* for his work.[269] *The Times'* report sparked a controversy in the medical world. Many in the medical profession were merely upset that so distasteful a topic had been aired in the press in the first place. Other medical colleagues accused Brown, a fellow of the Royal College, of being a quack. But the Church sprang to his defence. Both the Archbishop of Canterbury, the head of the Anglican Church, and the Archbishop of York praised his work.

Though clitoridectomy was eventually frowned upon in the West, female masturbation did not lose its power to frighten the medical profession. Dr Block, who mutilated the nine-year-old girl, called it a 'moral leprosy'. Fortunately, he was among the last American doctors to carry out such operations.[270] However, to this day the genital mutilation of girls and women remains common, even routine, in certain mainly Moslem parts of Africa and is also practised in the Arabian Peninsula and in areas of Asia (see Chapter 8).

It is not surprising that a culture that at one level worshipped woman as a neutered 'angel' should actually denature her, nor that it developed a cult of the little girl. Nothing could be less sexually threatening to a Victorian gentleman than a pretty female child frolicking among the meadow flowers, the picture of innocence. Among the period's most successful painters was Kate Greenaway, described as a 'gentle, bespectacled, middle-aged lady garbed in black',[271] who devoted her life to painting cloyingly sweet watercolours of coy little girls sniffing flowers or staring longingly out of nursery windows. Misogyny has rarely manifested itself in such a sinister form, representing as it does the complete inability of men to relate to adult women. Inevitably, such a profound sexual disjunction found another outlet: the obverse to the worship of female innocence has always been the degradation and humiliation of women. The number of child brothels in London indicated that Victorian gentlemen were not content to swoon over sentimental portrayals of little girls. A reporter for the French newspaper *Le Figaro* on a single evening counted 500 girls aged between five and fifteen parading as prostitutes between Piccadilly Circus and Waterloo Place in the city's fashionable West End district. One madam advertised her brothel as a place where 'you can gloat over the cries of the girls with the certainty that no one will hear them besides yourself.'[272]

The inability of the Victorian male to relate to mature women at a sexual level is nowhere more evident than in the age's literature. It is no coincidence that the most celebrated scene in Victorian literature is the death of Little Nell, in Charles Dickens' novel *The Old Curiosity Shop*. The denial of women's sexual nature meant that for the first time in the history of English literature, a major literary period is almost entirely without representations of erotic relations between men and women. This area was abandoned to the pornographers and the music hall. The roots of this are actually pre-Victorian, and can be traced back to the mid-eighteenth century when the success of the novel *Pamela* reflected the rising middle-class's ideal of the virtuous woman who vanquishes the brutish male. In 1801, the Society for the Suppression of Vice and the Encouragement of Religion and Virtue was founded in England, and kept a wary eye on literary matters to make sure no author overstepped the mark of good taste, which was increasingly defined as an absence of any reference to bodily functions, especially sexual ones. Seventeen years later, Thomas Bowdler (1754–1825) published the first *Family Shakespeare*, with all rude, vulgar, or overtly sexual references cut out. The Victorians showed that they had a penchant for mutilating literature as well as women.

Charles Dickens, the greatest novelist of the period – and arguably the greatest in English literature – did not succeed, over the course of some fifteen novels and many short stories, in creating a portrait of a sexually mature woman. In *David Copperfield*, perhaps Dickens' greatest, and certainly his most autobiographical work, the child-like nature Victorians sought in their women is realized most fully in his portrait of Dora, the hero's first wife. Copperfield makes the mistake of marrying her because she so closely resembles his mother, Clara, who was also weak, ineffective and immature. The novel exposes the cruel reality behind the ideal of girlish innocence, which generates nothing but contempt for the woman and unhappiness for both her and her mate.[273]

Victorian misogyny created not only the childish woman – it also offered for our admiration the noble woman, driven only by her altruism. In the classic Victorian text, such as Charlotte Brontë's *Jane Eyre* or George Eliot's *Middlemarch*, the only vocation open to the heroine is self-sacrifice, usually to foster her husband's well-being or further his career. Her role is to act as a kind of spiritual helpmate to the male. She, through the example of her purity, can elevate his coarser, more physical nature, so he can appreciate the higher sentiments. This was the white woman's burden, to be shouldered at the cost of denying her a vital part of her human nature – her sexuality. When passionate desire is depicted, as that between Heathcliff and Catherine in Emily Brontë's masterpiece *Wuthering Heights*, it is demonic and its consequences are disastrous.

Banished from respectable literature, the depiction of sexual relations and sexual desire went underground to supply a flourishing trade in risqué novels and explicitly illustrated men's magazines. In 1857, a word was invented to describe this material – 'pornography', literally, writing about prostitutes or prostitution. But sex also enlivened the stage of the working class music halls, where the never-ending struggle between men and women continued to be celebrated in sentimental, comic and bawdy songs, sketches and recitals.

While Victorian women were expected to be above certain aspects of nature, they were also expected to submit to nature in ways deemed an essential part of a woman's lot. The pangs of childbirth were one. Christians had long taught that such suffering was the punishment visited upon all women because of Eve's sin. Two hundred and fifty years earlier, when James VI (1566–1625) was king, one Euphanie McCalyane, unable to bear the pain of labour, asked a midwife Agnes Simpson to give her something to relieve her suffering. The king was outraged and had her burned alive. Had he not authorized the English translation of the Bible so that the word of God would be clear to everyone, including women? And in the book of Genesis it was spelt out plainly when God said to Eve: 'Unto the woman . . . I will greatly multiply thy sorrow and thy conception; in sorrow thou shalt bring forth children . . .' (3:16). Just in case it was not clear, it was repeated in Isaiah (26:17): 'Like a woman with child, that draweth near the time of her delivery, is in pain and crieth out in her pangs . . .'

God had spoken. So when a Scottish doctor called James Young Simpson (1811–70) came along with a proposal that promised to end what God ordained, there was something of an uproar. As a child Simpson had listened to a vivid description of how his own mother almost died giving birth to him. Later, working as an obstetrician, he saw the suffering of women in labour for himself, and began to search for a remedy to alleviate it. In 1847, he administered ether to a woman with a contracted pelvis to ease her labour. He demonstrated that even when she was unconscious, the woman's uterus still went through contractions. Later, he discovered the anaesthetic properties of chloroform, and began using it on women giving birth.

Simpson was denounced from the pulpit. Chloroform was called 'a decoy of Satan, apparently offering itself to bless women; but in the end it will harden society and rob God of the deep earnest cries which arise in time of trouble for help.' The Calvinist Church of Scotland circulated pamphlets to doctors' offices in Edinburgh warning that Simpson's work would destroy people's fear of the Lord and bring about a complete collapse of society.[274]

The attacks, which also came from his medical colleagues, many of whom argued that you should not interfere with 'the providentially arranged process of healthy labour',[275] had little long-term effect on his popularity. When he died, more than 30,000 people came to his funeral, a large number of them women. By that time, Queen Victoria herself had been put under, during the births of her last two children, which silenced the critics. It earns that fierce defender of the status quo a place in the struggle to improve women's lot.

Misogynistic arguments based on what God wants, or what nature dictates, would be deployed with increasing frequency as the nineteenth century progressed and the status of women became a legal, political, as well as scientific battleground in Western Europe and North America. The century had begun in France where a legislative package was passed that curbed women's rights with a repressive thoroughness hardly equalled until the Taliban took over Afghanistan in the late 1990s. In 1804, Le Code Napoléon rolled back the advances that women had made during the revolution, which had passed legislation giving them the right to divorce. According to Napoleon 'the husband must possess the absolute power and right to say to his wife, "Madam, you shall not go to the theatre, you shall not receive such and such a person, for the children you shall bear shall be mine." '[276] It gave legal force to his view that 'women should stick to knitting,' leaving him free to soak the battlefields of Europe in blood. However, on this battlefield, the great general would be comprehensively defeated.

Just over fifty years after the passing of Le Code Napoléon, in 1857, English women finally won the right to file for divorce from their husbands. It was a limited victory – a man merely had to prove that his wife had committed adultery, but aggrieved wives had to show that their husbands were guilty of 'incestuous adultery, or of bigamy with adultery, or of rape, or of sodomy or bestiality, or of adultery coupled with such cruelty as without adultery would have entitled her to a divorce . . .' But over the course of the next three decades, further legislation was enacted that gave judges the power to grant separation to a woman if her husband assaulted her, and forced husbands who deserted their wives to pay maintenance. The Married Woman's Property Act of 1870 strengthened a wife's financial independence against the objections of Lord Shaftesbury who lamented that it 'jars with poetical notions of wedlock'.[277] However, among the very poorest of women the situation improved much more slowly. As Jack London observed in the East End slums, wives who were brutalized would not report their husbands to the police because they were financially dependent on them and could not survive without their income if they were sent to prison.

Reform of the laws on divorce in favour of women was viewed by many as much of a threat to civilization as was female masturbation. It challenged the misogynistic belief in the 'natural' inequality between men and women. According to the influential *Saturday Review*, 'the adultery of the wife is, and always will be, a more serious matter than the infidelity of the husband.'[278] The natural differences between men and women justified and explained differences in their treatment and responsibilities. This argument was gradually replacing that based on divine authority as Christianity beat an intellectual retreat in the face of scientific advances. It was monotonously repeated, with one or two variations, to refute campaigns for women's education and the right to the vote.

In this view of things, women's 'natural frailty' made them unfit for the rigours of an intellectual education. One contemporary philosopher warned that if girls' brains were over-exercised they would become flat-chested and unable to bear 'a well-developed infant'.[279] Was not Eve punished for knowing too much? Education might bring with it too much knowledge of the 'mass of meanness and wickedness and misery that is loose in the world. She could not learn it without losing the bloom and freshness which it is her mission in life to preserve.'[280] Clearly, the author had not visited the East End to witness how woman's bloom and freshness fared under the hobnail boots of her husband – less well, it is certain, than if she were reading Shakespeare or Plato.

Traditional misogynists were not alone in advancing the argument that nature, or God, made women different from men. Advocates for women's rights used the same reasoning. But they, of course, argued from the premise that women's nature made them superior, not inferior, to men. Both those who opposed extending the franchise to women, and those who advocated its extension, used the belief in the 'Otherness' of the female's nature to advance their cause. In Britain, Prime Minister William Gladstone (1809–98) opposed suffrage because to involve women in politics would be, he said, 'to trespass upon the delicacy, the purity, the refinement, the elevation of their nature'. At the same time, reformers argued that by extending voting rights to more men, the government was 'enfranchising the vast proportion of crime, intemperance, immorality and dishonesty' because 'the worst elements,' i.e. men, 'had been put into the ballot box, and the best elements,' i.e. women, 'kept out'. [281]

The struggle for the vote was complicated. It revealed, very starkly, that not only did some feminists' disapproval of men mirror misogynists' contempt for women, but also that some women's contempt for women echoed that of men. It was a woman, Queen Victoria, who led the charge against the women's rights brigade. In a letter to the biographer of her husband Prince Albert she wrote:

> The Queen is most anxious to enlist everyone who can speak or write or join in checking this mad, wicked folly of 'Woman's Rights', with all its attendant horrors, on which her poor feeble sex is bent, forgetting every sense of womanly feeling and propriety.[282]

She said that one Lady Amberley, who dared present a paper arguing in favour of votes for women at the Mechanic's Institute in Stroud, should be given a good whipping. Many women from the Queen down opposed change, highlighting the fact that the status quo did not seem as oppressive to some women as it did to others. This would be a continuing difficulty that campaigners for women's rights would face in the years that followed when among their most vociferous opponents were women themselves.

The age of revolution, however, had created a new nation in North America, where the idea of progress was an economic, social and cultural imperative that threatened to undermine many of the assumptions on which traditional misogyny had rested. The first European colonists in the northeast brought with them the Christian tradition in which woman was viewed as the source of temptation and sin. At the same time the Protestant Reformation had fostered a view of her as a valuable and respected helpmate. The harsh conditions of the early colonies might be imagined by recalling the fact that of the eighteen wives the Pilgrim Fathers took with them, only five survived the first winter in the New World. Women were an essential resource on the frontier, working alongside their men. Sexual transgressions were severely punished, often by flogging and branding, but penalties were inflicted on male transgressors as well as on female. It has already been noted that in New England, in the late seventeenth century, the witch craze ran its course very rapidly, and the belief in witchcraft was quickly discredited. The result was that even relative to the small population, a lot fewer women were condemned and punished as witches in New England than in Europe during the same decades (see Chapter 4).

Puritan hostility to the body manifested itself with the traditional misogynistic attacks on women for decorating themselves. Most influential among a series of early tracts on this old familiar subject was that of the Rev. Cotton Mather (1663–1728), who was pastor for the North Church in Boston for more than forty years. (He was also one of those who vigorously argued in favour of the belief in witches.) Entitled *The Character Of A Virtuous Woman*, this revisits the usual cliché, which equates love of adornment with sin or moral laxity: 'The Beauty whereof a virtuous woman hath a remarkable dislike is that which hath artificial painting in it.' Virtuous women kept their whole bodies covered except their face and hands, for to do otherwise 'would enkindle a foul fire in the male spectators for which cause even popish writers would have no less righteously than severely lashed them.'[283]

However, Mather is careful to temper his admonitions and

warnings with praise of women. He denounces as 'perverse and morose men' those who have subjected women to a catalogue of 'indignities'. Only bad men would claim *'femina nulla bona'* ('no woman is good'). 'If any men are so wicked . . . as to deny your being rational creatures, the best means to confute them, will be by proving your selves religious ones . . .'[284] He seems at times equally ashamed of men for attacking women as he is at women for putting on make-up. His strong advocacy of education for women also shows that in the New World, they were already held in higher esteem than was traditionally the case in Europe.

During the American Revolution, Tom Paine advocated rights for women (see above). The tradition was carried on by Abigail Adams (1744–1818), the wife of the second president of the United States, John Adams (1735–1826, president 1797–1801). She declared in 1777 that women 'will not be bound by any laws in which we have no voice'.

The eighteenth-century doctrines of equality and the right to pursue happiness were enshrined in the American constitution. They provided a crucial reference point for those who wanted to wage war against the political and social discrimination to which women were still subjected. Thus, the traditional misogynistic beliefs that lay at the root of such discrimination were inevitably brought into question. Misogyny was put on the defensive, intellectually, politically and socially.

Even before women's rights were achieved, the beneficial influence of American democracy on the status of women was obvious to visitors such as Alexis de Tocqueville, the liberal French aristocrat who visited the United States for eight months between 1831 and 1832. In 1835, he published his masterpiece *Democracy in America*. De Tocqueville notes that American women are better educated and more independent-minded, sometimes startlingly so, than their French and English counterparts. 'I have been frequently surprised and almost frightened,' he writes, 'at the singular address and happy boldness with which young women in America contrive to arrange their thoughts and their language amid all the difficulties of free conversation.'[285]

In Europe, he says, men flatter women more, but betray an underlying contempt, whereas in the United States, 'men seldom compliment women, but they daily show how much they esteem them.' In America, he observes, rape is still a capital offence, and 'a young unmarried woman may alone and without fear undertake a long journey.' De Tocqueville's experience in America prompts him to ask the most important question of all concerning the relationship between men and women. Will democracy 'ultimately affect the great inequality between man and woman which has seemed, up to the present day, to be eternally based in human nature?' It is a question that at the beginning of a new millennium is reverberating around the developing world, as the West exports its political and social model into cultures still hostile to notions of equality between the sexes. In 1835, de Tocqueville predicted confidently what the answer would be. Democracy he believed 'will raise woman and make her more and more the equal of man'.[286]

De Tocqueville had spent most of his time in the northeastern United States, and comparatively little in the slave-owning southern states where the prospect of equality between men and women would have seemed as improbable as that between African Americans and their white masters. Slavery, like poverty, while not creating misogyny, certainly provides it with the opportunity to thrive. Crucially, it removes any legal barrier to the sexual exploitation of women. 'From the time the first African American was raped by her American master,' wrote the legal scholar Leon Higginbotham, 'the message was even clearer – in the eyes of the law, an African-American slave woman was not regarded as a human being and had no rights to control even her own body.'[287] Since in slavery, people were held as the property of others, African women were often used as breeders to produce more property.

According to the historian Beverly Guy-Sheftall: 'The sexual exploitation of Black women during slavery was as devastating as the emasculation of the Black male slaves.'[288] Sojourner Truth, a former slave who became active in the early women's rights movement, had thirteen children, and testified that most of them were sold off as slaves.[289]

Early feminists saw a parallel between slavery and misogyny in that, like slaves, women were seen as property. Indeed, it was when Lucretia Mott (1793–1880), the Quaker abolitionist, was excluded from speaking at an abolitionist meeting in London in 1840 because she was a woman that she decided to organize for women's rights. Eight years later, in Seneca Falls, upstate New York, the first women's rights convention took place, organized by Mott and Elizabeth Cady Stanton (1815–1902). They declared, 'We hold these truths to be self-evident, that all men and women are created equal.' The following year, 1849, the first women doctors were licensed to practise in the United States. Twenty years later, Wyoming territory made political, social and gender history by becoming the first modern political entity to give women the right to vote.[290] It would take another fifty years for the 19th Amendment to the US Constitution to pass, extending the vote to women in every state.

In England, the empiricist philosopher John Stuart Mill (1806–73), a keen proponent of women's rights and the author of *The Subjection of Women*, tried in 1867 to include a provision in a bill in the House of Commons that would grant the vote to women, though it would have been restricted by educational qualifications. It failed, as did the French Socialist Congress's attempt to win political rights for women in 1879.

Mill was one of the first to apply to politics and social policy the so-called Blank Slate hypothesis – the idea that 'human nature' as such did not exist, and that all differences between races and individuals could be explained by circumstances. He argued that the belief in innate differences, including those between men and women, was the chief obstacle to social progress.

His opponents proved him right. As the empiricists' argument in favour of women's equality gathered strength, the backlash against it increasingly relied on deductions from Nature to refute such an outlandish notion. Did Nature not make women weaker than men? Did they not have smaller heads, as one Charles Darwin pointed out who argued that their brains were therefore 'less highly evolved'? [291] Did they not have periods? The level of scientific analysis might be judged by the fact that for six months in 1878 the *British Medical Journal* featured a debate as to whether or not a menstruating woman could turn a ham rancid by touching it.[292]

The backlash expressed itself philosophically. Misogyny has never lacked for philosophers, from Plato onwards. In the nineteenth century, among mainly German thinkers, it took the form of a reaction against empiricism, and helped create the Romantic movement, under the influence of Rousseau (see Chapter 5) and Immanuel Kant (1724–1804). It is somewhat ironic that the Romantics should be lined up on the side of the perpetuators of misogyny, since 'romantic' at least in popular thinking has an aura of being woman-friendly. But the Romantics (in poetry and philosophy) were to women's liberation what the black and white minstrels were to the civil rights movement.

The Kantian notion that the deepest knowledge is independent of experience (i.e. essentially intuitive) lent itself to a semi-mystical, pantheistic interpretation of the world. It became anti-rationalist, rejecting the intellect and elevating the will as a means of realizing the meaning of the world, which it saw as being composed of essences. Women were assigned certain qualities, men others. For Kant, woman was the essence of beauty and her only role in life is that of a glorified flower arranger best left undisturbed by man the thinker's travails, of which the less she knew the better. In the philosophy of Arthur Schopenhauer (1788–1860), who followed Kant, she is a grown-up child, a creature of arrested development, fitted only for taking care of men. Schopenhauer, the author of *The World as Will and Idea*, was a Buddhist, a believer in magic and mysticism, an animal lover who never married and who was thoroughly anti-democratic. He believed that 'women exist in the main solely for the propagation of the species.' Undoubtedly, his influence over Friedrich Nietzsche (1844–1900) was his most important contribution to the history of ideas.[293]

For Nietzsche, as for Schopenhauer, the only reality was the will. He admired Napoleon and the British poet Lord Byron (1788–1824). Napoleon seems more obvious a choice than Byron, the first literary celebrity in the modern sense. But Byron embodied what Nietzsche believed was the role of the '*Ubermensch*' – or 'Overman', more usually rendered into English as 'Superman'. He trampled on convention, defied prevailing moral standards, incarnating the will to power. In Byron's case, it was power over women – he was renowned as a living 'Don Juan'.[294]

'The happiness of man is: "I will." The happiness of woman is: "He will,"' Nietzsche wrote in *Thus Spoke Zarathustra*. And again: 'Everything in woman is a riddle, and everything in woman has one solution: pregnancy.' When not bearing Superman's babies, she dedicates herself to 'the relaxation of the warrior'. 'All else,' he declares, 'is folly.' In *The Will to Power*, he wrote of women, 'What a treat it is to meet creatures who have only dancing and nonsense and finery in their minds!'

Nietzsche's fantasies of power and violence are those of a sickly recluse, and his contempt for women is that of a man who fears them.[295] The frivolous female simpleton he depicted as his ideal woman is the daughter of Rousseau and Schopenhauer, a combination of innocence and ignorance, who is not unrelated to the Victorian 'Angel in the House'. But her direct descendant would be born later, in the mind of Adolf Hitler. In the twentieth century, she would take the shape of the pure-bred German maiden, the sexless mother of the master race.

Through his impact on Hitler, Nietzsche may well have been the most influential misogynist of the nineteenth century, but he was not the most famous. That dubious distinction must go to a man whose identity still remains as much of a mystery as it was just over a hundred years ago when he earned the nickname by which he is still known – Jack the Ripper, the first modern serial killer. Murder can speak as eloquently of a society's innermost fears, desires and preoccupations as does its poetry. In this way, there is no more chillingly eloquent expression of Victorian misogyny than the five murders Jack the Ripper carried out between August and November 1888. It was just one year after Queen Victoria celebrated her Golden Jubilee. The British Empire was at its peak, and Britain was the most confident and powerful nation on earth. Yet, the sordid, vicious murders of five working-class prostitutes would shake the imperial capital by providing it with a bloody mirror in which to behold frightening reflections of society's deep-seated hatred of women.

Certainly, Victorians were not strangers to violence against women, though they may well have chosen to ignore it when the victims were lower class, which the great majority of them were. When the reality of violence did not suffice, pornography provided it in generous helpings to stimulate the fantasies of middle-class gentlemen. The same year as the Ripper murders, the anonymously written *My Secret Life* was published. Its eleven volumes are the purported sexual autobiography of a married gentleman who is addicted to prostitutes and lower-class women. After one escapade, during which he thinks he contracted syphilis, he returns home to his wife, who refuses to have sex with him.

> But I jumped into bed and forcing her on her back, drove my prick up her. It must have been stiff, and I violent, for she cried out that I hurt her. 'Don't do it so hard – what are you about!' But I felt that I could murder her with my prick, and drove, and drove, and spent up her cursing. While I fucked her, I hated her – she was my spunk-emptier.[296]

The contempt for women so powerfully expressed in this passage results in a kind of psychic murder, with the penis wielded as a deadly weapon. The Ripper was more literal-minded, and used a knife. But it was the way that he used it that reveals how misogyny can transform itself. This time, it changed to suit the triumph of the new scientific paradigm, which was to a growing extent replacing religion, as the arbiter of what was right and wrong in sexual behaviour. Rather than overtly moral categories, it preferred the vocabulary of medical science. Jack the Ripper applied this paradigm in the most direct and brutal way imaginable: he reduced women to specimens fit only for dissection.

His five victims were Mary Ann Nichols, murdered on 31

August; Annie Chapman, murdered 8 September; Elizabeth Stride, murdered 30 September; Catherine Eddowes, murdered on the same date; and Mary Jane Kelly, murdered on 9 November.[297] All the victims were prostitutes who worked the streets, the cheap lodging houses and the pubs of the Whitechapel area of the East End. All were alcoholics. All were separated from their husbands. All were struggling desperately to survive.

Their murderer's modus operandi was to strangle his victim as she lifted her skirt to get ready of sex. Laying her on her back on the ground, he sliced her throat twice and then began his real work. Usually, he is described as mutilating his victims. But what he actually did is closer to a dissection, concentrated on the woman's pubic area. He removed the uterus, stabbed and/or removed portions of the vagina. (In the case of Stride, he was apparently interrupted and did not get this far.) He also took out the victim's entrails. The aim of the dissection was to expose women, from the inside out. The worst case was that of Mary Kelly who died in the dingy little room she rented. A reporter for *The Pall Mall Gazette* noted that her body resembled 'one of those horrible wax anatomical specimens'.[298] Being more secure from interruption than he had been on the street, the Ripper dissected her completely. According to the report of police surgeon Dr Thomas Bond,[299] her breasts were removed, one being placed under her head and the other by her right foot. Her uterus was found also under her head, as were her kidneys. Her genitals were denuded of flesh, as was her right thigh. Her face was mutilated beyond recognition. The flesh from the abdomen was left on the bedside table. One of her hands had been pushed into her abdominal cavity, which was empty. She was three months pregnant but the reports do not mention the foetus. The Ripper left her with her thighs spread in what was clearly a leering sexual gesture. All his other victims were found with their skirts hoisted up, exposing their genital areas. Yet the Victorians, though they famously covered table legs because they found them sexually provocative, did not categorize the Ripper's murders as sex crimes.

Like the witch craze of the late medieval and early modern period, the murders of Jack the Ripper tell us a lot about what was lurking in society's view of women. One widow of 46 wrote to a London newspaper that 'respectable women' like her need fear nothing because Jack 'respects and protects respectable women'.[300] Indeed, some respectable opinion in the upper class West End of the city held that the 'bad' women got what they deserved. The Victorian contention that good women were asexual beings and that therefore sexual desire on a woman's part was a sign of 'disease', had led to the practice of genital mutilation as a cure for masturbation, hysteria, nymphomania and other 'female' disorders. Prostitutes were commonly referred to as 'fallen women' or 'daughters of joy' since Victorian misogyny saw their activities as a result not of economic desperation but of uncontrollable sexual desire. Jack the Ripper took this to its logical, if psychopathic extremes. Since 'fallen women' suffered from a sexual disease he would operate upon them, laying them bare like any other diseased specimen for the world to behold.[301]

In the witch craze, misogyny had operated through a powerful institution, the Church. In the case of Jack the Ripper, it expressed itself at the level of a psychotic individual. Unfortunately, the twentieth century would provide too many opportunities for misogyny to assume both forms.

7

MISOGYNY IN
THE AGE OF SUPERMEN

When what we call history is actually being lived, there is rarely a neat dividing line between one epoch and another. We decisively separate our modern world from that of the Victorians, especially in sexual matters, forgetting that it was men rooted in the Victorian Age who helped shape the twentieth century and how it would view and treat women. Sigmund Freud (1856–1939), Charles Darwin (1809–1882) and Karl Marx (1818–1883) were nineteenth-century men who bequeathed us ideas the consequences of which were only fully realized in the century following it. The ideas of all three have had a (sometimes profound) bearing on the history of misogyny. With Marx and Darwin the influence is not at first immediately obvious. But with Freud it most certainly is.

By the beginning of the twentieth century, the ideals of the Enlightenment, with their emphasis on the individual's equality and autonomy, seemed secure throughout Western Europe, the United States and in nations that were their off-shoots. Linked to these was the idea of progress, also firmly embedded in the West. It seemed far more than merely an idea. It seemed a reality. A period of unparalleled industrial growth and economic expansion held out the promise of widespread prosperity. In Europe and North America, in states where democratic forms of government prevailed, women's rights were firmly on the political agenda, among them the right to vote. In 1893, New Zealand had become the first nation state to grant suffrage to women. Denmark, Finland, Iceland and Norway followed. The Bolshevik Revolution in Russia gave them that right in 1917. The next year, after a long and at times bitter campaign lasting the best part of a century, the United Kingdom granted women over 30 the right to vote and ten years later dropped the voting age to 21. The right to vote became the 19th amendment to the US constitution in August 1920. Meanwhile, women were an increasingly important part of the workforce. The public sphere was no longer an all-male preserve. Middle-class women had access to higher education and were entering professions hitherto thought of as for men only.

Not for the first time in the history of misogyny, women's progress provoked a reaction. It manifested itself at several different levels: scientific, philosophical and political. But if these reactions had a shared aim it was to demonstrate that men's contempt for women was justified. The ancient prejudice had to be reconfirmed, if not reinforced, to reassure men that regardless of equality and women's rights certain aspects in the male–female relationship would never change.

This emerges starkly enough in the work of Freud. He has been extraordinarily influential, so much so that in the words of the English poet W. H. Auden, he became 'a whole climate of opinion/Under whom we conduct our different lives'.[302] His work represents the first extensive and detailed 'scientific' examination of the psychological differences between the sexes. Freud attempted to find the psychoanalytical roots in the perceived differences in the nature of men and women. In his early years, he tended to stress the parallels between the development of boys and girls rather than the differences. At one point, he even entertained the notion that boys experienced 'womb-envy'. [303] However, as he grew older, he developed a more dualistic view. It was during this period, in the 1920s, that his more famous formulations about men and women were pronounced.

When probed, some of these findings turn out to resemble those held by African witchdoctors. That the witchdoctor makes his pronouncements dressed up in the shiny new white coat of science cannot disguise their remarkable similarities. Witness Freud's attack on the clitoris. In a paper written in 1925, he saw the clitoris as the 'masculine' element of female sexuality since it has erections, and masturbation of the clitoris as 'a masculine activity'. He claimed, 'The elimination of clitoridal sexuality is a necessary precondition for the development of femininity'.[304] Femininity is achieved through a sort of regime change, with the clitoris handing over 'its sensitivity, and at the same time, its importance, to the vagina'.

The Dogon tribe of Niger, in West Africa, believes that each person is born with a male and female soul. For girls to realize their true femaleness it is necessary to remove that part of them where their male soul resides, i.e., the clitoris, just as boys must undergo circumcision to remove their female soul hiding in their foreskin.[305] As we have seen, some Victorian medical experts advocated clitoridectomy to cure 'female diseases'. What is the difference between a quaint old African myth, Victorian clitoridectomy and the assertions of Sigmund Freud, other than that Freud proposes a psychic instead of a physical mutilation of the woman? He claims that true femininity comes about when the woman foregoes the sexual pleasure derived from 'masculine' activity, which is identified with the clitoris because it is the source of a pure pleasure unrelated to reproduction. Such selfishness is characteristic of the male, and therefore has to be abandoned if the female is to become fully a feminine creature, since femininity implies self-abrogation and self-denial for a higher purpose, which is identified with the vagina. And what, may we ask, could possibly inspire a girl to forgo her clitoral delights? Girls, writes Freud, 'notice the penis of a brother or playmate, strikingly visible and of larger proportions, at once recognize it as the superior counterpart to their own small and inconspicuous organ, and from that time forward fall a victim to envy for the penis.'[306] Clearly, for Freud at least, size matters. It also determines how men see women, and offers an explanation for misogyny:

'This combination of circumstances leads to two reactions, which may become fixed and will with other factors, permanently determine the boy's relations to women: horror of the mutilated creature or triumphant contempt for her.' According to Freud, this explains not only why men hold women in contempt but also why women themselves develop a contempt 'for a sex which is the lesser in so important a respect'.[307] This theory therefore predicts that misogyny is not an aberration but in fact a normal, universal reaction on the part of both men and women to the 'mutilated' female.

Freud's description of female development echoes not only that of African witchdoctors but also the views of Aristotle. Some 2,200 years earlier, Aristotle also saw females as 'mutilated' males, creatures that failed to realize their full potential (see Chapter 1). Like Aristotle, Freud's starting point is to assume that the male is the sexual norm against which the other is measured. This establishes a kind of duality – male-normality vs female-abnormality – that deepens in his thought as time

passes. He uses it in the end to repeat many of the old misogynistic prejudices against women, except that this time they
are justified in the name of science.[308] His theory that femininity
depended on a transfer of focus from clitoral to vaginal sex
could be seen as the 'scientific' justification for the prejudice,
expounded most vociferously in contemporary Nazi propaganda, that woman's role should be confined to being mothers.

By the time he had come to write one of his last works,
Civilization and its Discontents, in 1929, men were equated
with civilization itself and women with its opponents, a hostile,
resentful and conservative force driven by penis envy. His
conclusion was that female sexuality was a 'dark continent' – a
revealing metaphor that places women alongside Africans
firmly outside the realm of civilization, which is 'the business
of men'. [309]

Freud admitted in *Some Psychical Consequences* that his
theories of female sexuality were based 'on a handful of cases'.
Erecting big theories on small data is not good scientific
practice. Science is one of those areas where size (of the sample
of facts upon which theories are based) does matter. Freud's
willingness to advance his views despite lack of sufficient
evidence says more about the size of his own ego than about
the nature of female sexuality.

'I always find it uncanny,' he wrote, 'when I can't understand someone in terms of myself.' [310] Remarks like this have
led some to put him in the tradition of the 'supermen' of
Nietzsche, those self-reverential monsters before whose great
male egos all else pales into insignificance.[311] Certainly,
Freud's dualistic view of the sexes fits very well into that
tradition though it is not derived from the same irrational,
romantic tenets. Nietzsche saw woman as the enemy of truth,
whereas Freud saw her as the enemy of civilization.

The Nietzschean tradition of the essential dualism of male

and female provided one of the chief bases for the philosophical, and later the political, backlash against women in the twentieth century. In the autumn of 1901, Freud made the acquaintance of one of its lesser known, but nonetheless significant exponents. A twenty-one-year-old graduate from the University of Vienna called Otto Weininger approached him with the outline of a book he planned to write entitled *Sex and Character*. Freud read the outline and was unimpressed, remarking – ironically enough considering his own habit of making do with small data – 'The world wants evidence, not thoughts.' He told the young man to spend ten years gathering evidence for his theories. Such an undertaking was alien to Weininger's nature. In any case, he did not have that long left to live.[312]

Otto Weininger (1880–1903) was by all accounts a brilliant student who by the age of eighteen could speak eight languages. He was deeply influenced in his thinking by Schopenhauer and Nietzsche. That is, he inherited a tradition deeply hostile to women, and brought it to its philosophical climax in *Sex and Character*, published in 1903. In it, his misogynistic dualism takes on an almost mystical quality. Every positive achievement in civilization is associated with men – Aryan men. Women are its negation. Weininger goes to the extreme of denying women their humanity and reduces them to nonentities: 'Women have no existence and no essence; they are not, they are nothing.'[313] He invokes the Platonic distinction between matter and form, between the mutable, transient world of the senses and the ideal. Woman is matter, and man is form. Claiming that woman has no 'essence' means that she does not exist at the highest level of pure form, and therefore, for Weininger, her actual material existence is of no consequence.

Weininger repeats the Fall of Man myth at a philosophical level. 'For matter is in itself nothing, it can only come into existence through form,' that is, through desiring a woman who is 'the material on which man acts.' She is 'sexuality itself'. According to Weininger:

> The dualism of the world is beyond comprehension: it is the plot of man's Fall, the primitive riddle. It is the binding of eternal life on a perishable being, of the innocent in the guilty.

Plato, Genesis and the Doctrine of Original Sin are combined in Weininger's thought, as woman binds man into perishable matter, and the eternal form degenerates into the transient world. He concludes that as the instrument that brings about this Fall, 'Woman alone then is guilt.'[314]

Weininger was Jewish, but his anti-Semitism is as much a characteristic of his work as is his misogyny, though he dissociates himself from anything as vulgar as advocating persecution 'practical or theoretical' of the Jews. He draws parallels between women and Jews. Like women, Jews are 'without any trace of genius'. Jews and women are similar in 'their extreme adaptability' and 'their lack of deeply-rooted original ideas, in fact the mode in which, like women, they are nothing in themselves, they can become everything'. Both too are 'double-minded', never truly believing in anything and therefore entirely untrustworthy.[315]

Not surprisingly, Weininger also regards the empiricists as contemptible. No true Aryan, he asserts, would build a system of thought based on anything so superficial as the evidence of the senses or the need to validate theories by experiment. He despises the English because of their reliance on empirical thought, which he scorns as shallow.

The ultimate aim of *Sex and Character*, as stated by the author at the beginning of the book, is to deal with the question of woman's emancipation, which fills him with anxiety, since he views it as a threat to the concept of humanity. He returns to the question in his conclusion and laments the fact that New Zealand has granted women the right to vote, putting it on a par with enfranchising imbeciles, children and criminals. He relates emancipation to prostitution and the Jews' pernicious influence. Not surprisingly, he arrives at a position similar to that of the Christian ascetics of the fourth century, and concludes 'coitus is immoral'.

Not long after *Sex and Character* was published in 1903, Otto Weininger committed suicide. The book had generally received scant or unfavourable attention. But the young man's death cast a tragic aura over him and his work, and his ideas soon took on the status of a cult in Viennese circles where, according to sexologist Ivan Bloch, even heterosexual men began to 'renounce women in horror'.[316] His impact spread to France, Germany, England and America, where his work was hailed by the prestigious literary critic Ford Maddox Ford, who declared that a 'new gospel had appeared' among men.[317]

Weininger influenced such thinkers as the philosopher Ludwig Wittgenstein, also a Viennese, and has more lately impressed a handful of feminists. Germaine Greer praises his work in *The Female Eunuch*, arguing that his theories of women were merely based on what he saw around him. In this she carries on a long tradition within feminist thought that shares some of the assumptions of traditional misogyny, including contempt for aspects of the feminine, such as concern for beauty.

However, his true significance in the history of misogyny is found elsewhere. At the level of ideas, he vividly and powerfully crystallizes the main currents of contempt for women flowing from traditional Judaeo-Christian and Greek philosophical thought. More importantly, he is the expression of a worldview that is both anti-Semitic and misogynist, which found a powerful resonance in another young man who haunted the cafes and streets of turn-of-the-century Vienna and absorbed its fetid atmosphere of prejudice and hatred – Adolf Hitler (1889–1945).

There are remarkable similarities not only in the thought but also in aspects of the lives of Hitler and the three philosophers Schopenhauer, Nietzsche and Weininger. All were alienated, sexually insecure men who (as far as is known) never formed mature, stable relationships with women, or enjoyed steady home lives. Their sense of isolation was accompanied by an overwhelming belief in their own destiny. When Weininger declared after his book was published, 'There are three possibilities for me – the gallows, suicide or a future so brilliant that I don't dare think of it,' Hitler would have understood. Their misogyny, based on fear of women (and perhaps of an underlying fear of intimacy itself), was also linked to other prejudices, especially anti-Semitism.[318] To paraphrase Hamlet, rarely do prejudices come as single spies, but rather in battalions. The atmosphere of Vienna at the turn of the last century was poisonously anti-Semitic.[319] In the mind of Weininger, women's emancipation, prostitution and Jews were all linked. He writes that what the women's movement is about is 'merely the desire to be "free", to shake off the trammels of motherhood; as a whole the practical results show that it is a revolt from motherhood towards prostitution, a prostitute emancipation rather than the emancipation of womanhood as a whole is aimed at.' He claims that it is only because of the cunning influence of the Jews, that we 'bow before it' and see it as other than it really is.[320]

Hitler echoed these ideas, denouncing women's rights as a 'phrase invented by the Jewish intellect'.[321] In his warped vision, Jews, prostitutes, Marxists and modern women were part of a sinister plot against motherhood and 'Teutonic' civilization.

Hitler arrived in Vienna in 1908 as a nineteen-year-old aspiring artist but failed in his attempt to gain entrance to the Academy of Fine Arts. In his ample spare time, he used to lecture his friend August Kubizek, with whom he for a time shared a room, on the evils of prostitution. Occasionally he took Kubizek on tours of the city's red-light district, which inspired further rants about sex and moral decadence. Later, he would blame the Jews for the spread of prostitution, as well as for the spread of liberal ideas. He once launched into a furious diatribe when Kubizek, who was studying piano, brought a woman home to give her piano lessons. He told his friend women were incapable of benefiting from such learning.[322] Like Weininger, Hitler advocated abstinence from sex (as from alcohol and meat). He was also against masturbation. Another friend said of him that he 'had very little respect for the female sex, but very austere ideas about the relations between men and women'.[323] His ideal woman was, in his own words, 'a cute, cuddly, naïve little thing – tender, sweet and stupid'.[324] All sorts of mostly lurid rumours have accumulated over the years about Hitler's sexuality. He obsessed about women, Jews and syphilis in his autobiography, *Mein Kampf*, and five of the six women with whom he had any kind of relationship committed suicide, including his twenty-three-year-old niece Geli Raubal, about whom he was pathologically jealous. 'My uncle is a monster,' she once said.[325] In September 1931, she was found dead in his Munich apartment, shot in the head with his pistol. He was almost certainly asexual, and while he seems to have derived some pleasure from the company of pretty young women, his behaviour indicates a tremendous fear of women in general.[326] He liked to refer to the malleability of the masses as 'feminine', showing his contempt for both the mobs that he roused with his speeches and woman with whom he compared them. Tragically, he would leave the bloody stamp of his obsessions, misogynistic as well as racial, on the history of the twentieth century.

With the rise of the National Socialist movement, out of which the Nazis sprang, Hitler went from being a vagrant with fanatical ideas to a charismatic leader with the power to turn them into political reality, in all their murderous horror. From the beginning, the Nazi party was a powerful engine of misogyny as well as of racial hatred. It came out of the all-male culture of the trenches, beer-halls, the paramilitary organizations and ex-servicemen's associations set up by former German soldiers, embittered and angry at Germany's defeat in the First World War. There was also a distinct homosexual trait running through the Nazi cult of the warrior and 'superman'. (This became especially noticeable in the Nazi Party's original paramilitary organization, the SA.) Hitler's own contempt for women fitted well with the fledgling party's prevailing attitude. At the very first general meeting of the National Socialist German Workers' Party in 1921, party members passed a unanimous resolution that 'a woman can never be accepted into the leadership of the party and into the governing committee.'[327]

More broadly, Nazism's misogyny was one expression of a deep-seated paradox that it shares with many fundamentalist and conservative movements, including those that Islam, Christianity and Orthodox Judaism have more recently produced. While exploiting technological progress, without which it could not fight its wars, or maintain its dominance, at the same time National Socialism remained fiercely hostile to modernity. To the Nazis, no more blatant and worrying expression of modernity could be found than the emancipated woman of the 1920s, with her high heels, lipstick and cigarettes. Between the years 1918 and 1933, Germany had developed a modern hedonistic culture, where nightclubs flourished, Hollywood movies were the rage and sexual experimentation was rife. The Nazis' rigid exclusion of women from its power structures, and their long-term goal to remove them altogether from public life, did not prevent women from supporting the up-and-coming agitator. As Hitler himself recognized, women had 'played not an insignificant part' in his political career.[328] A few even worshipped him as a new messiah.[329] In some ways, the National Socialist line followed the same theme of 'kinder, küche, kirche' – 'children, kitchen, and Church' – that the other conservative parties extolled. At first German women gave their support to these more traditional rightwing parties. But in the election of November 1932, women voted Nazi in as large numbers as did men.[330] Given what happened later, it is surely one of the great ironies that women proved so crucial to Hitler's success. However, it is hardly surprising that in an age of uncertainty, rapid change and threatened communist revolution, Hitler's message was for many German women reassuring in its emphasis on the timeless values of home and family. As one sentimental Nazi poem expressed it:

> Mothers, your cradles
> are like a slumbering army
> Ever ready for victory,
> They will never be empty.[331]

Most women probably did not take the militarization of motherhood seriously or see its sinister metaphor directly linking the cradle to war as a prediction of what was to come. But Hitler took it very seriously. German women were an essential part of his war machine's production line. However, Nazi propaganda managed to disguise the brutal reality as it conjured up an Arcadian vision of lost innocence, a time when the world was a simpler place, and women were purer, content to be mothers, without perverse social or political ambitions. Two of the party's most notorious misogynists, Julius Streicher and Ernest Rohm, chief of the SA, helped propagate a cloyingly sentimental vision of German motherhood. Not surprisingly, both men were fixated upon their mothers. Streicher edited the lurid weekly *Der Sturmer*, which at its height had a circulation of nearly 1,000,000. It combined anti-Semitism with violent, pornographic depictions of helpless German maidens being raped by demon-like Jews. Streicher's excesses embarrassed even some Nazis, who wanted *Der Sturmer* suppressed. But Hitler tolerated Streicher and his obsessions, perhaps because they resembled one of the Führer's own recurring nightmares: a naked German woman chained and helpless as a Jewish butcher creeps up upon her from the rear and a watching Hitler is unable to save her.[332]

Streicher furiously protested in 1923 that the French army that occupied the Rhine in the post-war settlement employed black soldiers. He wrote: 'When a Negro soldier on the Rhine misuses a German girl, she is lost to the race forever.'[333] He also believed that a single act of intercourse between a Jew and a German woman would prevent her from ever having a 'pure-blooded Aryan child' and campaigned (successfully) to have marriages between the races outlawed.

Misogynistic cultures dwell on such fantasies of rape or seduction of 'their women' by alien forms. In the phantasmagorical minds of Nazi and inquisitor, the demon Jew played the same perverse role to the purebred Aryan maiden as the incubus did to the witch. It repeats a common misogynistic obsession linking something seen as crucial to male security, such as honour, to a woman's virtue. In Nazi ideology, preserving the German woman's virtue was identified with preserving racial purity. Frighteningly, this pathology became a social policy. The Nazis passed laws forbidding German women to have sex with the 'lesser' races, such as Jews or Slavs. During the war, in the absence of German men, thousands of Poles were employed to work on farms to help the lonely and no doubt often frustrated German wives and widows. From denunciations made to the German secret police, the Gestapo, it appears that even in cases where a German woman was raped at the hands of a Polish worker, she was publicly punished. Her head was shaven and she was pilloried. The men were hanged, whether the relationship was consensual or not. In contrast, when German men slept with Polish women the Gestapo merely noted it.[334]

Hitler saw the problem of women's position in modern society as a direct result of the 'stupid' notion of the equality of the sexes. Modern women were held to be responsible for 'the twilight of the family'. They were guilty of 'treason against nature' for not having children. 'But German men want German women again,' declared a National Socialist pamphlet. 'Not a frivolous plaything who is superficial and only out for pleasure, who decks herself with tawdry finery and is like a glittering exterior that is hollow and drab within. Our opponents sought to bend women to their dark purposes by painting frivolous life in the most glowing colours and portraying the true profession allotted to women by nature as slavery.'[335] The true German woman rejected lipstick, high heels, and nail varnish in favour of becoming a sort of primordial milkmaid, according to the ideal of party experts. They held that women will only be happy again when the natural differences between men and women are reinstated. Alfred Rosenberg, the party 'philosopher', claimed that women think 'lyrically' not 'systematically' as men do. One Nazi slogan declared, 'Women must be emancipated from women's emancipation.'

Hitler promised to 'do away with the idea that what he does with his own body is each individual's own business'.[336] It was the state's business, and the state knew what it wanted to do with German women's bodies. Hitler declared:

If in the past the liberal-intellectual women's movements contained in their programs many, many points arising out of the
so-called 'mind', then the program of our National Socialist
women's movement really only contains one single point and
that point is: the child.[337]

His words echo Nietzsche's proclamation that the answer to
the riddle of woman is pregnancy. Hitler reflects the mother-
fixation of those mystical misogynists, Schopenhauer and
Weininger. One of the practical consequences of this for
German women was that in 1938, childlessness was restored
in law as grounds for divorce. Abortion and contraceptives
were also banned. In this case at least, Hitler was on the pro-
life side of the argument.

The state awarded women a decoration, the 'Motherhood
Cross Award', mimicking those given to men for courage in
battle, according to 'their child-bearing achievements'.[338] Hitler's vision of a post-war world included a law that would
force every woman single or married under the age of thirty-
four who had not already borne at least four children to mate
with a purebred German male. If he was already married, he
would be set free for the purpose. According to Heinrich
Himmler, the head of the elite SS Troop, 'Nietzsche's Superman could be attained by means of breeding.'[339] Thus did the
Nazis envision Germany's future as one vast stud farm that
would supply Hitler's divisions with fresh canon fodder. The
racially pure studs were to be called 'conception assistants'.
But misogyny under the Nazis was unfortunately not confined
to the familiar obsessions with German woman's virtue or to
perpetuating sentimental though self-serving illusions about
motherhood. No more horrifying contrast with these cloying
fantasies could be found than in the murderous brutality meted
out to Jewish women during the reign of the Third Reich.

The Nazis placed all Jews outside any normal ethical code in their pursuit of the genocidal solution to the 'Jewish problem'. Some scholars have objected that anti-Semitism did not distinguish its victims on gender lines. 'The Holocaust happened to victims who were not seen as men, women and children, but as Jews,' wrote Cynthia Ozick.[340] But as is nearly always the case, when persecution is inflicted upon any hated group, the women of that group are singled out for particular humiliations and cruelties. When racial or religious hatreds are let loose, the underlying misogyny is usually given free reign.

When Hitler annexed Austria in March 1938, and the German army marched in, a series of brutal attacks were unleashed upon Austrian Jews. In a wealthy suburb of Vienna called Wahring, the Nazis ordered Jewish women to dress in their fur coats. They gave them small brushes and forced them to scrub the streets. As a joke, acid was often put in the pails of water. Then as the women knelt on the pavement, to the cheers and jeers of the large crowds of onlookers, Nazi soldiers urinated on their heads.[341] It is somehow grotesquely appropriate that the city, which had a few years earlier produced a Weininger, who denied women their very existence, and had nourished the virulent misogyny and anti-Semitism of Hitler himself, should have witnessed the disgusting reality behind those fantasies. Nietzsche's 'superman' was revealed as bigoted, beer-hall bully.

When the Nazi war machine swept through Poland and the Soviet Union three years later, genocidal acts became the norm. Huge numbers of Jewish men, women and children were rounded up and massacred. During the purges of the ghettos, before being massacred Jewish men were usually stripped to the waist, left with what little dignity a pair of pants affords a man. Not so the Jewish women. They were more often than not stripped naked before being driven like cattle into the streets to be mocked and humiliated. We know this, because German soldiers frequently took snapshots of these events, sometimes to send them to the folks back home, sometimes for the historical record. Two grey, grainy pictures from the Polish ghetto of Mizoc taken on 14 October 1942 show a line of sixteen naked women huddled together, supervised by two soldiers. Heaps of clothes are piled or scattered on the short grass around them. There are three children among them – one a baby in its mother's arms, the other two, little girls, holding on to older women, probably their mothers or sisters. At a guess, the women range in age from their late twenties to their early forties. Many cover their breasts in a futile attempt at protecting their modesty. They are obviously cold. They are being shunted down the line to death. The next grainy shot, taken minutes later, reveals a promiscuous pile of white bodies, and one woman, still alive, her back to the camera, raising herself up on her elbows next to the corpse of a little girl, while a German soldier stands over her, taking aim with a rifle, ready to finish her off.[342] Such scenes were replayed again and again wherever the Nazis took power in the east. They were regarded as so normal that the soldiers involved in the killings felt happy to record them to share with their families, wives and girl-friends, as if they were vacation snaps.

Even in the midst of the horrors of the concentration camps, Jewish women were frequently singled out for special treatment and subjected to grotesque 'gynaecological' experiments. In the concentration camp at Ravensbruck, Germany, Professor Carl Clauber carried out sterilization experiments on women. Using hundreds of Jewish and Gypsy women as guinea pigs, the notorious Nazi doctor, Joseph Mengele, injected chemicals into the uterus to block their fallopian tubes.[343] Younger women were forced into camp brothels set up for the sexual amusement of the guards.[344] Public nakedness was used as a tool for their constant sexual humiliation. It was also used as a tool of elimination. In the death camp at Auschwitz, among new arrivals women seen to be pregnant were directed to the left as they entered, and shunted into the gas chambers. For Jewish women, the bearing of life had become a death sentence. To the very end, in the Nazi scheme of inhumanity, where for the first time in history, murder became an industrial process, misogyny still found a place.

Unlike Nazism and other forms of fascism, socialism and the ideology that developed out of the ideas of Karl Marx were from the beginning very much on the side of women's emancipation. The goal of the Marxists was to eradicate differences whereas the Nazis saw them as essential. Marxism's relation to misogyny is therefore a more complex one.

In the nineteenth century, early socialists firmly supported women's rights. Marx and Friedrich Engels (1820–95) produced scorching critiques of the position of women, which they saw as stemming directly from the development of a property-owning society. Patriarchy and women's oppression in this analysis is a direct result of property relationships. According to Engels, 'monogamous marriage comes on the scene as the subjugation of one sex by the other'[345] and the relationship between man and woman provides a prototype for the class struggle, which Marxists saw as the driving force behind historical change. Woman's full emancipation could only come about when the property relations that underlay her subjugation were abolished. This, in turn, would only be achieved with a socialist revolution, the overthrow of capitalism and the bourgeoisie, and the triumph of the proletariat. It was another dualistic ideology, in which – at least in the more simplistic versions that prevailed – the bourgeoisie represented corruption, greed, and decadence, and the proletariat, progress, freedom, and decency. History teaches us that women generally do not do well under dualistic ideologies in which the world is viewed as the battleground for two conflicting forces or principles.

The philosophical framework for Marxist thought owes much to that of the eighteenth century empiricists. It shared their belief that social conditioning explains differences in people's characters and talents, including those found between classes, races and genders. Woman's oppression was 'a problem of history, rather than of biology, a problem which it should be the concern of historical materialism to analyse and revolutionary politics to solve'.[346] It accepted the 'blank slate' hypothesis that consciousness was determined by social being. Marxists were confident that given the right economic circumstances upon that slate they could draw a portrait of the new, Communist Man and Woman, in whom the old divisions that so troubled human relationships over the centuries would no longer be evident. But where that left sexual differences was to prove problematic, especially if it were argued (as it would be) that social circumstances produced such differences and not nature. Nature had become a 'bourgeois' and 'reactionary' concept, one that was identified with those who wished to keep women enslaved.

The opportunity to apply these beliefs first came in 1917 in Russia, when a demonstration during International Woman's Day sparked off a series of political upheavals that within six months had led to the overthrow of the Tsar and the coming to power of the Bolsheviks led by Vladimir Lenin (1870–1924). Lenin declared: 'The proletariat cannot achieve complete freedom, unless it achieves the complete freedom for women.'[347] The new government moved quickly on women's issues and within months of taking power passed legislation declaring the absolute equality of men and women. Women were granted the vote. They were given the right to divorce their husbands. In 1920, the Union of the Soviet Socialist Republics, as the new state was called, legalized abortion – the first modern state to do so. By then, the Bolsheviks had become the Communist Party of the Soviet Union. In the belief that the only way woman would achieve freedom from what Lenin described as 'her daily sacrifice to a thousand unimportant trivialities' was for her to be 'liberated' from the home and drafted into the 'large-scale socialist economy' as a member of the proletariat.[348] Since the home was identified with woman's 'slavery', it would be abolished. Large public dining halls, crèches, communal kitchens and laundries were established to integrate the private world of the family into the world of the new social order. The despised bourgeoisie was identified with selfishness, luxury and love of decoration. As usual in dualistic ideologies, anything associated with artifice – such as make-up – becomes demonized. In the new world order of communism, it was a symbol of what Lenin called the 'old bourgeois humiliation of women'[349] – a symbol of their sexual and domestic slavery from which Marxism had rescued them. In some ways, the Leninist utopia is similar to that of Plato's Republic (see Chapter 1) in which women were integrated into the ruling community as Guardians only at the cost of denying important aspects of human sexuality, such as the love of beauty.

In the aftermath of the Second World War, Soviet troops imposed the political, social and economic model established in the Soviet Union on Eastern Europe. Mao Zedong (1893–1976) followed that model when the communists fought their way to power in China in 1949. Similar systems were established in North Korea and North Vietnam. Hundreds of millions of men and women effectively became the guinea pigs in the greatest experiment in social engineering of all time.

Ironically, the egalitarian promise contained in communism, and expressed in the term 'comrade' that was theoretically applied to all, regardless of rank, became instead an ideological steamroller that attempted to reduce individuals to products of social engineering, in which human nature played no role. Had Marx not declared that, 'The real nature of man is the totality of social relations'?[350] Hitler had declared that the age of the individual was over. On this the communists, his main ideological enemies, agreed with him.

Of course, as in Plato's Republic, males and females had different biological functions and therefore anatomical differences but these were regarded as relatively unimportant in terms of behaviour and psychology. Any attempt on the part of women to highlight or draw attention to sexual differences was at best frowned upon, and at worst among the more fanatical regimes punished as evidence of possessing vicious bourgeois tendencies. In Maoist China, during the Cultural Revolution (1962–76 or so), women were forbidden to wear skirts, which were a sign of their sexual slavery, and forced into the same uniform-style clothing as men – a sort of boiler suit with a peaked cap. Make-up was strictly forbidden. Neighbourhood committees (set up by the local communist party) policed their periods to make sure they were not trying to violate the strict limits placed on the size of their families, which allowed only one child per couple. Experimental drugs were used on female comrades to control their fertility in the name of 'revolutionary science'.[351]

Needless to say, the great experiment to remodel human nature according to the dictates of Marxist social theory failed. After Mao's death in 1976, as soon as more liberal policies began to be tolerated, beauty parlours began to appear, and Chinese women flocked to them. By the late 1990s, a sexual revolution was sweeping China in reaction to the decades of repression. Bars with lap dancers and go-go dancers began to open. The Chinese say: 'The Cultural Revolution is the father of the sexual revolution.'[352]

In China, women were often forced to have abortions in order to keep the size of their families down to prescribed limits. Meanwhile, in the Soviet Union, in 1936, just sixteen years after abortion had been legalized, it was banned under Joseph Stalin. To say Stalin like Hitler before him was pro-life is perhaps to miss the point. What is more important is what both have in common with the Chinese communists, and indeed with today's so-called 'pro-life' movement in the United Sates: they are all anti-choice, believing that a woman's right to control her own fertility must be subordinated to goals more important than any notions she may have of her autonomy. That in itself is a form of contempt.

Both right wing and left-wing forms of totalitarianism are in many ways so profoundly alike that their ideological differences are mostly irrelevant. Both set out to reverse the political and moral revolution of the Enlightenment, which for the first time in history enshrined the idea of the individual's autonomy, his right to liberty and to pursue happiness, rights that have gradually been extended also to women. The totalitarian assault on the Enlightenment is nowhere more clearly illustrated than in its utter disregard – indeed contempt – for the rights of the individual, and the horrifyingly brutal manner with which totalitarian states treat their citizens. 'The extreme violence of totalitarian systems,' wrote the novelist Vasily Grossman, 'proved able to paralyse the human spirit throughout whole continents.'[353] It might be argued, as it has been in relation to the Holocaust, that considering the horrors inflicted upon both men and women who fall foul of these regimes there is little point in distinguishing them in terms of the suffering that both endure. Inhuman acts by their very nature deny or ignore the humanity of their victims. However, there is always room for misogyny. Indeed, in such regimes cruelty against women based on misogynistic feelings is often the norm.

Women are frequently punished for their femininity, and for performing their biological role as mothers. Through its systematic mistreatment of women, the totalitarian state often reveals itself at its most frightening.

In May 2002, a group of three defectors offered us a terrifying glimpse of life inside a women's prison in North Korea, part of a gulag of camps and jails, which currently is estimated to hold about 200,000 people. Human rights organizations believe that about 400,000 prisoners have died in custody there since 1972. The three defectors testified in May that year before the House International Relations Committee in Washington DC. They spoke about their experience as political prisoners in what is the last truly totalitarian state on earth. Created in 1948 as the People's Democratic Republic of Korea, the country has been ruled by a sort of communist dynasty under Kim Il-sung and his successors since then.

The defectors described how it was common practice to inject pregnant women with abortion-inducing shots. Guards and prison doctors forced mothers who gave birth in custody to either kill their babies themselves or watch as others killed them.[354] One of the defectors, Sun-ok Lee, a fifty-four-year-old economics researcher now living in Seoul, South Korea, has written a book about her time in prison, *The Bright Eyes of the Tailless Beasts*. She was held in Kaechon political prison where, she said, 80 per cent of the prisoners were housewives.[355] She was one of eighty to ninety women held in a cell 19 feet long by 16 feet wide. They slept with no bedding on the floor. They were allowed to shower twice a year. They were permitted to go to the toilet twice a day, at fixed times, and in groups of ten. The special punishment cell was less than two feet wide and just over three feet high, too small to stand upright or to lie down and stretch your legs. If a woman was seen looking at her reflection in a window, she was punished for the bourgeois crime of vanity and sent to the 'drop-out team' for three months or one year.

'Their main job is to collect dung from the prison toilet tanks and dump it into a large dung pool for supply to the farming teams working at the prison farm outside the wall,' Mrs Lee told the committee. 'Two women wade knee-deep at the bottom of the toilet tank to fill a 20-litre rubber bucket with dung using their bare hands. Three other women pull up the rubber bucket from above and then pour the contents into a transport tank.' The tank was then brought and emptied into a large dung pool. One rainy day in 1991, a housewife from Pyongyang named Ok-tan Lee who had been on the toilet detail all day climbed on to the top of the tank when its lid became stuck. As she tried to force it open, 'she slipped from the rain-wet surface and plunged into the ground dung-pool. It was so deep she disappeared into the dung. A guard some distance away (they always keep their distance because of the stink from the prisoners) shouted, "Stop it! Let her die there unless you want to die the same way yourself!" She was left to drown there in the dung.'

After recovering from a bout of paratyphoid in 1989, two years after she arrived in the prison, Mrs Lee was told to report to the medical room. 'When I arrived at the medical room, I noticed six pregnant women awaiting delivery,' she said. 'While I was there, three women delivered babies on the cement floor without any blankets. It was horrible to watch the prison doctor kicking the pregnant women with his boots. When a baby was born, the doctor shouted, "Kill it quickly. How can a criminal in the prison expect to have a baby? Kill it." The women covered their faces with their hands and wept. Even though deliveries were forced by injection, the babies were still alive when born. The prisoner/nurses, with trembling hands, squeezed the babies' necks to kill them. The babies, when killed, were wrapped in a dirty cloth, put into a bucket and taken outside through a backdoor. I was so shocked with that scene that I still see the mothers weeping for their babies in my nightmares. I saw the baby-killing twice while I was in the prison.'

Other defectors told the HIRC that on other occasions, the mothers themselves were forced to smother their babies with pieces of plastic, after giving birth in their cells, and if they did not, the guards threatened to beat them. They said that there was special animosity towards women who had been made pregnant by Chinese men. Between March and May 2000, 8,000 North Korean defectors, most of them women, were deported from China back to their homeland as part of a crackdown on prostitution and forced marriage. Estimates are that up to one-third of them were pregnant. The vast majority of them were imprisoned on reaching North Korea. A former factory worker, identified only as Miss Lee (no relation to Mrs Lee) told the HIRC: 'The guards would scream at us: "You are carrying Chinese sperm, from foreign countries. We Koreans are one people, how dare you bring this foreign sperm here." '[356]

Patriotic feelings about sperm may be thought of as a rather extreme example of nationalism, that mainly twentieth-century phenomenon that has sparked so many wars and conflicts. But unfortunately those wars and conflicts have taught us that it is not so unusual. Nationalism, one of the most divisive forces in history, overlaps with racism, religious sectarianism and tribalism. At times it has reached genocidal proportions as it did in Rwanda in the spring of 1994. Women of the hated group are usually treated with the special contempt born out of misogyny, and subjected to sexual tortures and rape before being murdered. In this dualistic vision of the world, the hated group represents 'the Other', and the women of that group are usually seen as the most contemptible aspect of the perceived 'Otherness'. That is, its feminine form.

The history of the last hundred years is a depressing

chronicle of atrocities carried out under the influence of this intoxicatingly simple view of the world as being divided into 'us' and 'them'. From the Rape of Nanking, then the capital of China, by the Japanese in December 1937, to the Hindu nationalist massacre of Moslems in western India in March 2002, vulnerable women have suffered from the misogyny that always accompanies the racial or religious hatreds stirred up by nationalism. The grotesque mutilations that accompanied these attacks on women were of a sexual nature so that it appeared as if ordinary men had been transformed into so many Jack the Rippers. Behaviour that would be normally seen as proof of psychosis became acceptable. Of course war sanctions acts such as killing of which society normally strongly disapproves. So in some sense the Japanese soldiers and Hindu nationalists, who gang raped and then ripped open the wombs of pregnant Chinese and Moslem women to tear out their foetuses, must have seen their behaviour as sanctioned. And it was, by the profound contempt for women enshrined at some deeper level in their cultures. The Japanese military used thousands of Korean women as 'comfort women' during the war, a euphemism for forced prostitution. The soldiers' name for them was as direct as it was contemptuous: they were called 'toilets'. In Nanking no one knows the exact number of women raped often as a prelude to being mutilated and murdered. But one figure puts it as high as 80,000. In actions reminiscent of serial killers of women such as Jack the Ripper, the Japanese left the bodies of their victims lying in the streets with their legs splayed open, their vaginas pierced with bamboo canes, sticks, bottles and other objects.[357] The Germans claimed that during the Soviet army's advance across East Prussia in 1945, 'all German women who stayed behind were raped by Red Army soldiers.' One Soviet tank officer later boasted '2 million of our children were born' in Germany.[358] If true, this would make the Soviet invasion of Germany the occasion of the biggest mass rape in history.

Rape in war is as old as war itself, both as a way of taking revenge on the enemy population and as sexual relief for frustrated soldiers. But in the civil wars that followed the break up of Yugoslavia in the early 1990s it acquired a sinister dimension. It became a weapon of ethnic conflict as the Serbian majority launched attacks on the Croat and Moslem minorities. During 1992, Serbian authorities established rape camps, where Moslem and Croatian women were systematically raped and impregnated.

The Serbian Orthodox Church taught for years that the Serbs' low birthrate was because Serbian women were selfish. They declared it a sin against the Serbian race. Propagandists warned the Serbs that fundamentalist Moslems were kidnapping 'healthy Serbian women between the ages of seventeen and forty . . . to be impregnated by orthodox Islamic seed . . .'[359] The Serbs believed (as did Moslems and Croatian Catholics) that it was the male who determined the child's identity, with the female playing no more than the role of incubator to his seed. As we have seen, this misogynistic fantasy goes back to Aristotle. The Serbs therefore saw forced impregnation as a means of reproducing the ethnic group. At the same time it was a means of profoundly humiliating their enemies, especially the Moslems who have a saying: 'As our women are, so also is our community.' [360] Therefore these unfortunate women were made to carry a double burden, which made their bitter personal humiliation also a devastating humiliation for their community. Their families and husbands often rejected those women who survived the rapes. The all-too familiar identification of a woman's virtue with the honour of the family or nation or race always means that women are punished twice over for acts over which they have no control. To the trauma of rape is added the trauma of communal rejection. Many women went mad, and some committed suicide. It is not known exactly how many women suffered sexual violence at the hands of the Serbs. Figures vary from between 20,000 and 80,000.[361]

The wars in the former Yugoslavia brought up the whole question of rape as a war crime. Traditionally rape in wartime is the least punished offence and women began campaigning to redress this injustice.[362] In 1993, at the UN conference on human rights held in Vienna, rape and other forms of sexual violence were recognized as war crimes. Further conferences in Beijing and Cairo, which addressed the issue in the context of women's rights in general, reiterated the declaration, though not without considerable opposition on some issues from representatives of the Vatican and Moslem states. Undoubtedly, this represents a moral advance. But its practical effects will almost certainly be limited.

The problem is the nature of war itself in which the most important moral prohibition of all, that against killing fellow human beings, is removed. Never was this more emphatically the case than in the total wars fought in the twentieth century, which saw the near extermination of entire communities, and not only at the hands of Nazis and communists. Between 1943 and 1945, Allied bombers systematically obliterated German cities, killing about 700,000 men, women and children. When such monstrous violations of ordinary human decency are accepted as legitimate, then it should not be surprising if rape is ignored. Realistically, the only way to abolish rape during war is to abolish war itself.

As we move into the second millennium, that seems extremely unlikely. Indeed, with the rise of nationalism and other dualistic ideologies which dehumanize the hated group on racial, ethnic or religious lines, rape and the sexual degradation of women if anything would seem to be encouraged.

8

BODY POLITICS

In the 1960s, the politics of the body entered the body politic.
For the last several thousand years, control of the body –
that is, woman's body – has been a central concern of many of
the religious, social and political doctrines and institutions
created by man. There would have been no need to write a
history of misogyny if this were not the case. However, deep
within the male psyche are the wellsprings of fear and fascination that contemplation of woman causes. Her dehumanization, either through elevation or denigration, was always
(broadly speaking) a political matter. That is, the politics of
the body was not invented in the 1960s. But it was not until the
middle of the twentieth century that women themselves had
the power to shape how the politics of the body would be
defined. At that point, a technological breakthrough and the
resurgence of feminism combined to force the issue into the
public sphere as never before.

The first half of that century had seen in the Western and developed nations (outside of the totalitarian sphere) women winning political, legal and social rights. In the decades following, the struggle would shift to a far more profound arena – the right of women to control their own fertility as the technology to do so became increasingly sophisticated, reliable and available. It was a battle for the ultimate mechanism of control within a woman's body – her reproductive cycle. For a woman, this right is the most crucial of all, and the key to achieving real autonomy. Misogyny denies her that autonomy; her subordination depends on her lack of it. As the sexual revolution unfolded in the West, misogyny was faced with its worst nightmare. It would not be found wanting in the virulence of its response to the challenge.

The idea of women having sex without risking pregnancy is deeply disturbing to the vision of woman's role that Western civilization has inherited from the Judaeo-Christian tradition, which at its heart is profoundly misogynistic. In Britain, the Anglican Church denounced it as 'the awful heresy'.[363] As families grew smaller in the US during the early years of the twentieth century, with the average woman bearing around three children by 1900 as compared with seven in 1800, the moral reaction mounted. There was opposition from women themselves to contraception based on moral grounds. Elizabeth Blackwell, the first woman in the US to earn a medical degree, claimed that using contraceptives to 'indulge a husband's sensuality while counteracting Nature is on the one hand most uncertain of success and on the other hand is eminently noxious to woman'.[364] Theodore Roosevelt attacked the use of condoms as 'decadent'. Anticipating the terms later used by the Nazis in their campaign to keep women barefoot and pregnant in the kitchen, he declared women who used contraceptives as 'criminals against the race . . . the object of contemptuous abhorrence by healthy people'.[365]

Pregnancy, with its pains and sufferings, was preordained by God as part of the punishment, along with work and death, which Eve had incurred for her wicked inquisitiveness. Without the threat of pregnancy, women would have sex for pleasure and abandon their maternal responsibilities, becoming as selfish as men or worse, since the thought that women were sexually insatiable had never gone away and remained a source of male anxiety. The family and therefore civilization would collapse. For some, it was that simple. It made the demand for effective birth control far more threatening than the demand for the vote. Without effective birth control, equality for women would always be highly qualified. Opponents to the demand in both Church and State were happy that it should remain so; they might trust woman with the vote but not with the power to decide her reproductive fate.

However, the demand for access to birth control would not become a major threat to society's domination of women as long as birth control methods remained clumsy, unreliable, unrefined, or just too plain embarrassing to use, as they were for most of human history – until, that is, the invention of the contraceptive pill in 1955. Before, men had women more or less at their mercy in deciding whether or not to employ condoms, the most common contraceptive device. In theory, of course, a woman could refuse to have intercourse with a man unless he wore one, but in practice men bullied, coerced, blackmailed or otherwise pressurized women into taking risks for the sake of the man's pleasure. They still do. But when the pill became widely available in the early 1960s, it meant that for the first time in human history women could choose for themselves whether or not they wanted to regulate their fertility without having to consult the man with whom they were having sexual relations.

The old system of male dominance, with its theories of misogyny, was more than just a reflection of property relationships as Marx and Engels crudely maintained. It also rested on the biological subjugation of women to men, which was maintained in the absence or refusal of birth control measures to regulate the woman's fertility. This patriarchal system was remarkably successful (and still is in many parts of the world), and gave men the kind of sexual freedom that was denied to women. As the philosopher Bertrand Russell wrote, 'men, who dominated, had considerable liberty, and women, who suffered, were in such complete subjection that their unhappiness seemed not important.'[366] For the first time, in the 1960s, the contraceptive pill threatened this ancient hierarchy and opened a vista of sexual equality.

Traditionally, the women's movement had shied away from arguing for sexual equality for fear of deterring support among the respectable classes. In fact, birth control advocates in the early 1900s were more concerned with population control and regulating the poor, whose increasing numbers were viewed as a threat to social stability, than they were with levelling the sexual playing field between the sexes.[367] If women's rights advocates argued in favour of sexual equality between men and women, it was generally to stress the need for men to respect the morality of monogamy that they had imposed upon women. They were firmly within the Christian moral tradition, which had, 2,000 years earlier, attracted women by regarding the adulterous husband as being as much of a sinner as the adulterous wife. The notion that equality could be secured through allowing women to behave as promiscuously as men was so defiant of the traditional code, as well as of certain biological realities, that the women's movement feared it would mark their own endeavours with the taint of bohemian radicalism. But with the advent of the pill, it now became

physically possible for women to have sexual intercourse as
casually as men without the fear of pregnancy, if they so chose.
The right to choose is as always the key to progress for women,
as it is for men. Within fifteen years of its introduction, 20
million women were exercising that right by taking the pill and
another 10 million were using the Intra Uterine Device or
IUD.[368]

Misogyny seeks to dehumanize women through restrictive
definitions of what their 'true' role supposedly is and in
making sure they are confined to it. In Western civilization,
there had been no more powerful apparatus for imposing such
a definition than the Christian churches. But by the middle of
the twentieth century, their influence had considerably weakened in most parts of the West. Beginning in the eighteenth
century, the Catholic Church, which perhaps has done more
than any other institution in history to fashion how men
viewed and treated women, went on an irreversible intellectual
retreat. It had seen off the threat from the Reformation, but
not the challenge of the Enlightenment and the subsequent
scientific revolution. Instead of mounting a serious philosophical response to the scientific worldview, it sought refuge in
saccharin simplicity. The Church's most effective propaganda
weapon in the war to keep women in their place, the Virgin
Mary, suddenly began appearing before the astonished eyes of
peasant girls and boys in Portugal, France and Ireland. Over
two hundred such visitations occurred, beginning in the nineteenth century, of which the Church authenticated only a
handful, such as that in Lourdes, southern France. It continues
to draw millions of believers every year. The Virgin was
supposedly distressed by the lack of faith in the modern world,
and her message was that only the Rosary can save mankind.
The sightings followed Pope Pius IX's 1854 declaration of the
dogma of Mary's Immaculate Conception, hailing her as the

only human being ever conceived without Original Sin, and making this belief one of the essentials of the Catholic faith. The Church's response to the scientific revolution was to trust in a sentimental credulity and to proclaim its dogmas to be beyond and above reason. It was from this position that it would launch its attacks on contraception and abortion.

The Church may have lost the intellectual argument with science, but it still wielded enormous moral influence over millions of believers, especially in the developing world, as it does to this day. It has used that influence to try and prevent women from gaining access to birth control measures, even in the poorest countries where such access is essential if there is to be some hope of escaping from the cycle of poverty and deprivation. 'The unnatural practice known as birth-control is working havoc in the United States,' wrote Fr Orville Griese in 1944, a Jesuit and an authority on canon law and married life. 'If it continues at its present rate, the American people will not long survive. Unfortunately, most Americans are indifferent to the harmful effects of this loathsome vice. Indeed, the only organized attack on the crime of contraception is that which is being made by the Catholic Church.'[369] Fr Griese argued that even if it meant certain death for the woman, it is undoubtedly sinful for her to 'perform the marriage act in a manner contrary to nature', that is, use a contraceptive device.[370] In the early 1960s, in response to the call of many millions of Catholic women, especially in the US, who wanted to limit the size of their families through the use of contraception, a papal commission was set up to look at Catholic teaching on birth control in the light of current scientific knowledge. It found that there was no scriptural, theological, philosophical reason, or basis in natural law for the Church's prohibition on birth control.[371] Millions of Catholic couples heaved a sigh of relief in the expectation of the Church adopting a more liberal attitude. However, in 1968, Pope Paul VI responded instead with an encyclical *Humanae Vitae*. The encyclical reaffirmed the Church's rejectionist stance: Contraceptives were evil and against God's law. Ten years later, Pope John Paul II declared that *Humanae Vitae* was 'a matter of fundamental Catholic belief'.[372]

In the West, many if not most Catholics ignored the ban. For them, however painful, the decision of whether to conceive or not was rarely a life-or-death issue. Unfortunately, for women in the poorest parts of the world, it often is. There, the right to choose whether or not to conceive was vitally linked to a woman's prospects for freeing herself and her family from poverty. It is in this context that the inherent and deeply rooted misogyny of the Church has taken its greatest toll on the lives of women. Pope John Paul II spent a considerable part of his pontificate propagandizing on behalf of a doctrine that tells poor and illiterate women that to use a condom is the moral equivalent of murder and that each time they use contraceptives they render Christ's sacrifice on the cross 'in vain'. He said: 'No personal or social circumstances have ever been able, or will be able, to rectify the moral wrong of the contraceptive act.'[373] Underlying this attitude is the assumption that when it comes to having a baby, a woman's consent is not necessary and that once made pregnant, accidentally or not, her own will is rendered irrelevant. The moral implications of this are interesting when compared with those governing our attitudes to rape. All civilized societies accept that a woman's consent is necessary in order to have intercourse with her. Not to seek that consent and to coerce her into intercourse is to commit rape, which is a serious crime. But yet according to the Church, in the vital matter of pregnancy, a woman's consent is beside the point. She can be made pregnant against her wishes, and without her consent. The inexorable law of God overrides her will and the fact that she is pregnant determines her fate. Her personal autonomy is denied her.

To deny the need for her consent in this the most important aspect of a woman's life is surely the moral equivalent of justifying rape. It reminds us once more of the profound contempt that has underpinned Catholic attitudes towards women and that has been responsible for so much suffering down the centuries. Millions of women in the poorest countries, who are the most vulnerable, continue to suffer because of it. The Church discourages governments in Catholic countries from developing family planning facilities, which are desperately needed where the population growth outstrips their economic development. In 1980, the Pope visited Brazil, the world's most populous Catholic country. For years Brazil followed the Catholic doctrine and was opposed to family planning. Abortion was outlawed, with sentences ranging from six to twenty years for anyone convicted of carrying it out. As a result, millions of Brazilian women were forced to go to back street abortionists or to resort to knitting needles or coat hangers to terminate their unwanted pregnancies. It is estimated that about 50,000 women die each year there in botched efforts to end their pregnancies.[374] However, two years after the Pope's visit, the government reversed its previous position and asked for help from the United Nations Population Fund, which aims to expand family planning aid to the poor nations who need it most. But abortion is still outlawed in Brazil, and still kills more Brazilian women than anything else. Of course, it is the poorest women who suffer most. Brazil's rich elite has access to abortion without fear of arrest or social stigma. 'Our law serves only to punish the poor,' commented Elsimar Coutinho, the head of the Brazilian Family Planning Association.[375]

The Catholic Church is not the only powerful, worldwide body or institution that is campaigning to curtail the access of the poorest and most vulnerable women to family planning facilities. In the 1980s, the United States government under President Ronald Reagan adopted a policy of denying funding to family planning groups that carry out abortion services or provide information about abortion. The policy was urged upon the government by lobbyists for fundamentalist Protestant organizations, which have grown in influence since the 1980s in US politics. They are part of a conservative and religious backlash against the gains that women made in the 1960s and 1970s (see below). By the congressional elections of 1994, two out of every five votes for the Republican Party came from the Christian right.[376] President George W. Bush, whose core supporters are fundamentalists, revived the policy and declared 'war' on abortion before his 'war' against terrorism. On his very first day in office in 2001, he reinstated the 'gag rule' against funding going to groups that provide abortion services and information about them. Hundreds of women's health organizations in some of the poorest countries in the world had to make the difficult choice of dropping their abortion services and counselling or lose their funding. One of those who refused to sign the gag rule was Amare Badada, of the Ethiopian Family Guidance Association. He said that because of his refusal forty-four of the fifty-four family planning clinics in his region would probably be closed by 2004. Each serves about five hundred women, some of whom have to walk six miles to reach them. The problems that his clinics deal with on a day-to-day basis include rape, forced marriage and genital mutilation. 'Under the gag rule, I can treat a woman who comes bleeding after an illegal abortion but I am not allowed to warn her of the dangers before she goes,' Mr Badada said. 'We should not be told what to think and say.' He concluded: 'The US is driving women into the hands of back-street abortionists.'[377]

As of 1999, abortion was illegal in most Central and South American nations, except in cases of rape or incest or where the woman's life was at stake. The same restrictions apply in a majority of African states, and in a large number of Middle Eastern and South Asian nations. In the mainly Catholic Irish republic in 1983 an anti-abortion clause was put into the country's constitution.[378] As a result of such restrictions, the World Health Organization estimates that around 70,000 women die every year because of having unsafe abortions, and many hundreds of thousands more suffer terrible infections or loss of fertility.[379] This means that as many if not more women die each year because they are denied the right to choose than were murdered annually at the height of the European witch-hunts in the sixteenth and seventeenth centuries. As then, the misogyny of Christianity is directly responsible for the major part of this unnecessary suffering.

It may seem somewhat ironic that the Catholic Church finds itself advocating the same position against abortion as its severest Christian critics, the Protestant fundamentalists. In fact, it is no more surprising than finding the so-called pro-life movement keeping company with Adolf Hitler, Joseph Stalin and Chairman Mao, all of whom at one time or another banned abortions. What they have in common is their belief, rooted in misogyny, that the woman's right to choose – a fundamental aspect of her autonomy – must be crushed in order to achieve what they have deemed a 'higher' religious, moral or social goal.

The campaign for the woman's right to choose has been among the most bitter and controversial struggles in the United States in the twentieth century. It provoked the misogynistic backlash of the 1980s and 1990s, which at its most fanatical led to attacks on family planning clinics and the murders of doctors and health care workers.

The ideological justification for this campaign sprang from the traditional misogyny of Christianity and its basic tenet that woman's subordination, her perceived inferiority, is God's judgement on her for her guilt in bringing about the Fall of Man (see Chapters 3 and 4). However, even the Catholic Church has not always been as completely intolerant of abortion as it is currently. Until 1588, the Church followed Aristotle's dictate that the foetus was not 'ensouled' until 40 days after conception if it was male, and 60 days if female. So abortion could under certain circumstances take place up until then. However, in that year Pope Sixtus V decreed that abortion at whatever stage of conception was murder. The dogma of the Immaculate Conception proclaimed in 1854 further strengthened the Church's anti-abortion position because it assumed that Mary was 'ensouled' as the only human free from Original Sin from the very first moment of her conception, which means that from that second onwards she was fully human. Pius IX reiterated that teaching in 1869. Just to make sure that there was no argument to the contrary, the next year he proclaimed the dogma of Papal Infallibility. Undoubtedly, the curve of rising intensity with which the Church proclaimed that abortion was murder kept pace with the rise in demands from women for birth control and the right to choose. It became the battlefield where the fate of the family itself would be determined: '. . . from the standpoint of the union of husband and wife, statistics have been gathered which show that divorce is practically non-existent among parents of large families, and they multiply as the number of children decrease . . . nothing so develops the solidarity of husband and wife as the multitude of their children.'[380] Learned theologians would argue that without a large family to look after, a wife would become selfish, devote herself to gossip, to reading dangerous books, and hanging around with bad company.[381]

With the death of Stalin, abortion was legalized again in the Soviet Union in 1955 (having been outlawed in 1936), and throughout the Soviet dependencies around the same time. Abortion was legalized in Britain in 1967, in the US six years later, in France in 1974, and in Italy in May 1978. However, it has mainly been in the US that the ruling in favour of choice has been met with such fierce, violent and fanatical resistance involving both Protestant fundamentalists and conservative Catholics. In the 1980s, when the number of abortions in the US peaked,[382] an organization called Operation Rescue emerged to stage protests outside family planning clinics where abortion services were provided. Its members were mostly middle-aged or elderly men. Some protestors recited the Rosary as women made their way into the clinics; others waved models or pictures of mutilated foetuses. They chanted 'abortion is murder', 'don't kill your baby', or screamed 'baby killers' at doctors and staff. They made frequent comparisons between abortion and the Holocaust. The millions of aborted foetuses were compared to the mass murder of Jews under the Nazis. For many women already suffering stress because of the difficult decision they had made to end their pregnancy, to be exposed to this barrage of intimidation and abuse could be agonizing and traumatic.

Religious authorities from the pope down had for years been denouncing abortion as murder. Virtually every time a Catholic priest spoke from the pulpit about abortion the words 'murder' and 'murderer' were heard issuing from his mouth. Protestant preachers were not far behind in the race to see who could come up with the most sensational, obscene and cruel comparison between abortion and some real or imagined horror. Both Protestant and Catholic religious authorities frequently poisoned their rhetoric against a woman's right to choose with allusions to the Holocaust. The hysterical rhetoric of the protestors merely followed the example set by their mentors, as their verbal attacks on women took on the intensity of hate speech. The logic of this is inescapable. If women exercising their right to end a pregnancy and the medical staff who aide them are the moral equivalent of murderers and concentration camp administrators, then it follows that they should be punished as such – at least it did in the minds of those who took the hate-speech literally.

Among them was Michael Griffin, who shot dead Dr David Gunn at an abortion clinic in Pensacola, Florida, in 1993. He inspired Paul Hill, a forty-year-old father of three and former Presbyterian minister, who was a frequent protester outside abortion clinics where he would scream through the window 'Mommy don't kill me!' Hill appeared on television, arguing on programmes such as *Nightline* and *Donahue* where he compared killing an abortion doctor with killing Hitler.[383] On 29 July 1994, as sixty-nine-year-old Dr John Bayard, his driver James H. Barrett, a retired Air Force lieutenant aged seventy-four, along with Mr Barrett's wife, pulled into the parking lot of the other abortion clinic in Pensacola, Hill opened fire on them with a twelve-gauge shotgun. He killed Barrett first before shooting Dr Bayard in the head. Hill explained later that he deliberately took aim at Dr Bayard's head, knowing that the doctor was probably wearing a bulletproof vest. He also wounded Mrs Barrett who was crouching in terror in their vehicle.

Hill surrendered, was tried, convicted and sentenced to death. On the evening of his execution, 3 September 2003, a crowd of protesters gathered outside the prison in Starke, Florida. Some were opposed to the death penalty, some were there to support Hill, and others the right to choose. Some of the pro-Hill crowd's placards were an incitement to murder, if not hatred. 'Dead Doctors Can't Kill', said one. 'Killing Baby Killers is Justifiable Homicide', proclaimed another. A protester told the *New York Times* that Hill had 'raised the standard' for the anti-abortion movement. 'Some day I hope I will have the courage to be as much of a man as he was,' he said. At a news conference before he was executed, Hill spoke of his belief that the state 'will be making me a martyr'. His last words were: 'If you believe abortion is an evil force, you should oppose the force and do all you have to, to stop it.'[384]

Between 1993 and 1998, those who like Hill followed the logic of the anti-choice campaign's violent rhetoric claimed the lives of seven abortion providers and employees of family planning clinics. In 2001, 'pro-life' terrorists in Australia emulated their attacks, and killed a security guard outside the Fertility Control Clinic in East Melbourne. Of course, the Protestant and Catholic churches, as well as the mainstream anti-abortion organizations, were understandably quick to distance themselves from the killings. The paradox of an organization claiming to be pro-life yet being identified with murder was a bit too glaring for all but the most fanatical to ignore. However, the 'pro-life' movement cannot escape the moral consequences of the hate-speech they commonly employ against the staff of the clinics and the women who use them. Nor can the fundamentalist Protestant and conservative Catholic leaders whose rhetoric describing abortion in terms of the Holocaust was surely instrumental in sending the killers out to murder in the name of life. Hill compared killing a doctor to killing Hitler. James C. Kopp, a forty-eight-year-old convert to Catholicism, was convicted in May 2003 of the October 1998 murder of Dr Barnett A. Slepian at his home near Buffalo, New York. In his statement to the court, Kopp compared Margaret Sanger, the founder of Planned Parenthood, to Hitler and said that abortion was 'the continuation of the Holocaust. It didn't end in 1945.'[385] He went on: 'I hope that my younger brothers and sisters in the movement know that we can still cut some holes in the fences of the death camps and let a few babies crawl to safety.'[386]

The image of babies (surely it should be foetuses) crawling through barbed-wire fences is as bizarre as it is ludicrous, but given the context, not a surprising fantasy. 'Pro-life' terrorism attracted an unsavoury collection of bigots and misfits that throws light on the links between misogyny and other forms of hatred. In June 2003, Eric Robert Rudolph was charged with four bombing attacks between 1996 and 1998. They include a pipe bombing in a park hosting the Summer Olympics in Atlanta, Georgia, which killed a woman and injured a hundred people, and a bombing outside an abortion clinic in Birmingham, Alabama, which took the life of an off-duty police officer who was acting as a guard. He was also connected to the bombing of a gay bar in Atlanta. Rudolph was a member of a white supremacist organization, and an anti-Semite who complained that Jews had taken over the world. Rudolph remains something of a folk hero to the community of Murphy, North Carolina, where he was raised and where many people express support for his views. One resident of the town was quoted as asserting: 'Rudolph's a Christian and I'm a Christian and he dedicated his life to fighting abortion. Those are our values.' [387] John A. Burt is a well-known anti-choice activist who has been charged on several occasions with organizing violent protests at birth control clinics in Florida. The family of Dr Gunn, murdered in 1993, won a civil action against Burt claiming that he prompted the man convicted of the murder, Michael Griffin, to carry out the killing. Burt is also a member of the Ku Klux Klan. In 2003, he was charged with sexually abusing a teenage girl.

Thirty years after the Supreme Court's Roe vs Wade ruling secured the right to choose for US women, the so-called 'pro-life' movement is still active in trying to roll back that victory and force women to return to the days of the coat hanger and the knitting needle. That some in that movement have at times resorted to terrorism is a reminder that misogyny like any hatred or prejudice can result in extreme violence. It is tempting to dismiss those who murder in the name of the 'pro-life' movement as insane extremists. But comparing a desperate woman in need of an abortion to a genocidal Nazi as Church leaders have done does not pass the test of sanity either. Yet such invidious comparisons remain essential to the dehumanizing rhetoric of right-wing religious and conservative spokespersons determined to keep women in their subordinate position.

The politics of the body had even more deadly consequences in those areas of Africa, Asia and the Middle East where the influence of the West had been felt since the nineteenth century. But paradoxically, it was frequently because of the West's attempt to impose more progressive and liberal values that challenged indigenous practices. In the wake of the Second World War, opposition to colonialism began to mount. Often, that opposition took the form of defending customs and traditions that the colonialists attacked. Unfortunately, these were frequently customs that were injurious to women or that expressed indigenous misogynistic beliefs. Britain's efforts to prohibit sati, or widow burning, in India had created intense hostility to its rule (see Chapter 6). In the 1950s, in Kenya, the British government's attempt to ban the tribal practice of clitoridectomy led to a rise in support for the anti-colonial movement known as the Mau Mau. Independence was achieved in 1962, and the practice of female genital mutilation continues.

It does so too in Egypt where it was condemned at a UN conference on Population Control held in Cairo in September 1994 as a violation of the basic human right to bodily integrity. After two little girls bled to death following botched clitoridectomies in 1996, President Mubarak's government banned it. But popular support for mutilating girls remains strong. 'Am I supposed to stand around while my daughter chases men?' Said Ibrahim, a farmer, was quoted as saying. 'So what if some infidel doctor says it is unhealthy? Does that make it true? I would have circumcised my daughter even if they passed a death sentence against it. You know what honour is in Egypt. If a woman is more passive it is in her interest, it is in her father's interest, and in her husband's interest.'[388] A seventeen-year-old teenager agreed. 'Banning it would make women wild like those in America,' he was reported as saying.[389] It is estimated that between 80 per cent and 97 per cent of girls have undergone some form of genital mutilation in Egypt. About 100,000,000 women worldwide have suffered the procedure, and 2,000,000 more undergo it each year, including 40,000 in immigrant communities in the United States, according to the Egyptian feminist Nawal Assaad.[390] However, the most momentous opposition to Western influence manifested itself in the Middle East in opposition to governmental efforts to outlaw the Islamic practice of veiling women.

Misogyny is rarely noticed as a historical catalyst, yet it has played a sometimes profound role in helping to determine the course human affairs would take. It would not be an exaggeration to say that the long and bloody sequence of events that led to the September 11 attacks on the United States began forty years earlier in a college in Afghanistan when an angry male student hurled acid in the face of a young woman student because she was not wearing the veil. His name was Gulbuddin Hekmatyar, and he would go on to help foment a rebellion against Afghanistan's reforming government that would first draw the Soviets and eventually the Americans into a brutal war against Moslem fundamentalists in which the US is engaged to this day.

From the nineteenth century onwards, when Western influence on the Arab world began to challenge Moslem customs, the practice of veiling women has been at the centre of a contentious debate involving Westerners, Islamic reformers, Islamic nationalists and Islamic fundamentalists. It has frequently provoked revolution, violence and bloodshed. The West in its drive to dominate and control Arab nations held up veiling as proof of the backwardness and inherent inferiority of Islamic cultures. In response, those who fought against the colonial powers often seized on the custom as fundamental to the preservation of a Moslem identity as it confronted the overwhelming political, economic and cultural might of the West. Meanwhile, women, whose welfare and status was supposedly at the heart of this battle, were ordered to veil or unveil at the dictate of whichever tendency had achieved hegemony. The West's concern for their treatment has usually not been allowed to interfere with the more important goal of domination.

And always behind this and other arguments looms the question of Islam's inherent misogyny. It would indeed be a miracle if a religion so closely related as Islam is to both Christianity and Judaism did not exhibit powerful misogynistic tendencies. Islam after all accepts the Biblical tradition as one of divine revelation, including its misogynistic stories about women. The Fall of Man myth is as important in Islam as it is in Judaism and Christianity as the key to explaining woman's lower status.

While early Islam accorded women some rights that were

denied them under Christianity, such as the right to inherit property, Mohammed (570–632) adopted other practices, including polygamy, seclusion and veiling, that adversely affected how women were viewed and treated. In the years following the death of Mohammed, as Arab armies swept as conquerors into the Middle East and North Africa, women were removed from public life, segregation was instituted during prayers and stoning introduced as a punishment for adultery. At the same time, Islamic civilization was reaching a peak of intellectual, scientific and artistic splendour. It preserved the learning of the Ancient World and transmitted it back to the barbarians who had triumphed in the West after the fall of Rome. Sir Richard Burton, the nineteenth-century explorer and translator of the Arabic erotic masterpiece, *The Perfumed Garden*, described Baghdad, which stood at the heart of this culture, as 'the centre of human civilization, which was then confined to Greece and Arabia, and the metropolis of an empire exceeding in extent the widest limits of Rome . . . essentially a city of pleasure, a Paris of the ninth century.'[391] As in the *Kamasutra* of India (see Chapter 6), woman in *The Perfumed Garden* is celebrated for the beauty of her sexuality, and the book, like the earlier Indian and Chinese works on eroticism, is a guide to achieving sexual satisfaction for both men and women. 'Praise be given to God,' it begins, 'who has placed man's greatest pleasure in the natural parts of woman, and has destined the natural parts of man to afford the greatest enjoyment to woman.'[392] This unashamed and explicit recognition of woman's sexuality puts Islam, erotically speaking, closer to the Eastern tradition than to Christianity, with its consistent repression of the body.

But it would not be the first time that such recognition as well as respect for learning and the arts coexisted alongside intellectual, spiritual and social contempt for women. From the eighth century onwards, the word for 'woman' became synonymous with the word for 'slave'. However, Islam absorbed many local customs and traditions as it expanded, so that scholars argue that it is difficult to isolate misogynistic or discriminatory practices that are specific to Islamic cultures. For instance, polygamy, veiling and seclusion were long-established features of the higher echelons of Byzantine society.[393]

The Islamic medieval theologian Ghazali (1058–1111) expressed the same familiar misogyny as his Christian and Jewish counterparts when he stated: 'It is a fact that all the trials, misfortunes, and woes which befall men come from women.' He lists the eighteen punishments women must suffer as a result of Eve's disobedience. Among them are menstruation, childbirth, and pregnancy. But he is careful to go beyond the biological to include in the list purely social customs deeply prejudicial to women, such as 'not having control over her own person . . . her liability to be divorced and inability to divorce . . . its being lawful for a man to have four wives, but for a woman to have [only] one husband . . . the fact that she must stay secluded in the house . . . the fact that she must keep her head covered inside the house . . . that two women's testimony [has to be] set against the testimony of one man . . . the fact that she must not go out of the house unless accompanied by a near relative.'[394] By making a social custom an expression of the will of God, Ghazali gives it the power of religious sanction. Some but not all of these customs have been traced back to Mohammed. But Ghazali represents a conservative consolidation of Islamic thinking about women. One leading Arabic historian can name only one major Moslem scholar, Ibn al-Arabi (1165–1240), as being sympathetic to women, and calls him 'probably unique'.[395] With the decline of Arab power, and the growing penetration of the Middle

East by Europe and then the United States, such practices – or 'punishments' as Ghazali has it – represented the lowly status and cruel treatment of Middle Eastern women. They became part of the propaganda war that was and is being waged between the West and its Islamic opponents

Contradictions, inconsistencies and at times downright duplicity have ever been a part of the West's engagement with Moslem nations. The British, who occupied Egypt in 1882 condemned veiling as part of the backwardness from which they were trying to rescue Egyptians, yet at the same time cut funding for education for girls.[396] Efforts at economic reform in Iran in 1951 fell victim to Cold War rivalries when the CIA and Britain orchestrated a coup that restored dictatorial power to the Shah. Egypt gained independence from Britain in 1953 after a political uprising in which women played a prominent role. It brought President Gamel Abdel Nasser (1918–70) to power. In 1956, he granted a limited form of suffrage to women. The same year, the British, French and Israelis invaded Egypt after Nasser nationalized the Suez Canal. Though he became increasingly dictatorial, Nasser remained a figure of popular esteem because he was viewed as someone who stood up to Western aggression. The opposite was true of the Shah of Iran. After 1951, Islamic fundamentalists saw his modernizing programme, which included banning the veil, as a sell-out to the Western powers. This provoked a huge demonstration of women in Tehran in 1979 demanding the right to wear the veil. The same year, the Islamic revolution in Iran put the Ayatollah Khomeini in power. He imposed severe restrictions on women, removing them from public life as he pursued his aim of reversing the gains made under the Shah's reign. The new laws included a punishment of seventy-four lashes for defying the new dress code requiring them to be veiled at all times when in public. They reduced Iranian women to 'the status of privatized sex-objects required to be at the disposal of their husbands at all times'.[397] Women accused of violating the restrictions were exposed to male violence and gangs of fundamentalists attacked them in the street if they were judged inadequately covered. The legal system was overhauled and became a codified misogyny. Women judges were dismissed, and evidence from women witnesses was not allowed unless corroborated by men. Women were barred from attending law school. The marriageable age for a girl was dropped from eighteen to thirteen. Since the Ayatollah was an enemy of the United States, his conduct towards women was held up as an example of the barbarism of Islam and proof of the need for a strong Western deterrent in the Middle East, while it was conveniently forgotten that the West's complicity in supporting the Shah's dictatorship against its democratic opponents was at least partly to blame for the Islamic backlash.

Further east, in Pakistan, a similar reaction to Westernization was under way. In 1980, under the dictatorship of General Zia ul-Huq, veiling was enforced. Women were declared to be 'the root and cause of corruption' and working women were especially condemned for being responsible for a collapse in morality and the disintegration of the family. The new regime wanted them retired and pensioned off.[398] The pronouncements have a familiar ring, echoing the propaganda of the Nazi Party in Germany in the 1930s in its drive to force women back to their 'proper' sphere of domestic imprisonment. An Islamic adviser to the government advocated that women 'should never leave the confines of their homes except in an emergency'. The state came close to abolishing rape as a crime when its expert on Islamic law argued that while women are visible in the public sphere, no man should be punished for rape. In other words, it is understandable if a man seeing a woman in public is overcome with lust and rapes her since she has no business being seen outside her home in the first place. If rape did occur, then a woman needed four male witnesses before she could bring a case to court. Women's testimony and that of non-Moslems are not admissible. The misogynistic bias of the court is blatant, since it has to be supposed that any woman who brings a rape charge must have been outside the control of her male guardian when attacked, which immediately puts her behaviour in a suspicious light.

Though the harsh government of General Zia is over, its misogynistic legacy lives on. In May 2002, a twenty-six-year-old woman was sentenced to death by stoning after she had brought a charge of rape against her brother-in-law. Zafran Bibi, who gave birth to a baby girl while her husband was in jail, told the court that she was repeatedly sexually assaulted by his brother Jamal Khan either on the hillside behind her home in the remote mountain country of Pakistan, near the Afghan border, or in her farm when she was alone. Applying Islamic law, the judge said:

> The lady stated before this court that, yes, she had committed sexual intercourse, but with the brother of her husband. This left no option to the court but to impose the highest penalty.[399]

Mr Khan walked free without being charged. Human rights workers said that even if the death penalty was annulled, Ms Bibi faced a term of between ten and fifteen years' imprisonment for having illegal sex.

Pakistan courts make little distinction between consensual sex and rape. Up to 80 per cent of all women in Pakistani prisons are there because they have been convicted under Islamic laws against adultery.[400] It is reported that girls as young as twelve or thirteen face conviction and a public whipping if convicted of illegal sexual relations.[401] Nearly half of all women who report rape end up convicted of adultery. The law actively discourages women from bringing a charge of rape, but if they do not, and become pregnant, they can be convicted of adultery. A few weeks after the Zafran Bibi case caught the eye of the media, that of Mukhtaran Bibi (no relation) came to light on the other side of Pakistan, in the Punjab district. She was gang-raped on the orders of the local village council because her younger brother had been accused of forming a relationship with a higher-caste woman. After a public outcry, however, the police charged six men in connection with the rape.[402] The state awarded Mukhtaran Bibi just over $8,000 in compensation.[403] Normally, the vast majority of cases such as this go unreported.

However brutal and repressive to women Iran and Pakistan were, events there would prove merely a prelude to what was to happen in Afghanistan, where perhaps for the first time in history a state came into being the primary purpose of which was to enact, politically, socially and legally, a misogynistic vision of terrifying cruelty.

Afghanistan has impressed itself upon the imagination of the West because the men who flew their hijacked aircraft into the World Trade Center, the Pentagon and a field in Pennsylvania, were largely products of the training camps established there over the last few decades by fundamentalist Moslems. Mohamed Atta, believed to have crashed Flight 11 into the Trade Center's north tower just before 9 a.m. on the morning of 11 September 2001, stipulated in his will that no women would be allowed to touch his body or even attend his last rites. In fact his inhuman crime, with ghastly irony, ensured that his atoms intermingled with those of many hundreds of women in the conflagration and collapse that the crash caused. That Atta was a misogynist is no coincidence. Misogyny is an essential part of the worldview of the Moslem terrorists trained in the mountains of Afghanistan with whom America is now at war, just as it is a crucial ingredient in the recent history of that unhappy land.

The thread that runs through the recent history of Afghanistan, linking it to the attacks of 9/11, is the ferocious resistance to any attempt to have women treated as human beings. Since 1959, when a reforming government decreed that women were no longer required to veil, Islamic fundamentalists have been at the centre of that resistance. Sometimes they have collaborated with various nationalist groups, as well as a patchwork of tribal alliances – these have united periodically to fight a common enemy – before invariably turning their weapons on each other. Afghan women obtained the vote in 1964. At this point, Afghanistan was more progressive than most Moslem nations: In cities such as Kabul, some girls were allowed to attend school. Nonetheless, the vast majority of women remained illiterate. And those who did dare seek an education faced fundamentalist fanatics such as Gulbuddin Hekmatyar, whose first memorable action as a mujahideen or holy warrior was when he commanded a group that threw acid in the faces of young women who attended school unveiled. Later, his men crucified a young woman student, whose naked and bisected body was found nailed to the doors of a classroom in Kabul University.[404]

The United States only really began to pay attention to Afghanistan when pro-Soviet socialists staged a coup against the government in 1978. The new regime's efforts at reform, often aimed at bettering the position of women, were fiercely resisted, and support for Islamic fundamentalism grew. This prompted the Soviet Union to intervene in late 1979. From this point, the United States firmly supported Hekmatyar, who by that time was a puppet of the fundamentalist Pakistani regime of General Zia ul-Huq. Under the Reagan administration, billions of dollars were funnelled through the Pakistani secret service to Hekmatyar and his supporters.[405] More moderate mujahideen were never bankrolled to the same extent. The Soviets were forced to withdraw in 1989 after a bloody war, though Hekmatyar's contribution to their defeat has been disputed.

US policy-makers obviously assumed that communists were more dangerous than misogynists. History would prove them wrong. The movement known as the Taliban emerged out of the chaos that followed the Soviet withdrawal. It was made up mainly of religious students trained in the madrassas or Koranic schools of Pakistan. Its roots lay in Deobandism, an ultra-conservative tendency in Islam that dated back to the nineteenth century and came from Northern India. It taught a strict, literalist reading of the Koran.[406]

Misogyny was to the Taliban what anti-Semitism was to the Nazis: the very core of their ideology. As they spread their rule from Kandahar in the south, to Kabul in the north, women were systematically driven from the public sphere. In a long series of decrees, the misogynistic equivalent of the Nazis' Nuremberg Laws against German Jews, women were forbidden to work, go to school, attend male doctors, wear make-up or any form of decoration, appear in public unless accompanied by a male relative and completely covered from head to toe in a burka – the dark veil of opaque cloth, attached to a close-fitting cap – which completely encloses a woman's body. Only a peephole at eye level allows any light into this walking tomb. Television was banned, as was music, dancing and any form of entertainment. The radio droned out Koranic prayers and what seemed like a never-ending stream of restrictions and edicts such as:

Public transport will provide buses reserved for men and buses reserved for women . . . Women and girls are forbidden to wear brightly coloured clothes beneath the chadri [dark veils] . . . A woman is not allowed to go to a tailor for men. A girl is not allowed to converse with a young man. Infraction of this law will lead to the immediate marriage of the offenders. Women are not allowed to speak in public because their voices arouse men. Women engaged to be married may not go to a beauty parlour, even in preparation for their weddings . . . Merchants are forbidden to sell female undergarments.[407]

Men too were targeted. They were forced to grow beards and wear a white cap or turban. Nobody was allowed to display photographs, or have their photograph taken, even at festive occasions such as weddings. It was against the law to whistle. The Taliban even found Koranic justification for banning whistling kettles. This was literalism gone mad.

But however absurd or insane their decrees, the Taliban enforced them with frightening cruelty. Their moral police, under the aegis of the Ministry for the Promotion of Virtue and the Prevention of Vice, patrolled the streets. They attacked two women on a Kabul street and beat them senseless with whips. Their crime: wearing white shoes under their burkas, a gesture seen as an insult to the flag of the Taliban, which is white. Another Kabul woman was seized in the street and denounced. Her crime: wearing nail polish. Her fingers were cut off on the spot. Women were flogged for going out alone. Two women convicted of adultery were dragged to the Sports Stadium in Kabul, which had become a public execution ground. Before a large crowd, they were shot in the back of the head. As one young woman who lived through this nightmare expressed it: 'Even though they seem to follow one another without rhyme or reason, these decrees have a certain logic: the extermination of the Afghan woman.' The Taliban, she wrote, 'tried to steal my face from me – to steal the faces of all women.'[408] Women fought back. One woman opened a secret beauty salon in Kabul. Her patrons came and went with the surreptitiousness of conspirators bent on some dreadful revolutionary act: in fact, that is what putting on make-up had become. Others opened schools for girls in their apartments. Girls were advised to carry some religious tract with them at all times, and if the apartment was raided, religious works were always on hand in the hope that the morals police could be persuaded that the children were undergoing only religious instruction.[409]

Shortly after the occupation of Kabul, in September 1996, the Taliban debated whether or not the peepholes in the chadri were too big. The veil had turned a woman's face into a sexual organ, and it has to be negated, denied, and repressed at all costs. Not only woman herself, but anything to do with her is infused with her sexuality, especially her clothes, which the Taliban will not touch. A man, his wife and daughter were fleeing the country. He avoided having his suitcases searched simply by telling the Taliban guards: 'This is my wife's suitcase, and these belong to my daughters,' and the guard steps back.[410] Rarely has the horror and fear of the female body expressed itself so eloquently, or manifested itself so explicitly.

Some have sought explanations for this misogyny in the nature of Islam itself. It is easy to dig out quotations from various mullahs condemning women's beauty as evil and the work of the devil. But in this the Islamic tradition is in fact little different from that of Christianity and Judaism. It shares with them a common inheritance rich in misogyny (though in works such as The Perfumed Garden it incorporated the erotic influence of the East in a way the Christian tradition never has). The historical traditions to which Islam is heir were no doubt influential, but an explanation for such unrelenting misogyny as the Taliban embodied must be sought elsewhere.

The Taliban have been compared to an all-male brotherhood of holy warriors like that of the Medieval Crusaders.[411] A more recent parallel might be drawn with the origins of the Nazi party, whose policy towards women was aimed at driving them out of the public sphere into a domestic prison where they were expected to perform their only true function: reproduction.

Both the Taliban and the Nazis were products of war, disillusionment, and frustration. The Taliban emerged from the Pakistani refugee camps, where millions of Afghanis had fled during the war against the Soviets, and the all-male world of the religious schools that wealthy Saudis set up and funded in Pakistan to teach a reactionary form of Islam deeply hostile to the West. Many who flocked to these schools were orphans, with little or no contact with women. In the Taliban, this all-male world would consolidate into one that was profoundly antagonistic to women, and not a little afraid of them.

Both movements attracted men brutalized by years of death and destruction, men whom humiliation had embittered. For the Germans who joined the National Socialists, Germany's defeat in the First World War was the catalyst of their anger; for those who joined the Taliban, it was the humiliation of their country and its traditions at the hands of lawless brigands funded by America, and more broadly, the humiliation of Islam, as the influence of the West spread throughout the Middle East. The Nazis had the beer halls, an all-male domain like that of the trenches, the veterans and paramilitary associations that they created after the war. For the Taliban, the Koranic schools exercised a comparative function, where their anger and frustration could coalesce into an ideology whose misogyny is so extreme that it does not pasts the test of sanity. Had an individual expounded such doctrines, he would have been regarded (quite rightly) as insane. But, as has been noted before, once religion sanctions a belief, our ordinary notions of what distinguishes the insane from the sane are thrown out the window.

As in the all-male milieu of the Nazis, it is not surprising to find also a strong homoerotic element among the Taliban. Shortly after the fall of the Taliban in late 2001, an American journalist visiting their stronghold of Kandahar was surprised to find a photography shop with photographic portraits of Taliban fighters, some of whom were wearing eyeliner. He learned that it was not uncommon for these fundamentalists to do what was utterly forbidden to women: paint their finger and toe nails with henna. Some even wore high-heeled sandals, which gave them a mincing, feminine gait. These 'Talibanettes' were tolerated in the capital of a state that brutalized and mutilated women for putting on make-up and where the official punishment for homosexuals was to use bulldozers to crush and bury them alive.[412]

Hypocrisy is inevitable when moral restrictions defy human nature.

Unfortunately, hypocrisy also remains a fundamental part of the West's relationship to the Moslem world. Until after 9/11 the governments of the West largely ignored the Taliban's violations of human rights and the many atrocities that they were responsible for that were specifically aimed at women. In February 1997, the French government invited the Taliban Minister for Health, Mullah Mohammed Abbas, to Paris where on the very day that two women were executed in Kabul for committing adultery he was received by the Ministry of Foreign Affairs and the President of the National Assembly. 'A "Minister for Health",' commented one Afghan woman, 'who bars women from hospitals,' who forced women doctors and nurses out of work, and closed day-care centres. Abbas was an 'uneducated mullah' who was not even a doctor. The invitation caused some Afghan women to despair that 'if France is welcoming a talib, that means the Taliban propaganda has worked.'[413] In May 2001, just four months before the attacks on the United States, President George W. Bush congratulated the Taliban because they had cracked down on opium production and compensated them for the loss of revenues with a check for $43,000,000.[414] All this time, the Taliban were providing facilities for training the men, followers of Osama bin Laden, who would attack the United States and its allies.

There was some satisfaction in knowing that in the American air strikes against Taliban targets that began in October 2001, at least one of the pilots involved was a woman. But it is, in the end, small compensation for the decades of misguided policies the West has pursued that helped create the Taliban in the first place.

In the years since the fall of the Taliban, the United States and its allies have been funding health and education schemes for women in an attempt to repair the havoc the years of war and fundamentalism have wrought on the medical and school systems. 'Maternal mortality in Afghanistan is at catastrophic levels,' a UNICEF official reported a year after the Taliban had fled. In one province, between 1998 and 2002, 64 per cent of women of reproductive age who died did so from complications associated with pregnancy.[415] The efforts to educate girls has seen improvised schools opening in remote rural areas, as well as a resurgence of schools in the big cities. However, Afghanistan remains unsettled and the fundamentalist threat still thrives. In late 2002, four girls' schools were attacked in villages south of Kabul. Near one a message was left which warned: 'We call on all our countrymen to save their clean sisters and daughters from this infidel net. Stop carrying out the plans of the Americans or you will face further deadly attacks.' Local police said the attackers were either Taliban supporters, or those still loyal to Hekmatyar.[416]

One of the lessons of Afghanistan, and of the Middle East in general, is that the treatment of women is not a foreign policy issue for the United States unless, as under George W. Bush, there is the prospect of aid money going to family planning clinics that offer abortion services. Misogyny, unlike racism, is never an issue when Washington's foreign policy hawks survey the global balance and pick their allies and their enemies. Women's rights continued to be denied systematically in states such as Saudi Arabia and Pakistan that are close allies to the United States. Yet, unlike racism, misogyny is regarded as a quaint if sometimes upsetting cultural trait, with which outsiders do not interfere. It is like the days, not too long ago, when wife beating was a domestic dispute that was nobody's business.

Our recent history should have made one thing clear. Women's rights are human rights. Any foreign policy that fails to recognize this effectively dehumanizes half the human race.

9

IN CONCLUSION:
MAKING SENSE OF MISOGYNY

When I told people I was writing a history of misogyny I got two distinct responses and they were divided along gender lines. From women, came an expression of eager curiosity about what I had found. But from those men who knew what the word 'misogyny' meant, there came a nod and a wink in an unspoken assumption that I was engaged in justifying it. If I had said I was writing a history of racism, I do not think anyone would have concluded automatically that I was a racist. It suggests that unlike racism, misogyny is not seen by many men as a prejudice but as something almost inevitable.

For much of human history, misogyny has been part of what the holocaust historian Daniel Goldhagen has called (in reference to anti-Semitism) 'the common sense of society'.[417] It was a prejudice that was too obvious to be noticed. In different civilizations, at different times, the historical record is clear: it was regarded as perfectly normal for men to condemn women or express outright disgust at them simply because they were women. All the world's major religions, and the world's most renowned philosophers, have regarded women with contempt and a suspicion that sometimes amounted to paranoia. In Classical times, when Athenian women were forced to stay in doors for most of their lives, or when during the end of the Middle Ages, women were being burned alive as witches, it was not seen as the result of a prejudice against women, in spite of the fact that both societies had a long history of denigrating and demonizing them.

A prejudice can exist a long time before it has a name.

Today, in many parts of the world, practices such as veiling, seclusion and clitoridectomy are still accepted as part of society's 'common sense'. According to the Humphrey Institute of Public Affairs, women still own less than 1 per cent of the world's property. UNICEF reports that 120,000,000 children do not go to school, 80 per cent of them in sub-Saharan Africa and Southeast Asia, the vast majority of them girls. In early 1993, it was reported that a clinic in Bombay, India aborted 8,000 foetuses, 7,999 of them female.[418] As George Orwell has said, 'To see what is in front of one's nose needs a constant struggle.'[419]

Misogyny still flourishes in some corners of Western culture. Where males feel humiliated and angry, women still provide the universal scapegoat. A 1990 rap song by the group called Geto Boys declared, 'She's naked, and I'm a peeping Tom/Her body's beautiful so I'm thinking rape/Shouldn't have had her curtains open, so that's her fate.' In the verbal currency of rap, women are 'bitches' and 'hoes' (whores). Rappers are not the only proponents of misogyny in popular culture, and far from the first. Even during the 1960s and 1970s, a period remembered by many for its celebration of love and sexual freedom, pop groups such as the Rolling Stones had hits with songs like 'Under My Thumb' and 'Stupid Girl'. In 1976 the Stones released an album called 'Black and Blue' which was advertised with a picture of a beaten woman tied to a chair. However, hostility to women seems to be at the very core of rap culture. A young black man from a ghetto in Chicago, speaking about the rapper Ice Cube who was notorious for his hostility to gays as well as women, commented that he liked his music because it is 'talking the truth, that's the way it is in my neighborhood. There's a lot of tension between women and men in the neighbourhood, a lot of guys who act like pimps and a lot of women who act like bitches and whores.'[420] Even though rap's blatant contempt for women has come under attack, both from black women and others, it is clearly the product of a culture of alienation and frustration where misogyny still remains part of the society's 'common sense'. It is yet another reminder of the power of contempt for women to replicate itself in different cultures like an almost indestructible virus.

What history teaches us about misogyny can be summed up in four words: pervasive, persistent, pernicious and protean. Long before men invented the wheel, they invented misogyny, and today, as our wheels roll over the plains of Mars, that earlier invention still blights lives. No other prejudice has proved so durable, or shares those other characteristics to anything like the same extent. No race has suffered such prejudicial treatment over so long a period of time; no group of individuals, however they might be characterized, has been discriminated against on such a global scale. Nor has any prejudice manifested itself under so many different guises, appearing sometimes with the sanction of society at the level of social and political discrimination, and at other times emerging in the tormented mind of a psychopath with no sanction other than that of his own hate-filled fantasies. And very few have been as destructive. Yet, these very features that should have made misogyny stand out have rendered it in a strange way inconspicuous. In the case of misogyny, we have too often relinquished the struggle to see what is in front of our noses.

In November of 2003, the latest in a long line of American serial killers, Gary Ridgeway, stood in a Seattle court and repeated 'guilty' over and over again to charges of strangling forty-eight young women, mostly prostitutes, during a period of two decades.[421] Had the victims of his murderous rampage been Jews or African Americans, there would have been a national alarm sounded, and acres of print covered with soul-searching questions about the state of race relations in the United States as we enter a new millennium. But the actions of a Ridgeway, or a Jack the Ripper, are usually left to a psychiatrist to explain. Their urge to kill women is seen as an aberration when in truth it is simply an intensification of a commonplace prejudice. The spectrum of misogyny, which runs from the contempt of 'cunt' scrawled as a curse word on bathroom walls to the murderous rage of a serial killer, seems too wide, too extreme, to lend itself to any one easy explanation, though that has not stopped people from trying. Indeed, surely one of the main justifications for writing a history of any hatred or prejudice is to uncover its source in order that we may find a way of ending it. It must be more than just a collection of acts and words that display men's contempt for women.

As I have already suggested, the history of misogyny shows that this is an especially difficult task. The reason is obvious. It lies in the complexity of the relationship between women and men. It is biological, sexual, psychological, social, economic and political. It is a Gordian knot of interwoven dependencies, involving our very existence both as individuals and as a species. If we cut through that knot, where among the tangled skeins will we find the source of men's contempt for women?

Every level from the biological to the political at which women and men relate to each other has generated a theory of misogyny. All of them assume that at the core of this contempt is men's fear of women stemming from the recognition that women are different from men in potentially threatening ways. The history of misogyny certainly confirms men's obsessions with how women differ from them in a manner real or merely perceived as real. For men, women are the original 'Other' – the 'not you'. People have an alarming tendency to convert any category of persons designated as such into scapegoats. And before there were different races, religions or classes, there were women and men. But woman presents a more complex problem for those who designated her as 'the Other'. She is 'the Other' that cannot be excluded. Racists can avoid interaction with the despised group. But intercourse with women is in the end unavoidable, even for misogynists. Tribesmen in the highlands of New Guinea and aborigines in the Amazon basin may bar her from their sleeping quarters, Athenian gentlemen may lock her in the remotest part of the home, Catholic theologians seclude her behind convent doors, and Moslem fanatics hide her behind the head-to-toe veil, but intimacy with her is as unavoidable as it is essential. The very maintenance of human life and society depends upon it.

Dependency, fear . . . contempt. The theories that attempt to explain this bundle of conflicting feelings generally suffer from one of two failings: they are either overly ambitious or not comprehensive enough. In the first category, that of overly ambitious theories, are the biological, sexual, psychological and psychoanalytical explanations. The biological theory declares that 'essentially, the female is the primordial or basic form of the foetus' that undergoes transformation into a male foetus with the release of the androgen testosterone from the sixth week to the third month of pregnancy.[422] Maleness is seen as a superimposition upon primordial femaleness back into which men fear they will return. That is, ontogeny repeats phylogeny – the development of the individual duplicates that of the species to which he or she belongs. Misogynistic characterizations of women as swamps, bogs, miasmas, pits and so forth, are common enough, and are said to be an expression of this dread of engulfment. Sexual theories of men's fear of the vagina as an engulfing and/or castrating organ also reflect this notion of engulfment. Equally ambitious are the psychological and psychoanalytical hypotheses, Freudian and otherwise. These blame early dependency of the male infant upon his mother, or his unrequited love for her, as the culprit. In later life, this supposedly creates anger and resentment towards all women. Freud's theory that misogyny is based on the boy's contempt for the girl's 'puny' clitoris also fits into the category of ambitious explanations that seek a universal scope (see Chapter 7).

That is precisely their weakness. Since all males arise from female foetuses, and all boys are dependent on a mother during their most impressionable and formative years, and all men who have sex with women experience 'engulfment', these theories predict that all men must be misogynists. But the fact is that not all men are misogynists. Misogyny is only a part of the history of woman's relationship to man. If it were the entire story, then the progress that women have made towards equality in Western or Western-style democracies over the last two centuries, which has been achieved with the advocacy and support of men, would hardly have been possible. Nor would books such as this get written. It suggests that the fear of the primordial female within, or the desire for revenge on the pre-Oedipal all-powerful mother, are not universal determinants of how men relate to women.

Theories in the second category, those that are not comprehensive enough, tend to see the world mainly in social, economic and political terms, as a never-ending power struggle. Most derive from Marxist thought (see Chapter 7). They are broadly speaking rationalist in approach. When they see a prejudice, they ask, what purpose does it serve? In this view, prejudices arise from the need to justify the economic, social and political exploitation of one race or class or ethnic group of another. Many feminists have found this model or something like it strongly appealing and developed it as a critique of what they term 'patriarchy' – a system where all power lies in men's hands and where women are victimized as the permanent underclass. Misogyny springs up as the ideology that denigrates women in order to justify their lowly status.

However, there are two problems with Marxist or Marxist-based theories of misogyny. The first is that there is fairly compelling evidence that misogyny is found in cultures where the kinds of property relationships and economic conditions that are said to be at its root do not exist. According to some anthropologists, such as David Gilmore, it is even found in cultures in which women have relatively high social status and which could not be described as patriarchal. The second objection arises from an element within misogyny itself – its hallucinatory aspect. Capitalists may indeed feel the need to prove that the working class is mentally inferior, and slave owners sought to denigrate Africans as being less intellectually developed, but there was no equivalent to the phantasmagoria associated with misogyny, in which women had the power to cause other women to miscarry, fly through the air on broomsticks, make men's penises disappear, with a mere touch blight men forever with ill fortune, suckle cats, have intercourse with multi-pronged demons and give birth to the Devil's off-spring. There is only one prejudice that makes similar claims on a consistent basis over the centuries, and that is anti-Semitism.

Though anti-Semitism has been a prejudice largely limited to the Christian civilization that developed in Europe during the centuries following the fall of Rome, it bears more than a passing resemblance to misogyny, to which it offers some interesting parallels as well as contrasts. For about 1,500 years, anti-Semitism was part of the 'common sense' of society – a belief that was taken for granted as part of the cosmic and social order, so much so that it was hardly commented upon. Jews like women were held 'to violate the moral order of the world' mainly because of their role in the death of Jesus. Jews were deemed responsible for denying his divinity and women, because of Eve's role in the Fall of Man, were blamed for necessitating the Incarnation in the first place. Both Jews and women through the late Middle Ages and early modern period in Europe were attributed incredible powers to blight crops, poison wells, force cows and other men's wives to miscarry. Both Jews and women were ascribed these powers though the vast majority of them occupied the lowest and weakest rungs of society. Clearly, neither represented a real threat to anyone.[423] This did not save either from vicious outbursts of communal violence. For Jews, it occurred on a fairly regular basis. For women, it took this form during the witch craze, which persisted with peaks and troughs of intensity for almost 300 years (see Chapter 4).

Anti-Semitism shares another characteristic with misogyny and that is its protean nature. It flourished in Europe, especially in Germany, long after the religious reasons behind it had become part of history. It was transformed from a religious into a secular prejudice. Race replaced religion as the motivation for the persecution of Jews. In this form it thrived with peculiar intensity, as we have seen, in the intellectual circles of early twentieth-century Vienna. There, in the first decades of the last century, anti-Semitism and misogyny came together in a lurid alliance in the minds of people like Otto Weininger and Adolf Hitler. The two streams of hatred flowed together throughout the horrors of the Nazi period.

Malleable as always, misogyny likewise underwent a secularization process from the seventeenth century onwards as the power of Christianity declined among the intellectual elite. So-called 'scientific' explanations for what were viewed as women's intellectual and moral inferiority replaced those derived from religious authority, as they did as justification for early twentieth-century anti-Semitism.

The caricature of the demon Jew is largely confined to Christian anti-Semitism. But the hallucinatory character of misogyny is a characteristic of it wherever it manifests itself. The demon or devil woman in various guises is found in many very diverse cultures, including Jewish, Hindu, Germanic, Burmese Buddhism, Moslem, and in many African tribal beliefs. They are most famously represented in the monstrous female creatures of Classical Greek myth – the Gorgon, the Furies, Charybdis and Scylla. Unlike the Demon Jew, the Devil Woman remains a popular motif, finding its way into mass culture in songs like 'Devil Woman', by Marty Robbins, which begins:

> Devil woman, you're evil,
> Like the black coral reef . . .

Misogyny, like anti-Semitism, is 'out of proportion to any objective or social conflict'.[424] Yet, even anti-Semitism, for all its irrationality, has origins in a time and a place, however remote and irrelevant today. It can be traced to the struggle from the late first century AD onwards over who would be the inheritors of the revealed truth of the scriptures, Jews or Christians, and how that truth should be interpreted. But there is no social or political or ideological conflict in which men and women automatically find themselves on opposite sides, their opinions determined solely along gender lines. History proves that women can be as pro-war as men, even though the lives of their sons are at stake, and despite the fact that women are the most vulnerable when social order breaks down as the result of prolonged or traumatic conflict. Indeed, women sometimes incite violence against other women. During the Rwandan massacres, Pauline Nyiramasuhuko, a member of the government, allegedly incited Hutu men to rape Tutsi women before killing them. Ironically, she had been the Minister for Women's Affairs. The *New York Times* called her 'the minister for rape'.[425] She is currently standing trial for genocide, the first woman in history to face this charge.

Even on issues involving women's rights, many women were on the side of the men who opposed them, including the right to vote. Today, women are often the most vociferous opponents of the pro-choice movement. Their identity as women carries no ideological imperative. It is subsumed by another category, more important to their sense of themselves. So clearly as history shows and commonsense suggests, misogyny cannot be explained as an outgrowth of any social, political or ideological dispute that is somehow innate to the relationship of women and men. Undoubtedly some social, economic or political problems can exacerbate the conflict between women and men, like the economic dependence of the one upon the other. But such circumstances cannot account for its origins. In this, it is unlike any other prejudice that we know of.

I began this history in the world of the eastern Mediterranean as it was almost 3,000 years ago where a complex belief system originated that has been more decisive than any other in influencing our views of woman and her role and status. I believe that this system, a product of Greek and Judaeo-Christian thinking and mythology, carries an important clue to the origins of misogyny in general that takes us beyond the level of social structures in our search for an explanation.

In the dominant version of the Fall of Man myth common to both Greek and Judaeo-Christian creation myths, man came before woman, created autonomously by the gods or God. Man therefore was seen not only as having a special relationship to the Divinity, but also as being somehow separate from the rest of nature itself. He was a separate creation, set apart from nature, with a unique relationship to his creator. The creation of woman ended that relationship, and introduced into man's world all the features associated with nature. Man was suddenly subjected to the same needs and limitations as any beast, including copulation, the pangs of birth, the struggle for existence, the experience of ageing and of pain, the debilitation of various illnesses and finally the ignominy of death. In the words of the French novelist Louis-Ferdinand Céline, this was 'the horror of reality'.[426] But the true horror was the realization that man was not autonomous, rather he was dependent. 'There is also our mother, Eve, who wakes Adam from his dream of paradise and obliges him to confront the real world: work, history, death,' wrote the poet Octavio Paz.[427] Pandora, in the Greek myth, performs the same disillusioning role. As both Eve and Pandora remind us: autonomy is not an option.

At a less sophisticated level, the fear of the loss of autonomy, of being no longer distinct and separate from nature, is mirrored in the phobias of engulfment through the agency of women that are common to many cultures throughout the world.

Men do not surrender their illusion of autonomy easily. The solitary God of the Jews, Christians and Moslems, created the universe out of nothing, without the agency of any female being. Of all gods, he is the only one without any sexual feelings for the creatures he has created and rarely shows appreciation of their beauty. On the contrary, women's beauty often angers him. The creator has no link to his creatures other than his need to have them enhance his own sense of uniqueness in the cosmos or to punish them if they fail to do so. He is always there as a role model, albeit one that has proven to be impossible to emulate, though that has not stopped some men from trying. In a sense all misogynists, from Plato and Aristotle, to Tertullian and St Thomas Aquinas, to Rousseau, Nietzsche, and Hitler, have in one way or another sought to prove that it is possible for man to reassert the uniqueness of his relationship to God or to the cosmos – or however he chooses to describe the ultimate truth he identifies with his destiny. It creates a kind of dualism in which woman is the lesser truth, tethered to sexuality that keeps getting in the way. She has to be rejected and denigrated as the ambassador of the mutable world from which he seeks to assert his independence and over which he strives to establish his superiority. They would agree with Katharine Hepburn who proved herself a Platonist in *The African Queen*, when she remarks to the character played by Humphrey Bogart: 'Nature, Mr Allnut, is what we are put in this world to rise above.'[428]

But 'rising above' nature consists of understanding it and humankind's relationship to it. Although we are the only species capable of that understanding, we still can neither rise above nor sink below nature. We are still inseparable from it.

The myth of autonomous man has been a long time falling.

Ironically, it was revived at a philosophical level in the very theory that has done so much to provide an intellectual basis for the attack on misogyny that has its roots in the Enlightenment. The Blank Slate theory tried to banish human nature through its claims that all differences between individuals were social inscriptions, including all sexual differences other than those that were anatomical and biological. This allowed reformers seeking to improve women's status to argue that sexual differences often cited to prove women were somehow 'inferior' were in fact the product of her upbringing and education. Remove these obstacles, and women will prove to be the same as men. The Blank Slate hypothesis was based on a dangerous dualism that saw man as apart from the rest of nature. Human history was somehow separate from natural history. The behaviour of men and women was not rooted in anything innate – unlike the rest of the living world – but in social structures.[429]

The history of misogyny demonstrates that dualistic systems of thought tend to be unfavourable to women, none more so than the Fall of Man myth and its claim that man enjoys a privileged relationship to the rest of nature but one that woman undermined. The Blank Slate theory perpetuates this division at a philosophical level. Though it played a positive role during one phase in the struggle to end prejudice against women, in the end it is a disservice to women to argue for their equality based on its premises. There are two reasons why this is so. The first is that scientific developments since the nineteenth century have called into question some of its basic assumptions. We do not want to argue for women's equality based on false premises. And second, acting as if it were true leads to the denial or denigration of actual differences between women and men at the expense of our shared human nature.

Charles Darwin's theory of evolution radicalized how we

view nature and its role in shaping human behaviour, casting doubt on the Blank Slate theory. According to Bertrand Russell: 'The doctrine that all men are born equal, and that differences between adults are due wholly to education, was incompatible with his emphasis on congenital differences between members of the same species.'[430] Because of this unsettling claim, the theory of evolution, perhaps the most revolutionary scientific theory since the earth was displaced from the centre of the cosmos, has enjoyed the dubious distinction of being attacked from both the right and the left. The basis of their objections is fundamentally the same. Evolution denies that humankind stands apart from nature, either in terms of a special relationship to God, as stated in the Judaeo–Christian Fall of Man myth in Genesis, or as part of a special exemption from the natural processes that shape the rest of the living world, as implied by the Blank Slate theory.

The overwhelming evidence is that human behaviour is shaped by inherited characteristics as well as by social factors, and that as much as Galapagos tortoises we are a product of evolution. And that includes our sexual behaviour. What does this mean for misogyny? Some feminists fear that arguing that some differences between women and men are innate will lead to the justification of discriminatory behaviour towards women and therefore they cling to the Blank Slate hypothesis. By doing so they are, writes Pinker 'handcuffing feminism to railroad tracks on which a train is bearing down'.[431] In fact, the evolutionary view of human nature protects us from the misogynistic possibilities inherent in the Blank Slate theory. Those who believe that human nature is determined by social structures have often graduated from arguing that men and women can be the same to demanding that they should be the same. Social systems based on this model punish women for putting on make-up or any form of behaviour that is seen as refusing to conform to the asexual ideal. They agree with Plato that since mothering is merely a biological function with no behavioural consequences, babies can be taken from their mothers at birth to be raised by the state in communal nurseries.

If evolution helps explain why we are different both as men and women and as individuals, it does so without imposing any moral or legal imperative to discriminate based on difference. More importantly, if Darwin's theory helps us recognize the function of differences between the sexes then it can defend us against those who for whatever ideological reason want to ignore or eradicate them and in the process do violence to human nature. Ultimately, however, woman's equality is not derived from any theory of human nature but rather from concepts of justice, equality and the integrity of the individual based on philosophical and political principles that we have evolved since the Enlightenment.

'There is, in fact, no incompatibility between the principles of feminism and the possibility that men and women are not psychologically identical,' writes Pinker. 'To repeat: equality is not the empirical claim that all groups of human beings are interchangeable; it is the moral principle that individuals should not be judged or constrained by the average properties of their group.' That is, if it were found that most women spend more time in beauty parlours than in the library reading Plato, that is not an argument for depriving them of the vote – no more so than it would be if it were proven that a majority of men prefer to watch football and drink beer than to solve geometrical problems.

Evolution may not explain misogyny, but it can help us understand how women and men interact sexually. This in turn can lead to greater comprehension of the roots of some of the conflicts between the sexes that seem to transcend time and culture. Look, for instance, at the evolutionary reason for love poetry, which demonstrates that not every form of confrontation between women and men is necessarily destructive. At some point in our evolution as a species, the human female suppressed her oestrus cycle. Unlike nearly all the females of our closest relatives in the animal kingdom, the primate, ovulation is hidden in human females. 'So well concealed is human ovulation,' writes the physiologist and zoologist Jared Diamond, 'that we did not have accurate scientific information on its timing until around 1930. Before that, many physicians thought that women could conceive at any point in their cycle, or even that conception was most likely at the time of menstruation.'[432] Determining whether or not the female is receptive to sexual advances is much easier for the males of other primates. At the right time of her cycle, the buttocks of female primates turn a bright red and swell up. The males respond, and gather round, with the alpha males having first choice. But from pubescence onwards, human females maintain a constant display associated with sexual receptivity throughout their cycle. The human male's task is to decipher whether or not she is in fact ready to receive his attentions. Frequently she is not, and has to be convinced:

> Had we but world enough and time,
> This coyness, Lady were no crime.
> We would sit down and think which way
> To walk and pass our long Loves Day . . .
> An hundred years should go to praise
> Thine Eyes, and on they Forehead Gaze.
> Two hundred to adore each breast
> But thirty thousand to the rest . . .
> But at my back I alwaies hear
> Time's winged chariot hurrying near,
> And yonder all before us lye
> Desarts of vast Eternity.[433]

Had the oestrus cycle still been functioning, all the poet would have to do is show up at the right time of the month and his not-so-coy mistress would have felt compelled to mate with him or indeed, with any available male. But because of the nature of human sexuality, with us there is always doubt, and women have the power to choose the mate they think will be the most suitable. Men must seek to influence her choice. Some have produced great art in the process. So it is largely thanks to the suppression of the oestrus cycle that we have love poetry. Perhaps this is also why poets (and creative artists in general) come out of this confrontation between the sexes better than priests and philosophers. They bear witness that misogyny is only a part of the story of woman's relationship with man. For them, its conflict and its contradictions can be transcended through art.

It is no coincidence that central to this revolution within human sexuality is choice. The suppression of the oestrus cycle frees human females from the element of compulsion, keeps males attentive to her, and allows her greater opportunity to pick and choose a mate. Ovulation has been crucial to evolution. Just as importantly, it makes possible a wide variety of relationships between women and men that go beyond the purely procreative, allowing the complex social interactions that are characteristic of all human cultures where the sexes can relate to each other at many different levels – as lovers, friends, companions and work colleagues. It reminds us that women's right to choose is central not only to their own integrity, but to the very roots of what makes us human and distinguishes us from other primates.[434] It is no wonder then than the expansion of the right to choose has throughout history been crucial for women. The right to choose her mate, and control the circumstances under which she would mate with him, marked an important stage in women's history.

Now the battle for choice centres on her right to control her own fertility.

If choice is so central to woman's evolution (and therefore human evolution), then so too is her sexuality, and her right to display or emphasize it. It is one of the characteristics of cultures where misogyny is part of society's 'common sense' that they seek to suppress that right. In some cases, as with the Taliban in Afghanistan (see Chapter 8), it reached such levels of paranoia that anything associated with female sexual allure, such as lingerie, would inspire in them something akin to terror. This fear is usually associated with efforts to confine women's sexuality to its procreative role, so it is not surprising that mothers loom large in the minds of many misogynists. They have problems relating to a woman at any other level. Typically, of course, they disguise their opposition to women's sexual display patronizingly, in terms of 'protecting them' against exploitation by wicked chauvinists – both the Nazis and the Moslem fundamentalists followed that hoary tradition in the reasons they gave as they tried to suppress make-up and beauty parlours (see Chapter 7). But their actions and their obsessions reveal only their own inability to relate to sexually mature women.

A deep ambivalence towards women's beauty remains in our own culture as part of our inheritance of the Judaeo-Christian hostility towards the body. When Mary Wollstone-craft famously called on women to 'resign the arbitrary power of beauty' or they would 'prove they have less mind than man'(see Chapter 6) she was echoing that hostility. The vast majority of women rejected the dichotomy between mind and body, and more than two centuries later, they continue to do so. As the psychologist Nancy Etcoff has observed, 'the solution cannot be to give up a realm of pleasure and power that has been with us since the beginning of time.'[435]

The solution is not to reject beauty, but to reject misogyny. Since the Enlightenment, and the rise of modern democracy, with its emphasis on personal autonomy and the recognition of the right of the individual to pursue his or her happiness, both women themselves and men who have supported them in their struggle for equal rights have challenged the belief on which misogyny rests that women somehow violate the moral order of the world. Women are increasingly included and seen as an essential part of that moral order, even in cultures where traditional attitudes resist such change. Misogyny is no longer part of the 'common sense of society'. Man need no longer be at war with himself and at odds with the person with whom he can have the most productive, pleasurable and satisfying relationship.

Perhaps we are close to waking from the long-lived fantasy that is at the core of misogyny and are at last learning to treat it, the world's oldest prejudice, with the contempt that it deserves.

FURTHER READING

Ahmed, Leila, *Women and Gender in Islam*, Yale University Press, New Haven and London, 1992.

Anderson, Bonnie S, and Zinsser, Judith P., *A History of their Own, Volume I*, Oxford, 2000.

Balsdon, J. P. V. D. *Roman Women: Their history and habits*, Harper and Row, 1962.

Barrett, Anthony A., *Agrippina: Sex, Power and Politics in the Early Roman Empire*, Yale University Press, 1996.

Bauman, Richard A., *Women and Politics in Ancient Rome*, Routledge, New York and London, 1992.

Bishop, Clifford and Osthelder, Xenia, editors, *Sexualia: From prehistory to cyberspace*, Koneman, 2001.

Bloch, Howard, *Medieval Misogyny and the Invention of Western Romantic Love*, University of Chicago Press, 1991.

Blundell, Sue, *Women in Greece*, Harvard University Press, Cambridge, 1995.

Breslaw, Elaine G., editor, *Witches of the Atlantic World, A Historical Reader and Primary Source Book*, New York University Press, 2000.

Brown, Peter, *Body and Society: Men, women, and sexual renunciation in early Christianity*, Columbia University Press, New York, 1988.

Burleigh, Michael, *The Third Reich: A new history*, Pan Books, 2001.

Clack, Beverley, editor, *Misogyny in the Western Philosophical Tradition, A Reader*, Routledge, New York, 1999.

Clarke, John R., *Roman Sex, 100 BC–AD 250*, Harry N. Abrams, Inc., New York, 2003.

Davidson, John, *Courtesans and Fishcakes: The consuming passions of Classical Athens*, Harper Perennial, 1999.

Davis-Kimball, Jeannine, with Mona Behan, *Warrior Women: An archaeologist's search for history's hidden heroines*, Warner Books, New York, 2002.

Eller, Cynthia, *The Myth of Matriarchal Prehistory: Why an invented past won't give women a future*, Beacon Press, Boston, 2000.

Etcoff, Nancy, *The Survival of the Prettiest: The science of beauty*, Doubleday, New York, 1999.

Fest, Joachim C., *The Face of the Third Reich*, Pelican Books, 1972.

Freud, Sigmund, *Civilization and Its Discontents*, Dover Publications Inc., New York, 1994.

Friedan, Betty, *The Feminine Mystique*, Norton, New York, 1963.

Gay, Peter, editor, *The Freud Reader*, W. W. Norton and Company, New York, 1989.

Gilmore, David, *Misogyny: The male malady*, University of Pennsylvania Press, 2001.

Goldhagen, Daniel, *Hitler's Willing Executioners: Ordinary Germans and the Holocaust*, Vintage, New York, 1997.

Groneman, Carol, *Nymphomania, a History*, W. W. Norton & Co, New York and London, 2002.

Heer, Friedrich, *The Medieval World: Europe 1100–1350*, Welcome Rain, 1998.

Huizinga, J., *The Waning of the Middle Ages*, Peregrine Books, 1965.

Hunt, Lynn, editor, *The Invention of Pornography*, Zone Books, New York, 1993.

Johnson, Paul, *A History of Christianity*, Touchstone, New York, 1976.

Kaplan, Robert D., *Soldiers of God: With Islamic warriors in Afghanistan and Pakistan*, Vintage, New York, 2001.

Karlsen, Carol, *The Devil in the Shape of a Woman: Witchcraft in colonial New England*, Vintage, New York, 1989.

Keddie, Nikki, and Baron, Beth, editors, *Women in Middle Eastern History*, Yale University Press, New Haven and London, 1991.

Kendrick, Walter, *The Secret Museum: Pornography in modern culture*, University of California Press, 1987.

Keuls, Eva, *The Reign of the Phallus*, University of California, 1985.

Kleinbaum, Abby Wettab, *The War Against the Amazons*, New Press, New York, 1983.

Kofman, Sarah, translated from the French by Catherine Porter, *The Enigma of Woman: Woman in Freud's writings*, Cornell University Press, 1985.

Latifa, written with the collaboration of Shekeba Hacchemi, translated by Linda Coverdale, *My Forbidden Face, Growing up under the Taliban: A young woman's story*, Hyperion, New York, 2001.

Lea, Henry, arranged and edited by Arthur Howland, *Materials Towards a History of Witchcraft*, Thomas Yoseloff, 1957.

Levkowitz, Mary R. and Fant, Maureen B., editors, *Women's Life in Greece and Rome: A source book in translation*, John Hopkins University, 1982.

Llewellyn, Anne, editor, *War's Dirty Little Secret: Rape, prostitution and other crimes against women*, The Pilgrim Press, 2000.

McElvaine, Robert S., *Eve's Seed: Biology, the sexes and the course of history*, McGraw-Hill, New York, 2001.

Meacher, Robert, *Helen: Myth, legend and the culture of misogyny*, Continuum, New York, 1995.

Meyer, Johann Jakob, *Sexual Life in Ancient India: A study in the Comparative History of Indian Culture*, Barnes and Noble, 1953.

Miles, Rosalind, *Who Cooked the Last Supper: The women's history of the world*, Three Rivers Press, New York, 2001.

Moller Orkin, Susan, *Women in Western Political Thought*, Princeton University Press, 1979.

Moulton, Ian Frederick, *Before Pornography: Erotic writing in early Modern England*, Oxford University Press, 2000.

O'Shea, Stephen, *The Perfect Heresy: The revolutionary life and death of the medieval Cathars*, Walker and Company, 2000.

Paz, Octavio, translated from the Spanish by Helen R. Lane, *Conjunctions and Disjunctions*, Seaver Books, 1982.

Pearsall, Ronald, *The Worm in the Bud: The world of Victorian sexuality*, Pelican Books, 1969.

Pinker, Steven, *The Blank Slate: The modern denial of human nature*, Viking, 2002.

Pomeroy, Sarah, *Goddesses, Whores, Wives and Slaves*, Schocken Books, New York, 1975.

Rich, Adrienne, *Of Woman Born: Motherhood as experience and institution*, W. W. Norton, New York, 1986.

Russell, Bertrand, *The History of Western Philosophy*, George Allen and Unwin Ltd., London, 1946.

Shlain, Leonard, *Sex, Time and Power: How women's sexuality shaped human evolution*, Penguin Books, 2003.

Stark, Rodney, *The Rise of Christianity: A sociologist reconsiders history*, Princeton University Press, 1996.

Stephens, Walter, *Demon Lovers: Witchcraft, sex and the crisis of belief*, University of Chicago Press, 2002.

Tannahill, Reay, *Sex in History*, Abacus, London, 1979.

Trevor-Roper, Hugh, *The European Witch-craze of the 16th and 17th Centuries*, Penguin, Harmondsworth, 1966.

Warner, Marina, *Alone of all her Sex: The myth and the cult of the Virgin Mary*, Vintage, New York, 1983.

Willey, David, *God's Politician: John Paul at the Vatican*, Faber and Faber, London, 1992.

Wollstonecraft, Mary, *A Vindication of the Rights Of Woman*, with an Introduction by Miriam Brody, Penguin Classics, 1992.

Yalom, Marilyn, *A History of the Breast*, Ballantine Books, 1997.

NOTES

1. See the statistical evidence in *The Blank Slate: The modern denial of human nature*, by Steven Pinker, Viking, 2002.
2. *Hesiod: Theogony/Works and Days[elip]*, translated by Dorothea Wender, Penguin Classics, 1973.
3. Ibid.
4. *Helen: Myth, legend and the culture of misogyny*, by Robert Meacher, Continuum, 1995.
5. Wender, op. cit.
6. *Goddesses, Whores, Wives and Slaves*, by Sarah Pomeroy, Schocken Books, 1975.
7. *The Epic of Gilgamesh*, translated by N. K. Sanders, Penguin Classics, 1960.
8. *Women in Greece*, by Sue Blundell, Harvard University Press, 1995.
9. The seventh-century poet Semonides wrote, 'For Zeus designed this as the greatest of all evils: Woman/And bound us to it in unbreakable fetters.'
10. *The Tragical History of Dr Faustus*, by Christopher Marlowe.
11. *The Iliad*, translated by Richmond Lattimore, as quoted by Robert Meacher, op. cit.
12. *The Trojan Women*, translated by Gilbert Murray and George Allen, Unwin Ltd., 1905.
13. *Civilization and Its Discontents*, by Sigmund Freud, Dover Publications, 1994.
14. From the introduction to the *Larousse Encyclopaedia of Mythology*, Hamlyn, 1968.
15. Menander, quoted in *The Reign of the Phallus*, by Eva Keuls, University of California, 1985.

16. 'A Husband's Defense, Athens circa 400 B.C.', quoted in *Women's Life in Greece and Rome: A source book in translation*, edited by Mary R. Lefkowitz and Maureen B. Fant, John Hopkins University, 1982.

17. Pomeroy, op. cit.

18. Ibid.

19. *Courtesans and Fishcakes: The consuming passions of Classical Athens*, by James Davidson, Harper Perennial, 1999.

20. Keuls, op. cit.

21. 'Though wounded, battered, defeated and overcome by the javelins of the Classical heroes, by the moral indignation of the Fathers of the Church and numberless Christian defenders, by the fantastic spells and powers of Renaissance heroes, and by the boldness and greed of the early modern conquistadors, Amazons lived on to emerge again and again in Western culture,' writes Abby Kleinbaum, commenting upon the extraordinary persistence of this myth, in *The War against the Amazons*, New Press, 1983.

22. Blundell, op cit.

23. The comedies of Aristophanes, also written during the fifth century, often play upon similar themes, with women defying the prevailing moral, social and political order. His work without question reflects the concerns, obsessions and preoccupations of the contemporary world. Since both tragedies and comedies share similar themes, we can assume the contemporary relevance of both.

24. *Antigone*, translated by E. F. Watling, Penguin Classics, 1947.

25. Ibid.

26. *Hippolyta*, translated by Judith Peller Hallet, Oxford Classical Texts, 1902–13.

27. Plato's dualism was not new. In the sixth century BC, the philosophical school of Pythagoras drew up a Table of Opposites. The list comprised of ten pairs which Pythagoreans believed governed the Universe, such as good and evil, right and left, light and darkness, limited and unlimited, and male and female. The four elements into which the Ancients reduced all nature were also pairs of opposites: fire and air, earth and water. A habit of thinking viewed the differences between men and women as eternal and immutable opposites, and the source of an unending conflict.

28. As quoted in *An Introduction to Western Philosophy: Ideas and arguments from Plato to Popper,* Anthony Flew, Thames and Hudson, 1989. Popper's *The Open Society and Its Enemies* is a critique of the political and social thinking of Plato and Marx.

29. *The History of Western Philosophy*, by Bertrand Russell, George Allen and Unwin, 1946.

30. *The Republic*, translated by H. D. P. Lee, Penguin Classics, 1955. All quotes are from this edition.

31. In the parable of the prisoners in the cave he conveys his vision of the falseness of the world as perceived by the senses. Imagine that the prisoners have been there since childhood, chained together. Near the opening, a fire is blazing and people pass on a raised road between the fire and the prisoners. As the world goes by outside, the prisoners see nothing of it but its shadows flickering on the cave wall. Because they know no better, they mistake this for reality. In the same way as the prisoners are deluded by shadows of a reality they have never directly perceived, we who know the world only through the senses know nothing of the World of Perfect Forms, absolute and eternal, of which the world of the eyes and ears, of taste and of touch, is merely a shadow. The philosopher is equated with a prisoner who has escaped the cave and seen the world beyond it.

32. Russell, op. cit.

33. Keuls, op. cit.

34. 'On the Generation of Animals', quoted in *Misogyny in the Western Philosophical Tradition, A Reader*, edited by Beverley Clack, Routledge, 1999.

35. *Women's Life in Greece and Rome: a source book in translation*, by Mary R. Lefkowitz and Maureen B. Fant, John Hopkins University Press, 1982.

36. Pomeroy op. cit.

37. *Too Many Women?: The sex ratio question*, by Marcia Guttentag and Paul Secord, Sage Publications, 1983.

38. From *Lysistrata*, in *The Complete Plays of Aristophanes*, edited by Moses Hales, Bantam Books, 1962.

39. Lefkowitz and Fant, op. cit.

40. Ibid.

41. Ibid.

42. Ibid.

43. *The City of God*, translated by Gerald G. Walsh et al, Image Books, 1958.

44. *Roman Women: Their history and habits*, by J. P.V. D. Balsdon, Harper and Row, 1962.

45. Livy, *The Early History of Rome*, translated by Aubrey de Sélincourt, Penguin Classics, 2002.

46. *Civilization and Its Discontents*, Sigmund Freud, Dover, 1994. The flame survived until AD 394, when the Christians, now rulers of Rome, ordered it to be extinguished. It took sixteen years for the ancient prophecy to come true. In AD 410 Rome fell to an invading army of Visigoths.

47. *Jugurthine War, and Conspiracy of Catiline*, Sallust, translated by S. A. Handford, Penguin Classics, 1963.

48. Ibid.

49. Ibid.

50. Egyptian women, like those of Mesopotamia, were known for their elaborate make-up. Make-up is first mentioned in a Mesopotamian text dated to 3000 BC.
51. *Roman Women*, Balsdon, ibid.
52. Shakespeare, *Antony and Cleopatra*, Act 2, Scene 2.
53. Lefkowitz and Fant, op. cit.
54. Ibid.
55. *Women and Politics in Ancient Rome*, by Richard A. Bauman, Routledge, 1992.
56. Livy, op. cit.
57. Pomeroy, op. cit.
58. Bauman, op. cit.
59. Macrobius, quoted by Bauman, ibid.
60. The psychiatrist Frank Caprio, quoted in *Nymphomania: A History*, by Carol Groneman, W. W. Norton, 2000.
61. Groneman, ibid.
62. Ibid.
63. Translated by Rolfe Humphries, Indiana University Press, 1958.
64. Ibid.
65. Tacitus, *The Annals*, translated by Michael Grant, Penguin Classics, 1956. Outrageous marriages were far from unknown in Ancient Rome. In the reign of Nero, one aristocrat who had already shocked public opinion by fighting as a gladiator, married his boyfriend. Nero himself put on a bride's veil and married one of his male lovers.
66. Ibid.
67. *Agrippina: Sex, power and politics in the early Roman Empire*, by Anthony A. Barrett, Yale University Press, 1996.
68. Tacitus, op. cit.
69. Bauman, op. cit.
70. Agrippina wrote an autobiography, detailing her life and the misfortunes of her family, probably just a few years before her death. Unfortunately, we only know about this unique document from a few references in Tacitus and Pliny the Elder, both of whom used it as a source. We glean from this that Nero was a breach birth, probably the reason why his mother had no more children.
71. Juvenal, op. cit .
72. *Apulieus, The Golden Ass, A New Translation*, by E. J. Kennedy, Penguin Classics, 1998. The jackass, who is the human hero metamorphosed, afraid that once he has finished with the woman, he too will be eaten by the lions, decides to escape before he has to perform.
73. This comes from a Hebrew manuscript of Ecclesiastes, discovered in the twentieth century, and quoted by Russell, op. cit.
74. *A History of Christianity*, by Paul Johnson, Simon and Schuster, 1976.

75. There is some evidence that Pythagoras and the schools that he set up permitted women entrants.
76. Quoted by Pinker, in Pinker, op. cit.
77. Quoted in *Body and Society: Men, women, and sexual renunciation in early Christianity*, by Peter Brown, Columbia University Press, 1988.
78. Tacitus, *The Annals*. The accusation was investigated by her husband and she was acquitted.
79. A male relative of the emperor Domitian (AD 81–96) was a Christian who had worked alongside St Paul when the apostle came to Rome. According to legend, the beautiful church of San Clemente in Rome stands on the site of his family's villa.
80. The argument and evidence cited here is based on *The Rise of Christianity: A sociologist reconsiders history*, by Rodney Stark, Princeton University Press, 1996.
81. Women first took doses of various poisons to cause a miscarriage. If that failed, surgery followed, involving the use of blades, spikes, and hooks, to slice up and wrench out the foetus bit by bit. More often than not women were compelled to have abortions by lovers and husbands. The emperor Domitian's niece died following an abortion he forced her to have after impregnating her.
82. Stark, op.cit.
83. Guttentag and Secord, op. cit.
84. Stark, op. cit. He cites arguments that the infamous reference to women keeping quiet in church in Paul's Epistle to the Corinthians (14:34–6) is not Paul speaking but quoting a claim from an opponent that he is trying to refute.
85. 'Is Paul the Father of Misogyny and Anti-Semitism?' by Pamela Eisenbaum, *Cross Currents*, Winter 2000–2001. She argues forcefully that St Paul is neither.
86. This description taken from the apocryphal Acts of St Paul, is quoted by Johnson, op. cit.
87. Brown, op. cit.
88. Ibid.
89. De Ieuinion 5.1, Corpus Christianorum 2:1261.
90. 'On Female Dress', from *The Writings of Tertullian, Volume I*, translated by the Rev. S. Thelwall, Edinburgh, 1869.
91. 2 Corinthians, 6:16.
92. Ibid.
93. Quoted by Brown, op. cit.
94. Tertullian, op. cit.
95. This compares with fifteen in the first 130 years of imperial rule.
96. They were constructed during the reign of Aurelian (AD 270–275). It is still a prominent feature of Rome to this day.
97. The emperor Valerian, defeated by Shapur I in AD 260.
98. The first lasted from AD 165–180, and the second struck in AD 251.

99. Stark, op. cit.

100. In a particularly painful illustration of the dangers of literalism, Origen interpreted literally Matthew's words 'There be eunuchs, which have made themselves eunuchs for the kingdom of heaven's sake.' (19:12)

101. The Gospel of St Thomas quoted in Brown, op. cit.

102. Quoted in *A History of their Own, Volume I*, by Bonnie S. Anderson and Judith P. Zinsser, Oxford, 2000.

103. Brown, op. cit.

104. Ibid.

105. Ibid.

106. From a talk given by Fr Paul Surlis, 2002.

107. Brown, op. cit.

108. When Roman officials wanted to bring prosecutions for the attack on the Jews, Ambrose the Bishop of Milan and the man who was to inspire St Augustine, intervened to protect the anti-Semitic thugs on the grounds that they were good Christians

109. The doctrines of Mani were deeply dualistic, and held that all matter was inherently evil. His followers therefore regarded reproduction as a perpetuation of evil, so forbade it, and rejected the idea that God could have possibly allowed his Son to enter the material universe. Instead, they taught that Jesus was a phantasm. Mani was executed by the Persians in AD 276.

110. *Confessions*, translated by Henry Chadwick, Oxford University Press, 1991. All further citations come from this text.

111. *The City of God*, translated by Gerald G. Walsh, S. J., Demetrius B. Zema, S. J., Grace Monahan, O. S. U., Daniel J. Honan, Image Books, 1958. Further citations come from this text.

112. Russell, op. cit.

113. Walsh et al., op. cit.

114. In their compilation of inscriptions, letters and texts, *Women's Life in Greece and Rome*, the editors Lefkowitz and Fant include two, Hipparchia and Appolonia, from the third and second centuries AD respectively.

115. From Socrates Scholasticus' *Ecclesiastical History*.

116. Damascius' *Life of Isidore*, translated by Jeremiah Reedy, Phanes Press, 1993.

117. From the Chronicle of John, Bishop of Nikiu.

118. Ibid.

119. Socrates Scholasticus, op. cit.

120. *The Decline and Fall of the Roman Empire*, by Edward Gibbon, Penguin Classics, 2000.

121. There is some debate as to whether or not Moses might be there in body. Other Old Testament prophets Enoch and Elijah are also thought to have taken the direct route to Heaven, by-passing the long wait for the Resurrection.

122. Quoted in *Alone of All her Sex: The myth and the cult of the Virgin Mary*, by Marina Warner, Vintage Books, 1983.
123. *The Medieval World: Europe 1100–1350*, by Friedrich Heer, Welcome Rain, 1998.
124. Anderson and Zinsser, op. cit.
125. Quoted in *The Perfect Heresy: The revolutionary life and death of the medieval Cathars*, by Stephen O'Shea, Walker and Company, 2000.
126. Anderson and Zinsser, op. cit.
127. Heer, op. cit.
128. Ibid.
129. Ibid.
130. Warner, op. cit.
131. Attacks on the opulence of the Church and its growing distance from the faithful had formed the basis of other heretical movements, such as that inspired by Peter Waldo who preached a return to the poverty of Jesus.
132. O'Shea, op. cit.
133. Warner, op. cit.
134. Ibid.
135. *The Canterbury Tales*, by Geoffrey Chaucer, rendered into modern English by Nevill Coghill, Penguin Books, 1951.
136. Ibid.
137. Quoted in *Medieval Misogyny and the Invention of Western Romantic Love*, by Howard Bloch, University of Chicago Press, 1991.
138. In third-century Rome, execution by burning was prescribed for a witch who had caused the death of someone through magic. In the sixth century, Queen Fredegond of the Franks burned several women as witches after accusations were brought against them that they had caused the death of two of her young sons. The accused were tortured into confessing before being burned. The use of torture and the fact that it was a woman who accused other women of killing her children would become characteristic of the later witch-burning craze.
139. When in 1080 women were accused of being witches and blamed for causing storms and crop failures and put to death, Pope Gregory VIII complained to the Danish king forbidding such treatment. However, popular superstition persisted, often with cruel consequences. A mob burned three women to death in Bavaria in 1090. Ninety years later, a woman suspected of witchcraft was disembowelled on the orders of the local burghers and forced to walk through the streets of Ghent carrying her own intestines.
140. *The Waning of the Middle Ages*, by J. Huizinga, Peregrine Books, 1965.

141. *Demon Lovers: Witchcraft, sex and the crisis of belief*, by Walter Stephens, University of Chicago Press, 2002.
142. Later, there would be considerable learned speculation as to how and when this extraction occurred, and whether or not semen from 'nocturnal pollutions' or wet dreams could be used.
143. Stephens, op. cit.
144. Quoted by Stephens, ibid.
145. Even at the height of the witch-hunts, Ireland was largely un- affected. As has been noted before, Irish Celtic traditions lack many of the misogynistic elements common in Classical, Jewish and Christian worldviews.
146. *Europe's Inner Demons*, by Norman Cohn, University of Chicago Press, 2000.
147. Ibid. From the 1600s onwards, demonic possession became more common, frequently affecting large numbers of women at once. The most famous cases are the nuns of Loudun and the women of Salem. As with this Bohemian priest, possession often took the form of a revulsion towards attending religious ceremonies.
148. *Malleus Maleficarum*, by Henricus Institoris, translated with an introduction, bibliography and notes by the Rev. Montague Sum- mers, John Rodker, 1928. This quotation is from Summers' introduction. All quotations from *Malleus* that follow are from Summers' translation, unless otherwise indicated.
149. Accusations that witches steal penises still occur in Africa. In November 2001, the BBC reported that mobs in Cotonuo, Benin, attacked and killed five people, four of whom were burned to death, after men had reported that their penises had disappeared. It is believed that a man's penis can be made to disappear by a handshake or an incantation.
150. Stephens, op. cit.
151. Ibid.
152. *Materials Towards a History of Witchcraft*, Volume Two, by Henry Lea, arranged and edited by Arthur Howland, Thomas Yoseloff, 1957.
153. O'Shea, op. cit.
154. Summers, op. cit.
155. *The Encyclopaedia of Witchcraft and Demonology*, by Rossell Hope Robbins, Crown, 1959.
156. Lea, op. cit.
157. Jean Bodin, quoted in Lea, ibid.
158. Stephens, op. cit.
159. Cohn, op. cit.
160. *The European Witch Craze of the 17th Century*, Hugh Trevor- Roper, Penguin Books, 1966.
161. Lea, op. cit.
162. Sleep deprivation became the torture of choice during Stalin's

purges of the Bolshevik Party in the 1930s. In the show trials, leading party intellectuals confessed, like the witches three centuries earlier, to creeping about the countryside poisoning wells and killing cattle. The British in Northern Ireland used it in a modified form against suspected IRA activists in 1971.

163. *The Devil in the Shape of a Woman: Witchcraft in colonial New England*, by Carol Karlsen, Vintage Books, 1989.

164. *Democracy in America*, by Alexis de Tocqueville, Everyman's Library, 1994.

165. When she was canonized in 1920 it was because of her virtuous life, not her successful military career, according to the historians Bonnie Anderson and Judith Zinsser, op. cit.

166. Ibid.

167. In the *Oxford English Dictionary*, 'misogyny' first appears in a glossary in 1656 and is defined as hatred or contempt of women. 'Misogynist' had appeared in 1630 in a pamphlet entitled 'Swetman Arraigned'. Swetman was the author of a notorious tract attacking women (see below): 'Swetman's name will be more terrible in women's eares/than euer yet Misogynists hath beene.'

168. *The Weaker Vessel: Women in 17th century England*, by Antonia Fraser, Alfred A. Knopf, 1984.

169. *The Family, Sex and Marriage in England 1500–1800*, by Lawrence Stone, Pelican Books, 1979.

170. Quoted by Stone, ibid.

171. Ibid.

172. William Blackstone, Oxford Professor of Law, quoted in *A Vindication of the Rights Of Woman*, by Mary Wollstonecraft, with an Introduction by Miriam Brody, Penguin Classics, 1992.

173. Stone, op. cit.

174. Quoted in *Who Cooked the Last Supper: The women's history of the world*, by Rosalind Miles, Three Rivers Press, 2001.

175. Anderson and Zinsser, ibid.

176. Stone, op. cit.

177. Fraser, op. cit.

178. Ibid.

179. Stone, op. cit.

180. Ibid.

181. Russell, op. cit.

182. The fall myths of the Greeks and Jews had been predicated upon a concept of specifically male autonomy – the idea that men had been created before women, and had lived happily and autonomously without them, enjoying a privileged relationship with the deity or deities.

183. Quoted by Russell, op. cit.

184. This remains the dominant view of social scientists, though it is now being challenged by the findings of evolutionary biology.

185. Stone, op. cit.

186. Locke, op. cit.
187. Ibid.
188. The second step would have to wait for another three centuries, until the contraceptive pill became widely available in the 1960s.
189. 'The Poetry of the 18th Century', by T. S. Eliot, *The Pelican Guide to English Literature*, volume 4: *From Dryden to Johnson*, edited by Boris Ford, Pelican Books, 1973.
190. Quoted in *A History of the Breast*, by Marilyn Yalom, Ballantine Books, 1997.
191. *Ben Jonson's Plays*, vol. 1, with an introduction by Felix Schelling, J. M. Dent and Sons, 1960.
192. Quoted in *Before Pornography: Erotic writing in early modern England*, by Ian Frederick Moulton, Oxford University Press, 2000.
193. *William Shakespeare, The Complete Works*, General Editors Stanley Wells and Gary Taylor, Oxford, 1988.
194. *Misogyny: The male malady*, by David Gilmore, University of Pennsylvania Press, 2001.
195. *Selected Essays by T. S. Eliot*, Faber and Faber, 1969.
196. Ibid.
197. Othello makes the same lament about his wife Desdemona: as his jealousy deepens, he remarks (*Othello* Act 3, Scene 3):

> O curse of marriage,
> That we call these delicate creatures ours,
> But not their appetites!

198. Either that or, as T. S. Eliot has suggested, Shakespeare has simply failed in Gertrude to create a character capable of justifying her son's ferocious anger against her. It is another one of the many puzzles of the play.
199. *Shakespeare: A Life*, by Park Honan, Oxford University Press, 1998.
200. *The Complete Poems of John Wilmot, Earl of Rochester*, edited with an introduction by David M. Vieth, Yale University Press, 1968. This was the first complete uncensored edition of Rochester's poetry to appear. In another poem, personal hygiene seems to supplant misogyny as the theme as the poet pleads with his mistress

> Fair nasty nymph, be clean and kind
> And all my joys restore
> By using paper still behind
> The sponges for before.

Rochester was in this case simply reflecting the fact that English men and women of the period – of all classes – were notoriously dirty and lacking in personal hygiene, a reminder that in the aftermath of the fall of the Roman Empire, its wonderful public baths, its system of aqueducts, and constant running water to flush the gutters of the streets, was lost and Europe endured more than a thousand years of squalor. Personal hygiene in seventeenth-century London usually consisted of washing only the hands and face. The diarist Samuel Pepys (1633 –1703), who kept a famous account of his everyday life which included explicit descriptions of his multitudinous sexual encounters, had a sexual stand-off with his wife Elizabeth, after she had gone to a bath house (for the first time in her life) and then had refused to allow him to sleep with her until he did so too. After three days, his hostility to having a bath was overcome by his need for sex and he consented. But usually women were deemed to be the greater offenders.

201. Quoted in *Rochester's Poetry*, by David Farler-Hills, Rowman and Littlefield, 1978.

202. The resulting anxiety found an outlet in a stream of witty poetry. Among the most famous is Rochester's 'Signior Dildo'.

203. *The Secret Museum: Pornography in modern culture*, by Walter Kendrick, University of California Press, 1987.

204. *The Rise of the Novel*, by Ian Watt, University of California Press, 1957.

205. The other two are generally reckoned to be *Robinson Crusoe* (1719) and *A Journal of the Plague Year* (1722).

206. Stone, op. cit.

207. Defoe, 'Conjugal Lewdness', 1727.

208. *Roxana: The fortunate mistress*, by Daniel Defoe, edited with an introduction by David Blewett, Penguin Classics, 1982.

209. Ibid.

210. Another curious feature of *Roxana* is that it is a story about a whore but tells the reader almost nothing about her sex life. The only erotic scene in the book is in fact between Roxana and her devoted maid Amy. Roxana's lover has his eye on Amy, who returns his looks but is too coy and 'feminine' to take any initiative. Roxana invites Amy to go to bed with him and when Amy pulls back, insists upon it. When Amy still proves coy, Roxana begins to strip her. At first Amy resists, but after a tussle, she surrenders to Roxana who reports, 'she let me do what I would', using the phrase commonly employed when a woman surrenders to a man. Roxana then thrusts her naked into bed with her lover and watches while the two make love. The scene's purpose is to establish the heroine's ability to act decisively, in a way that defies the feminine stereotype of coyness. She masters Amy as decisively as would a man, just as she masters her money and her men, turning them to her own purpose.

211. It is interesting to compare these stale misogynistic stereotypes going back to Juvenal to Defoe's rich and original portrait of Roxana. The poetic outpourings about women of those such as Pope, who disdained the novel as literature for scullery maids, now seem pathetic, predictable, and outmoded.

212. *Pamela*, by Samuel Richardson, vol. 1, with an introduction by George Saintsbury, Everyman's Library, 1960.
213. The novelist Henry Fielding had no doubt as to what the answer was. In a pamphlet entitled 'Shamela' he attacked Richardson as a hypocrite. Fielding's first novel, *Joseph Andrews*, was a parody of *Pamela*, in which a handsome young footman is preyed on by a lascivious Lady Booby. Fielding thought it ridiculous to suppose that it is only men who lust and explored the same theme in his greatest work, *Tom Jones*.
214. *Emile*, by Jean-Jacques Rousseau, translated by Barbara Foxley, Everyman Library, 1911.
215. *Women in Western Political Thought*, by Susan Moller Orkin, Princeton University Press, 1979.
216. Rousseau, op. cit.
217. ibid.
218. Russell, op. cit.
219. *The Invention of Pornography: Obscenity and the origins of modernity 1500–1800*, edited with an introduction by Lynn Hunt, Zone Books, 1993
220. Kathryn Norberg, quoted in ibid.
221. *Justine: or, Good Conduct Well Chastised* and *The History of Juliette: or, The Fortunes of Vice* were banned in 1814 and 1815 respectively. They did not become widely available in English until 1965.
222. *The History of Juliette: or, The Fortunes of Vice*, Grove Press, 1968.
223. *The Golden Bough: The roots of religion and folklore*, by Sir James Frazer, Avenel Books, 1981.
224. *Sexual Life in Ancient India: A study in the comparative history of Indian culture*, by Johann Jakob Meyer, Barnes and Noble, 1953. Meyer's analysis is based on the old Indian epic poem *The Mahabharata*.
225. Similar figurines have been found throughout Western Europe and have been used as evidence for the existence of a matriarchal civilization predating recorded history – that is roughly between 8000 and 3000 BC. However, it is notoriously difficult to draw conclusions about social relations from artifacts. If all we knew about the Middle Ages were the portraits of the Virgin Mary, we might conclude that Catholic Europe was a matriarchy.
226. Quoted in *Sexualia: From prehistory to cyberspace*, edited by Clifford Bishop and Xenia Osthelder, Koneman, 2001.
227. *Conjunctions and Disjunctions*, by Octavio Paz, translated from the Spanish by Helen R. Lane, Seaver Books, 1982.
228. *Erotic Art of the East*, by Philip Rawson, quoted by Paz, ibid.
229. Paz, ibid.
230. Quoted in *Sex and History*, by Reay Tannahill, Abacus, 1981.
231. Ibid.

232. Ibid.
233. Paz, op. cit.
234. Ibid.
235. Bishop and Osthelder, op. cit.
236. Quoted in Tannahill, op. cit.
237. Reported in the *New York Times*, 20 July 2003.
238. Quoted in Bishop and Osthelder, op. cit.
239. Meyer, op. cit.
240. Reported by the Associated Press, 10 November 2002.
241. Quoted in Bishop and Osthelder, op. cit. It is to be hoped that the Abbé's indignation was also directed at the fact that the vast majority of the women of Western Europe were similarly barred from educational equality with men.
242. Ibid.
243. Ibid.
244. Meyer, op. cit.
245. Tannahill, op. cit.
246. Meyer, op. cit.
247. Tannahill, op. cit.
248. From 'An Occasional Letter to the Female Sex', quoted in Editor's Introduction to *Common Sense*, edited by Isaac Kramnick, the Penguin American Library, 1976.
249. From the Introduction to *A Vindication of the Rights of Woman*, by Mary Wollstonecraft, edited with an introduction by Miriam Brody, Penguin Books, 1992.
250. Brody, Introduction, ibid.
251. Brody, Introduction, ibid.
252. Brody, Introduction, ibid.
253. Ibid.
254. Russell, op. cit.
255. Quoted in *Of Woman Born: Motherhood as experience and institution*, Adrienne Rich, W. W. Norton, 1986
256. In an unpublished 1998 thesis for Trinity College, Dublin, Jenny E. Holland has argued that this tale of man creating life is an allegorical critique of science's takeover of the role of the midwife, which occurred during the nineteenth century with the rapid expansion of medical science.
257. Tannahill, op. cit.
258. Ibid.
259. *Charles Dickens: Selected Journalism, 1850–70*, edited with an introduction and notes by David Pascoe, Penguin Classics, 1997.
260. Hippolyte Taine, quoted in *The Worm in the Bud: The world of Victorian sexuality*, by Ronald Pearsall, Pelican Books, 1969.
261. *The People of the Abyss*, by Jack London, with an introduction by Brigitte Koenig, Pluto Press, 2002.
262. Ibid.

263. Mrs Elizabeth Fry, quoted by Pearsall, op. cit.
264. Ibid.
265. Ibid.
266. *Nymphomania: A History*, by Carol Groneman, Norton, 2001.
267. Quoted by Professor John Duffy, Tulane University School of Medicine, in 'Masturbation and Clitoridectomy', *Journal of the American Medical Association*, 19 October 1963.
268. The case is quoted in Groneman, op. cit.
269. Described in 'Women at our Mercy', by Peter Stothard, *The Times*, 27 March 1999. Brown later denied he had met with a reporter or made claims that surgery could cure mental illness. But the newspaper stood by its story. The *British Medical Journal* later produced female mental patients who had been operated upon by Brown. He lost his membership of the Royal College and left England to pursue his career in the United States.
270. Duffy, op. cit.
271. Quoted in Pearsall, op. cit. Ms Greenaway was also a huge success in France and Germany.
272. Ibid.
273. Dickens' work remains in stark contrast to that of his near-contemporary Emile Zola in France, whose novels abound with vivid portrayals of sexually mature women but who fails to give convincing depictions of children. His *La Terre* ('The Earth') was censored as obscene in England in 1888 when it became the topic of debate in the House of Commons. One outraged Member of Parliament declared that the moral fibre of England was being 'eaten out' by 'literature of this kind'. The English publisher went to jail for three months.
274. Rich, op. cit.
275. *The Lancet*, quoted by Pearsall, op. cit.
276. Miles, op. cit. According to Miles, the code allowed the husband to compel his wife to reside or move to any place he dictated, to acquire her property and earnings on divorce, to send her to jail for up to two years for adultery, while he was not liable to prosecution, and to deprive her children of all rights. She concludes 'Frenchwomen had been better off in the Dark Ages . . .'
277. Pearsall, op. cit.
278. Quoted in ibid.
279. Herbert Spencer, quoted in Miles, op. cit.
280. *Saturday Review*, February 1868, quoted by Pearsall, op. cit.
281. Tannahill, op. cit.
282. Quoted in Pearsall, op. cit.
283. Quoted in *Witches of the Atlantic World: A historical reader and primary source book*, edited by Elaine G. Breslaw, New York University Press, 2000.

284. Ibid.

285. De Tocqueville, *Democracy in America*, Everyman's Library, 1972.

286. Ibid.

287. *Shades of Freedom: Racial politics and presumptions of the American legal process*, by A. Leon Higginbotham, Oxford University Press, 1996.

288. Quoted in an interview on the *Essence Magazine* website. Sheftall is the author along with Johnetta B. Cole of *Gender Talks: The struggle for women's equality in African American communities*, Ballantine Books, 1999.

289. Miles, op. cit.

290. Even at the time, there was much speculation as to why the lawless frontier land of the far west should take such a progressive step. The cowboys and gunslingers seem to have concluded that Wyoming's image would benefit, since women represented all that was respectable and moral in the eyes of most Americans. Women also won the right to serve on juries. Chief Justice Hoyt who had opposed the move later concluded that 'these women acquitted themselves with such dignity, decorum, propriety of conduct and intelligence as to win the admiration of every fair-minded citizen of Wyoming'. See Tannahill, op. cit.

291. Miles, op. cit.

292. Tannahill, op. cit.

293. Russell, op. cit.

294. But Nietzsche misunderstood Byron as disastrously as he misunderstood women. Far from being like the Don Juan of legend, the heartless seducer, intent only on robbing women of their virtue, Byron was himself more often than not the seduced rather than the seducer. His greatest poem, the comic epic *Don Juan*, tells of a rather gentle, dreamy and good-natured young man, who finds it hard to say no to beautiful women.

295. Nietzsche's notions of power resemble in some ways those of Sade. But the 'Divine Marquis' would have regarded as ridiculous and infantile Nietzsche's view of woman. As Sade saw it, since women were human they were capable of inhumanity to the same degree as men, as he makes clear in *Juliette*.

296. Quoted by Pearsall, op. cit.

297. Jack the Ripper experts debate whether the number of murders attributed to the Ripper should be larger or smaller. There are as many as ten other killings, some before the first and some after the last generally accepted Ripper murder, which have been considered from time to time as the Ripper's work. But like so much else concerned with Jack the Ripper, the vast majority of the alleged links to him are based on pure speculation.

298. Quoted in *The Complete Jack the Ripper*, by Donald Rumbelow,

with an introduction by Colin Wilson, the New York Graphic Society, 1975.

299. His report is quoted on the *Casebook: Jack the Ripper* website, one of 178,000 entries relating to the Ripper murders as hosted by the Google search engine.

300. Rumbelow, op. cit.

301. Jack the Ripper's identity is puzzled over to this day. There have been about fifteen major suspects, ranging from the Duke of Clarence, a grandson of Queen Victoria, to a Polish barber. Several witnesses reported a 'shabby-genteel' man who looked 'foreign', speaking with several of the victims shortly before their deaths. Whitechapel was a Jewish area and police feared that such rumours would provoke anti-Semitic riots. For this reason they destroyed what may have been one of their few real clues. Shortly after the fourth murder, not far away a police constable came across graffiti that read: 'The Juwes are not the men that will be blamed for nothing'. It was fresh, and may have been the murderer's attempt to stir up feelings against the local Jewish population. Freud would later speculate on the relationship between misogyny and anti-Semitism,

302. *Collected Poems*, edited by Edward Mendelson, Random House, 1976.

303. *The Enigma of Woman: Woman in Freud's writings*, by Sarah Kofman, translated from the French by Catherine Porter, Cornell University Press, 1985.

304. *Some Psychical Consequences of the Anatomical Differences Between the Sexes*, The Freud Reader, edited by Peter Gay, W. W. Norton and Company, 1989.

305. Bishop and Osthelder, op. cit.

306. Gay, op.cit.

307. Ibid.

308. Kofman, ibid.

309. *Civilization and Its Discontents*, Sigmund Freud, Dover Publications, 1994.

310. Quoted by Betty Friedan in *The Feminine Mystique*, Norton 1963.

311. *Eve's Seed: Biology, the sexes and the course of history*, Robert S. McElvaine, McGraw-Hill, 2001.

312. Much of the information on Weininger was taken from the website *www.theabsolute.net/ottow/ottoinfo*, 5 November 2003. In turn, this material derives from *Sex, Science, and Self in Imperial Vienna*, a doctoral dissertation by Chandak Sengoopta, John Hopkins University, 1996.

313. *Sex and Character*, by Otto Weininger, *feastofhateandfear* website, 11 November 2003.

314. Ibid

315. Ibid
316. *www.theabsolute.net/ottow/ottoinfo*.
317. Ibid.
318. Freud theorized on an unconscious link between misogyny and anti-Semitism, at least as they manifested themselves in Western civilization. He speculated that they both sprang from a fear of castration. Circumcision inspired the same fear as the sight of female genitalia (see Chapter 9).
319. *Hitler 1889–1936: Hubris*, by Ian Kershaw, W. W. Norton, 1998.
320. Weininger, op. cit.
321. *The Face of the Third Reich*, by Joachim C. Fest, Pelican Books, 1972.
322. Kershaw, op.cit.
323. Ibid.
324. Ibid.
325. Ibid.
326. Ibid.
327. Fest, op. cit.
328. Ibid.
329. Ibid.
330. Kershaw, op. cit.
331. *The Third Reich: A New History*, by Michael Burleigh, Pan Books, 2001.
332. Ibid.
333. From the website *Truth at Last Archives*, 11 November 2003. Streicher was tried and executed by the Allies in October 1946.
334. Burleigh, op. cit.
335. Ibid.
336. *Mein Kampf*, quoted by Fest, op. cit.
337. Quoted by Fest, ibid.
338. Ibid.
339. Ibid.
340. *Women Writing the Holocaust*, website, 17 November 2003.
341. *Hitler's Willing Executioners: Ordinary Germans and the Holocaust*, by Daniel Goldhagen, Vintage Books, 1997.
342. The pictures are reproduced in Goldhagen, ibid.
343. *The Nazi Doctors*, by Rover Jay Lifton, quoted in the *New York Times*, 19 November 2003.
344. *Women in Concentration Camps* website, 17 November 2003.
345. *The Origins of the Family, Private Property and the State*, by Friedrich Engels, with an introduction by Michael Barrett, Penguin Classics, 1985.
346. Rosalind Delmar, quoted by Michael Barrett, ibid.
347. *The Woman Question: Selections from the writings of Karl Marx, Frederick Engels, V. I. Lenin, Joseph Stalin*, International Publishers, 1951.

348. Ibid. Lenin was following Engels who in *Origins* (Engels, op. cit.) had asserted that the liberation of the 'whole female sex' could only come about through integration in the general economy.
349. Ibid.
350. *Basic Writings on Politics and Philosophy*, Anchor Books, 1989.
351. Adrienne Rich, op. cit.
352. *The People's Daily Online*, 12 November 2003.
353. From *Life and Fate*, quoted in *The Fall of Berlin*, by Antony Beevor, Viking, 2002.
354. The North Korean government has called their allegations a 'whopping lie'. But credible human rights organizations substantiate the defectors' testimonies.
355. All following quotes and references to Mrs Lee come from the transcript of her testimony before HIRC.
356. *New York Times*, 3 May 2002.
357. Iris Chang, *The Rape of Nanking*, quoted in *War's Dirty Little Secret: Rape, prostitution and other crimes against women*, Anne Llewellyn, editor, The Pilgrim Press, 2000.
358. Beevor, op. cit.
359. Quoted in Llewellyn, op. cit.
360. Ibid.
361. Ibid.
362. One of the few instances of soldiers being punished for rape occurred during Alexander the Great's invasion of Persia in 334 BC. He ordered two soldiers executed for raping the wives of two Persians. Alexander compared them to 'brute beasts out to destroy mankind'. See *Plutarch's Life of Alexander*, translated by Thomas North, Southern Illinois Press, 1963.
363. Pearsall, op. cit.
364. Ibid.
365. Tannahill, op. cit.
366. *Why I am not a Christian: And other essays on religion and related subjects*, by Bertrand Russell, Simon and Schuster, 1950.
367. There were exceptions, such as the nineteenth-century birth control advocate and libertine Annie Besant who once declared: 'If the Bible and religion stood in the way of women's rights, then the Bible and religion must go.' See Pearsall, op. cit.
368. Miles, op. cit.
369. *The 'Rhythm' in Marriage and Christian Morality*, by Fr Orville Griese, Newman Bookshop, 1944.
370. Ibid.
371. *God's Politician: John Paul at the Vatican*, by David Willey, Faber and Faber, 1992.
372. Ibid.
373. Ibid.
374. Ibid.

375. Quoted in Willey, ibid.
376. Joan Didion, review of *Armageddon: The cosmic battle of the ages*, by Tim LaHaye and Jerry B. Jenkins, *New York Review of Books*, 17 November 2003.
377. BBC News World Edition website, 28 June 2003.
378. Fortunately for Irish women, England is only a short boat trip away. Thousands of Irish women go there every year to have the abortions denied to them at home. It allows succeeding Irish governments to be sanctimonious about their 'pro-life' credentials without having to face the consequences of their policies.
379. Bishop and Osthelder, op. cit.
380. Dr Jacques Leclercq, quoted in Griese, op. cit.
381. Ibid.
382. In 1981, according to a report in the *New York Times* of 20 January 2003, it reached just over 29 abortions per 1,000 women aged between 15 and 44. As of 2003, it stood at 21.3.
383. *New York Times*, 4 September 2003.
384. Ibid.
385. *New York Times*, 10 May 2003.
386. Ibid.
387. *New York Times*, 2 June 2003.
388. *Dallas Morning News*, 9 August 1996.
389. Ibid.
390. Quoted in *The Dallas Morning News*, op. cit.
391. *The Perfumed Garden of the Shaykh Nefzawi*, translated by Sir Richard Burton, edited with an introduction and additional notes by Alan Hull Walton, Gramercy Publishing Company, 1964.
392. Ibid.
393. *Women and Gender in Islam*, by Leila Ahmed, Yale University Press, 1992.
394. Tannahill, op.cit.
395. Ahmed, op. cit.
396. Ibid. Ahmed points out that Lord Cromer, the British Consul General in Egypt, campaigned against the veil while at home he formed an organization that was opposed to women's suffrage.
397. Haleh Afshar, quoted by Ahmed, ibid.
398. Ibid.
399. *New York Times*, 17 May 2002.
400. Ibid.
401. Ibid.
402. *New York Times*, 2 July 2002.
403. *New York Times*, 6 July 2002.
404. *My Forbidden Face: Growing up under the Taliban, a young woman's story*, by Latifa, written with the collaboration of Shekeba Hacchemi, translated by Linda Coverdale, preface by Karenna Gore Schifff, Hyperion, 2001.

405. *Soldiers of God: With Islamic warriors in Afghanistan and Pakistan*, by Robert D. Kaplan, Vintage, 2001.
406. Latifa, op. cit. There is a further irony in the fact that the British during their occupation of India encouraged Deobandism to offset the threat from Hindu nationalists.
407. Ibid.
408. Ibid.
409. Ibid.
410. Ibid.
411. Kaplan, op. cit.
412. John Anderson, *New Yorker*, 28 January 2002. Anderson also discovered that Mullah Omar, the head of state during the Taliban's reign, played secular music on the CD player of his Toyota Land Cruiser.
413. Latifa, op. cit.
414. *Los Angeles Times*, 4 November 2001.
415. *New York Times*, 27 October 2002.
416. *New York Times*, 31 October 2002. In December 2003, at a nationwide convention called to draft a new constitution for Afghanistan, one of the hundred women delegates spoke out against the mujahideen present at the meeting. 'Why have you again selected as committee chairman,' she asked, 'those criminals who have brought these disasters for Afghan people?' According to the BBC, 18 December 2003 she had to be placed under UN protection. No women were elected to any of the committees set up by the convention.
417. Goldhagen, op. cit.
418. *Washington Post*, 4 April1993.
419. *The Collected Essays, Journalism and Letters of George Orwell*, Volume 4: *In Front of Your Nose, 1945–50*, edited by Sonia Orwell and Ian Angus, Penguin Books, 1970.
420. 'Rock turns mean and ugly', by Greg Kot, rock music critic, *Chicago Tribune*, 18 November 1990.
421. *New York Times*, 6 November 2003. Ridgeway was known as 'The Green River Killer' and had been at large since the 1980s, when the first bodies of his victims began turning up on the banks of the Green River near Seattle.
422. Samuel Slipp, quoted in *Misogyny: The Male Malady*, by David Gilmore, University of Pennsylvania Press, 2001.
423. It is interesting to compare the treatment of the Jews under the Roman authorities, when they did pose a real threat to Roman control of Judaea, to their fate under the Christians. In spite of two serious Jewish uprisings, the first in AD 66, and the second in AD 132, both of which were only suppressed at the cost of considerable bloodshed, the Romans did not enact anti-Semitic laws. The sort of religious and racial intolerance, which became a feature of Christianity, was largely foreign to Roman thinking.

424. Goldhagen, op. cit.
425. *New York Times Magazine*, 15 September 2002.
426. *Fable for Another Time*, translated by Mary Hudson, University of Nebraska Press, 2003.
427. Paz, op. cit.
428. Quoted by Pinker, op. cit.
429. Ibid.
430. Russell, op. cit.
431. Pinker, op. cit.
432. *The Rise and Fall of the Third Chimpanzee: How our animal heritage affects the way we live*, Vintage, 1992.
433. 'To his Coy Mistress', by Andrew Marvell, the *Oxford Book of English Verse*, edited by Christopher Ricks, Oxford University Press, 1999.
434. The Bonobo, or pigmy chimpanzee, is the only other primate in which ovulation is hidden. Bonobos are constantly sexually active, and like humans use sex for a wide variety of reasons other than for procreation. See *Demonic Males: Apes and the origins of human violence*, by Richard Wrangham and Dale Peterson, Mariner Books, 1996.
435. *Survival of the Prettiest: The science of beauty*, by Nancy Etcoff, Doubleday, 1999.

INDEX